deepen. We view this First Edition from Talking Therapies UK as a contribution to the conversation, not the final word. We welcome feedback, recognise limitations, and commit to ongoing learning and revision in future editions.

Published by Talking Therapies UK www.talkingtherapies.co.uk

This manual is intended for use by qualified mental health professionals, skills trainers, and individuals participating in Dialectical Behavioural Therapy under professional guidance.

Disclaimer

This manual is designed to be used as part of a comprehensive Dialectical Behavioural Therapy programme, ideally under the guidance of a qualified mental health professional trained in DBT. Whilst every effort has been made to ensure the accuracy and completeness of the information provided, this manual is not intended as a substitute for professional mental health care, medical advice, diagnosis, or treatment.

The skills and techniques presented in this manual are based on evidence-based practice and research. However, individual results may vary, and no specific outcomes can be guaranteed. Always seek the advice of qualified health providers with any questions you may have regarding a mental health condition.

If you are experiencing a mental health crisis, thoughts of self-harm or suicide, or any situation that may require immediate attention, please contact emergency services (999 in the UK) or a crisis helpline immediately. Do not rely solely on this manual in crises. The Samaritans can be reached on 116 123 (free to call) at any time.

The case examples presented in this manual are composites drawn from clinical experience and do not represent specific individuals. Any resemblance to actual persons, living or deceased, is purely coincidental. Details have been modified to protect confidentiality.

Dedication

For Paul and Isabella James

"Still Here"
The weight is heavy, the path unclear,
But every breath says I'm still here.

Though tears may fall and hope feels thin,
There's quiet strength that stirs within.

You are not broken, just deeply made—
A soul that bends but won't be swayed.

Building a life worth living

How to Use This Manual

This manual has been designed to serve multiple audiences: DBT skills trainers and therapists who teach these skills, individuals learning DBT skills in a structured programme, and those seeking to understand and practice DBT skills independently. Each reader will naturally approach this manual differently, and this section provides guidance tailored to your specific role and context.

For DBT Skills Trainers and Therapists

If you are a mental health professional delivering DBT skills training, this manual serves as both a teaching resource and a client workbook. Each skills module follows a consistent structure designed to facilitate both teaching and learning:

Theoretical foundations are presented first, providing the rationale for each skill.

Understanding why a skill works increases motivation to use it and helps both therapists and clients adapt skills to unique situations.

Step-by-step instructions break down complex skills into manageable components, making them easier to teach and learn.

Multiple examples across varied contexts help illustrate how skills apply in real-life situations. Examples span different ages, relationships, and presenting problems. Case studies offer detailed narratives that demonstrate skills in action, making them effective for teaching key points and facilitating group discussions.

The "Common Problems and Solutions" sections address typical obstacles that arise when learning each skill. These sections draw from years of clinical experience and can save significant therapy time by pre-emptively addressing predictable difficulties.

Handouts and worksheets are integrated throughout, ready to be used directly with clients or adapted as needed.

Teaching Recommendations

When using this manual in skills training groups, we recommend the following approach:

Assigning a reading before teaching a skill and having participants read the relevant section before the group allows you to focus session time on practice, discussion, and problem-solving rather than on presenting basic information.

Begin each session with a brief review of key concepts from the reading, checking for understanding and addressing any questions that arise.

Use examples from the manual as discussion prompts, but also encourage participants to generate their own examples relevant to their lives.

Incorporate experiential exercises and role-plays. Skills are best learned through practice, not just discussion.

Review the common problems section together, inviting participants to identify which obstacles they anticipate encountering.

Assign specific homework using the worksheets provided, ensuring participants know what to practise before the next session.

Begin subsequent sessions with a review of homework, troubleshooting difficulties, and celebrating successes.

For individual therapy, this manual can supplement your work with clients as they learn DBT skills. You might assign specific sections for reading between sessions, use worksheets to structure practice, or refer to case examples to illustrate points. The extensive common problems sections can be particularly valuable in individual work, as they allow you to anticipate and address obstacles that commonly arise.

For Individuals Learning DBT Skills in a Programme

If you are participating in DBT skills training, whether in a group or individual format, this manual is your companion throughout the learning process. Your therapist or skills trainer will guide you through the material, but this manual provides detailed explanations, examples, and practice resources to support your learning between sessions.

Making the Most of This Manual

Read the assigned sections before group or therapy sessions. This preparation allows you to make better use of session time for practice and clarifying questions.

Bring this manual to every session. You will want to take notes, mark important passages, and refer to information during discussions.

Complete homework assignments using the worksheets provided. Skills are developed through practice, and homework completion is strongly linked to better treatment outcomes.

Review the common problems sections when you encounter difficulties. Often, the struggle you are experiencing is one that many others have faced, and solutions are already outlined.

Return to sections as needed. DBT skills build upon each other, and you may find it helpful to review earlier material as you progress.

Discuss questions and concerns with your therapist or skills trainer. This manual provides information, but your treatment providers can help you apply skills to your specific situation.

It is essential to understand that reading this manual alone, whilst valuable, is not the same as participating in DBT treatment. The skills are most effective when learned with professional guidance and when practised consistently over time. If you are using this manual as part of a DBT programme, you are receiving the best possible context for learning these life-changing skills.

For Self-Directed Learning

Whilst this manual is designed primarily for use within a therapeutic context, we recognise that some individuals may wish to learn DBT skills independently. Perhaps you do not have access to DBT services in your area, you are on a waiting list for treatment, or you want to supplement professional support with additional learning. This manual can support self-directed learning, though we offer some essential caveats and recommendations.

Essential Considerations for Independent Learning

Self-directed learning from a manual is not a substitute for professional treatment, particularly if you are experiencing significant mental health difficulties, thoughts of self-harm or suicide, or behaviours that put you at risk. In these situations, professional help is essential. Contact your GP, a crisis service, or call 999 if you are in immediate danger.

Learning skills without professional guidance can be more challenging. You will not have a therapist to help troubleshoot difficulties, answer questions, or provide personalised feedback on your skill use. The common problems sections in this manual can help, but they cannot replace individualised support.

Skills are most effective when practised consistently over a period of time. Without the structure and accountability of regular sessions, maintaining a consistent practice can be challenging. Consider finding ways to create structure and support, such as joining an online DBT community or finding a practice partner.

Some skills may be challenging or activating to learn without support. If you find yourself becoming overwhelmed or distressed whilst reading or practising a skill, take a break and consider whether you would benefit from professional guidance.

Recommendations for Self-Directed Learning

If you choose to use this manual for self-directed learning, we recommend the following approach:

Work through the modules in order. Skills build upon each other, and the sequence is designed to support learning. Start with Mindfulness, as these are foundational skills for all others.

Take your time. Do not rush through the material. Spend at least a week or two on each primary skill, practising consistently before moving on.

Keep a practice log or journal. Document your practice, what went well, what was difficult, and the questions that arise. This record will help you track progress and identify patterns.

Complete the worksheets provided. These are designed to structure your practice and deepen your understanding of the material.

Consider seeking support from Talking Therapies UK or another DBT service, even if only for periodic consultation. Even occasional professional input can significantly enhance your learning. Visit www.talkingtherapies.co.uk to explore options for support.

Connect with others learning DBT skills. Online communities can offer support, accountability, and shared learning opportunities. However, be cautious about taking advice from unqualified individuals, and remember that online communities are not a substitute for professional care.

Be patient and compassionate with yourself. Learning new skills takes time, and progress is rarely linear. Celebrate small successes and persist through difficulties.

Colour Coding Guide

This manual uses colour coding to help you navigate different types of content:

□ **Orange Text:** Chapter headers and major section titles - Use these to navigate the manual structure

□ **Magenta Text:** Worksheet titles - Identifies practical exercises and worksheets for skill practice

□ **Light Magenta Background:** Case studies and real-world examples - Learn how skills apply in practical situations

□ **Light Yellow Background:** Key learning points and important concepts - Pay special attention to these highlighted sections

These colour codes are used consistently throughout the manual to enhance your learning experience and help you quickly identify the type of content you're reading.

Introduction to Dialectical Behavioural Therapy

Welcome to this comprehensive guide to Dialectical Behavioural Therapy skills. Talking Therapies UK have created this manual to provide both mental health professionals and individuals learning DBT with an in-depth, practical resource for understanding and mastering these evidence-based strategies. This manual elaborates on previous iterations and various guides to provide a new, up-to-date, easier-to-understand, and engaging manual for all.

What is Dialectical Behavioural Therapy?

Dialectical Behavioural Therapy, also known as DBT, is a comprehensive, evidence-based treatment approach that combines cognitive-behavioural techniques with concepts derived from Eastern mindfulness practices. The treatment addresses the fundamental challenge many people face: how to change problematic patterns whilst accepting oneself and one's circumstances.

The word 'dialectical' captures the essence of this approach. In philosophy, dialectics refers to the process of integrating opposing viewpoints to arrive at a synthesis—a more comprehensive understanding that encompasses both positions. In DBT, the primary dialectic is between acceptance and change. You are doing the best you can, and you need to do better. Both statements are factual. This is not a contradiction; it is the reality of human growth and development.

Consider how this dialectical stance differs from other approaches. Traditional cognitive therapy might emphasise that your thoughts are distorted and need to be challenged and changed. Purely acceptance-based approaches might emphasise accepting your thoughts and feelings without trying to change them. DBT recognises that you need both. Sometimes your thoughts accurately reflect reality, and at other times, they do not. Sometimes your emotions fit the facts of a situation, and sometimes they do not. The skill lies in discerning which is which, accepting what cannot or should not be changed, and effectively changing what can and should be different.

This dialectical approach extends throughout all DBT. You focus on the present moment whilst planning. You accept yourself as you are whilst working to become who you want to be. You validate your own experiences whilst remaining open to others' perspectives. You maintain your own boundaries whilst being flexible in relationships. You use logic and reason whilst honouring your emotions. You hold firm to important positions whilst negotiating on less critical matters. Learning to navigate these dialectical tensions and find balance, rather than oscillating between extremes, is central to DBT.

The Development of DBT: A Story of Innovation

Understanding how DBT developed provides valuable context for understanding the treatment itself. In the late 1970s, Dr Marsha Linehan conducted research on treatments for individuals who were chronically suicidal, many of whom carried diagnoses of borderline personality disorder. This was, and in some ways still is, a population that many mental health professionals found challenging to work with.

Dr Linehan began by applying standard cognitive-behavioural therapy, which had demonstrated effectiveness for depression, anxiety, and various other difficulties. She was systematic and rigorous in her approach, as befitted someone trained in behavioural science. However, something was not working. Many clients found the change-focused approach invalidating. Being told to identify 'cognitive distortions' or modify 'maladaptive behaviours' felt to them like being told that their experiences and responses were fundamentally wrong. Some clients became more distressed rather than better. Dropout rates were high. Therapists, for their part, found the work exhausting and demoralising.

Dr Linehan realised that pure change strategies, whilst necessary, were insufficient. She began incorporating acceptance-based approaches, drawing particularly from her own extensive training in Zen meditation. She emphasised validation, working to communicate that clients' experiences made sense given their circumstances. She introduced mindfulness skills to help people observe and accept their experiences without being overwhelmed by them. She worked to create a treatment that would be acceptable to clients, sustainable for therapists, and effective in reducing life-threatening behaviours whilst improving quality of life.

The result was Dialectical Behavioural Therapy. Dr Linehan published her first randomised controlled trial in 1991, demonstrating that DBT was more effective than treatment as usual in reducing suicidal behaviour, decreasing therapy dropout, and reducing psychiatric hospitalisation amongst individuals with borderline personality disorder. These were remarkable findings. This population had been considered exceedingly difficult to treat, with many clinicians hesitant to work with them at all.

What made these results particularly impressive was not just the statistical outcomes, though those were significant. It was that clients stayed in treatment. They came to sessions. They practised skills. They formed strong therapeutic relationships. Therapists, supported by consultation teams and using a treatment model that balances acceptance with change, found the work to be sustainable rather than depleting. The treatment worked not only in efficacy trials but also in real-world clinical settings.

The Evidence Base: From Borderline Personality Disorder to Broader Applications

Since those initial studies in the early 1990s, the evidence base for DBT has grown substantially. Hundreds of research trials have examined the effectiveness of DBT across diverse populations and presentations. This research has established DBT as one of the most well-validated psychological treatments available.

The original focus was borderline personality disorder, and DBT remains a first-line treatment for this condition. Multiple randomised controlled trials have replicated the original findings, demonstrating that DBT reduces suicidal behaviour, self-harm, psychiatric hospitalisation, and treatment dropout. Studies have shown that these benefits are maintained over time, with follow-up studies demonstrating continued improvement even after treatment ends.

However, researchers and clinicians quickly recognised that the skills taught in DBT had broader applicability. The core problem that DBT addresses, emotional dysregulation, is not unique to borderline personality disorder. Many people struggle with intense emotions that are difficult to manage. Many people find themselves acting impulsively in ways they later regret. Many people have difficulty maintaining stable relationships or tolerating distress without resorting to destructive behaviours. DBT skills offer solutions to these universal human challenges.

Research has now demonstrated DBT's effectiveness with adolescents experiencing multiple problems, including suicidal thoughts, self-harm, and emotional dysregulation. Studies show that DBT helps reduce these dangerous behaviours whilst improving family relationships and overall functioning. This makes sense; many of the patterns that become entrenched in adulthood begin in adolescence, and intervening early can prevent years of suffering.

DBT has proven effective for eating disorders, particularly binge eating disorder and bulimia nervosa. The skills help individuals manage the intense emotions that often trigger binge eating or purging behaviours. Rather than using food or compensatory behaviours to cope with distress, individuals learn healthier ways to regulate emotions and tolerate discomfort.

In the realm of substance use disorders, DBT helps individuals reduce drug and alcohol use by addressing the emotional dysregulation that often underlies addiction. Many people use substances to numb painful emotions or to escape from distress. DBT teaches alternative skills for managing these emotional states, making it possible to maintain sobriety even when life is complicated.

Depression, particularly treatment-resistant depression, has also been successfully addressed with DBT. The behavioural activation components of DBT, combined with skills for managing painful emotions and tolerating distress, provide powerful tools for moving out of depression. Studies show that DBT can be effective even for individuals who have not responded to other evidence-based treatments.

Importantly, DBT skills have been found helpful for individuals without formal psychiatric diagnoses. These are simply life skills that anyone can benefit from. Schools have begun teaching DBT skills to students, seeing that they help with emotion management, peer relationships, and academic performance. Businesses have utilised DBT principles to enhance workplace culture and mitigate conflict. Parents have found DBT skills helpful in managing their own stress and responding more effectively to their children.

The research continues to expand. Recent studies examine DBT's effectiveness with post-traumatic stress disorder, where emotion regulation and distress tolerance skills are particularly relevant. Research explores adaptations of DBT for older adults, who face unique challenges related to loss, health problems, and life transitions. Studies investigate culturally adapted versions of DBT for diverse populations, ensuring that these valuable skills are accessible and relevant across diverse cultural contexts.

What makes this evidence base particularly strong is not just the quantity of research, although that is impressive, but also its quality. Many studies are randomised controlled trials, the gold standard for treatment research. Studies have been conducted by independent research teams, not just by Dr Linehan and her colleagues, demonstrating that the treatment works when delivered by diverse therapists in varied settings. Long-term follow-up studies show that benefits persist over time. Cost-effectiveness analyses demonstrate that DBT, whilst initially resource-intensive, saves money in the long run by reducing hospitalisations, emergency room visits, and other costly crisis interventions.

Core Principles and the Dialectical Stance

Understanding the core principles that underpin DBT helps make sense of why the treatment is structured as it is and why particular skills are included. These principles are not merely theoretical abstractions; they have direct practical implications for how therapy is conducted and how skills are taught and applied.

The Central Dialectic: Acceptance and Change

The primary dialectic in DBT, as we have discussed, is between acceptance and change. However, understanding this dialectic deeply requires exploring what acceptance and change mean in this context, because these terms are often misunderstood.

Acceptance, in DBT, does not mean resignation or approval. It does not mean giving up on change or deciding that things cannot improve. Instead, acceptance means acknowledging reality as it is, without judgement or resistance. It means letting go of the struggle against facts that cannot be changed, at least not in this moment. Acceptance is the recognition that suffering is increased when we fight against unchangeable realities.

Consider someone who has experienced a significant loss. They might spend enormous energy wishing the loss had not occurred, ruminating on what they could have done differently, or raging against the unfairness of what happened. All of this is understandable, but none of it changes the fact of the loss. Acceptance means acknowledging that the loss has occurred, that it cannot be undone, and that moving forward requires accepting this reality as it is. This acceptance does not mean the person is happy about the loss or thinks it was okay that it happened. It simply means they are no longer fighting against a fact that cannot be changed.

Change, on the other hand, focuses on modifying what can be different. Whilst the loss itself cannot be changed, how the person responds to it absolutely can be. They can learn skills for managing grief. They can build new sources of meaning and connection. They can create a life that honours what was lost whilst moving forward. Change is active and future-oriented; it is about building the life you want rather than the life you have.

The synthesis of acceptance and change means recognising when each is appropriate. Some things can and should be changed: behaviours that damage your health or relationships, thought patterns that perpetuate distress without serving any adaptive function, and ways of coping that provide short-term relief but long-term harm. Other things cannot be changed, at least not immediately, and require acceptance: past events, other people's behaviour, fundamental aspects of reality, and current emotional states before you have time to use skills to shift them.

This dialectical stance also applies to how you view yourself. You are acceptable as you are right now, with all your struggles and imperfections. At the same time, you need to change and grow. Both are true. You deserve compassion and respect whilst also working hard to develop new capabilities. This is the opposite of the harsh self-criticism many people engage in, where they believe they must berate themselves into change. DBT suggests that change is more likely when you accept yourself whilst working to grow and develop.

Additional Dialectics in DBT

Whilst acceptance and change are the primary dialectics, DBT recognises many others. Learning to navigate these dialectical tensions is a key skill.

One important dialectic is between nurturing yourself and pushing yourself. Sometimes you need to be gentle with yourself, to rest, to engage in self-care, to back off from demands. Other times you need to push yourself, to do things even when they are difficult, to persist despite discomfort. Neither extreme is always right; wisdom lies in knowing which approach is needed in each moment.

Another dialectic is between focusing on yourself and focusing on others. You need to attend to your own needs, emotions, and goals. You also need to attend to your relationships, to others' needs and perspectives, to your responsibilities to people you care about. Finding balance between self-care and other care is essential for healthy functioning.

There is a dialectic between structure and flexibility. You need structure, routine, and plans to function effectively. You also need flexibility to adapt when circumstances change, to respond to unexpected events, to adjust your approach when needed. Rigid adherence to structure can be as problematic as complete lack of structure.

In relationships, there is a dialectic between holding firm to your position and being willing to compromise. Sometimes you need to stand your ground, to maintain your boundaries, to refuse to budge on important matters. Other times you need to negotiate, to see others' perspectives, to find middle ground. Effective relationship management requires discerning which approach is appropriate.

Each of these dialectics reflects a fundamental truth about human experience: extremes are rarely effective. Wisdom lies in finding balance, in being able to move fluidly between positions as circumstances require, in holding both sides of an apparent contradiction simultaneously. This is not easy. It requires practice, mindfulness, and willingness to tolerate ambiguity. However, it is a skill that can be developed, and doing so is transformative.

NOTE: This represents substantial progress on the Introduction section. The document will continue with the remaining subsections, including detailed biosocial theory, treatment structure, skills module previews, and principles for learning.

Who Can Benefit from DBT?

One of the remarkable features of DBT is its broad applicability. Whilst the treatment was originally developed for individuals with borderline personality disorder who were chronically suicidal, the skills and principles have proven valuable for a much wider range of people and presentations.

At its core, DBT addresses emotional dysregulation, the tendency to experience emotions more intensely and more variably than others, combined with difficulty managing these intense emotional states effectively. Emotional dysregulation is not specific to any single diagnosis. Many people experience it to varying degrees, and DBT offers strategies that can help.

Individuals with borderline personality disorder remain a primary population for DBT. These individuals typically experience intense and rapidly shifting emotions, struggle with unstable relationships, have difficulty maintaining a consistent sense of self, and may engage in impulsive or self-destructive behaviours when distressed. DBT provides them with skills for managing emotions, improving relationships, tolerating distress without resorting to harmful behaviours, and developing a stronger, more stable sense of identity. The evidence for DBT's effectiveness with this population is particularly strong.

Adolescents represent another key group who benefit from DBT. The teenage years are characterised by intense emotions, developing identity, peer relationship challenges, and experimentation with various behaviours. For adolescents who are struggling significantly, perhaps engaging in self-harm, experiencing suicidal thoughts, having frequent conflicts with family or peers, or showing early signs of personality difficulties, DBT offers developmentally appropriate skills. Adapted versions of DBT for adolescents involve families more actively, recognise the developmental stage adolescents are in, and teach skills in ways that resonate with younger people. Research shows that adolescent DBT can prevent the progression of difficulties that might otherwise become more entrenched in adulthood.

People with eating disorders, particularly binge eating disorder and bulimia nervosa, often find DBT skills transformative. Many individuals with these conditions use food-related behaviours to manage difficult emotions. They might binge when feeling overwhelmed, restrict when seeking control, or purge to escape from intolerable emotional states. DBT helps them identify the emotions and situations that trigger these behaviours, develop alternative ways of managing distress, and build a more balanced relationship with food. The mindfulness and distress tolerance skills are particularly relevant, as they provide ways to experience and tolerate uncomfortable emotions without immediately acting to escape them.

Substance use disorders frequently involve attempts to regulate emotions through external means. Individuals might use alcohol to reduce anxiety, stimulants to improve mood, or opioids to numb emotional pain. Whilst substances may provide temporary relief, they ultimately perpetuate the problem by preventing the development of effective emotion regulation skills and creating additional difficulties. DBT helps individuals understand the functions their substance use serves, develop healthier ways to meet those needs, and build a life that is sufficiently rewarding that substances become unnecessary. The treatment addresses both the immediate challenge of remaining abstinent and the underlying emotional regulation difficulties that drive substance use.

Depression, particularly when it is chronic or treatment-resistant, can respond well to DBT. Depression is often characterised not just by sad mood but by difficulties with emotion regulation more broadly. People with depression may struggle to experience positive emotions even when positive events occur, may find negative emotions particularly persistent and difficult to shift, and may withdraw from activities and relationships in ways that perpetuate low mood. DBT's behavioural activation strategies, combined with skills for managing rumination, tolerating distress, and maintaining relationships even when depressed, offer a comprehensive approach. The treatment acknowledges the reality of depression whilst teaching skills for moving through it.

Post-traumatic stress disorder involves significant emotional dysregulation, with individuals experiencing intense fear, anger, shame, or other emotions in response to trauma reminders. They may use avoidance strategies to prevent triggering these emotions, but avoidance often restricts life significantly. DBT skills help individuals gradually build tolerance for trauma-related emotions, manage intrusive symptoms, and engage in life even whilst healing from trauma. The treatment can be used alongside trauma-focused therapies or as a preparation for trauma processing, helping individuals develop sufficient emotion regulation skills to engage in exposure-based work.

Importantly, DBT skills are not only for people with psychiatric diagnoses. These are life skills that anyone can benefit from learning. Many people experience occasional difficulties with emotions, relationships, or stress management without meeting criteria for any particular disorder. DBT skills offer practical strategies for handling life's challenges more effectively.

Healthcare workers, teachers, emergency services personnel, and others in high-stress professions have found DBT skills valuable for managing occupational stress and preventing burnout. The distress tolerance and emotion regulation skills help them cope with difficult situations at work, whilst the interpersonal effectiveness skills improve their interactions with colleagues and those they serve.

Parents often find DBT skills helpful both for managing their own stress and for responding more effectively to their children. The emotion regulation skills help parents remain calm during challenging parenting moments, whilst the validation and interpersonal effectiveness skills improve parent-child relationships. Many parents report that learning DBT skills has transformed their family dynamics.

Students facing academic pressures, social challenges, and the transitions of young adulthood benefit from DBT skills for managing stress, improving focus, handling relationship difficulties, and making wise decisions even when emotions are intense. Schools that teach DBT skills report improvements in student wellbeing, reduced behavioural problems, and better treatment outcomes.

The skills are also valuable for people navigating major life transitions, such as divorce, bereavement, career changes, or health challenges. These transitions often involve intense emotions, require adaptation to new circumstances, and may involve relationships that are changing or coming to an end. DBT skills provide practical tools for managing the emotional aspects of transition whilst building a satisfying new life.

In essence, if you experience emotions, face challenges in relationships, encounter stress, or wish to live more mindfully and effectively, DBT skills have something to offer. The treatment's principles of balancing acceptance with change, validating experience whilst encouraging growth, and building a life worth living resonate across diverse contexts and populations.

The Biosocial Theory

To understand why DBT works and why the particular skills included in this manual are so effective, it is essential to understand the biosocial theory. This theory explains how severe emotional dysregulation develops and, consequently, why a comprehensive treatment approach is necessary.

The biosocial theory proposes that severe emotional dysregulation results from the transaction, the ongoing interaction, between a biological vulnerability to emotional sensitivity and an invalidating social environment. Neither factor alone is sufficient. Instead, it is the combination of these factors, and particularly how they influence each other over time, which creates and maintains significant emotional and behavioural difficulties.

Understanding this theory helps explain why some individuals develop severe problems whilst others, facing similar environments or similar biological predispositions, do not. It also illuminates why effective treatment must address both acceptance and change, why validation is so critical, and why skills training alone is insufficient without the broader therapeutic context that DBT provides.

Biological Vulnerability to Emotional Sensitivity

The biological component of the biosocial theory refers to differences in how the emotional system functions. These are not chosen or caused by the individual; they are constitutional factors, likely influenced by genetics, prenatal environment, early life experiences, and other biological factors. Research has identified specific characteristics that define this biological vulnerability.

High Sensitivity to Emotional Stimuli

Individuals with emotional vulnerability notice and react to emotional stimuli more readily than others. Their emotional radar is highly sensitive. Where someone without this vulnerability might barely notice a slight change in another person's tone of voice or facial expression, someone with high sensitivity will immediately detect it and experience an emotional response.

This heightened sensitivity operates across all emotions. They notice subtle signs of disapproval, rejection, or criticism. They quickly detect when someone is upset or angry. They are attuned to nuances in social situations that others might miss entirely. Whilst this sensitivity can be a strength in some contexts, allowing for empathy and interpersonal attunement, it also means they are more frequently triggered into emotional states.

The sensitivity extends beyond interpersonal situations. Physical sensations, environmental stimuli, even memories or thoughts, can trigger emotional responses more readily. A song associated with a painful memory might provoke intense sadness. Physical discomfort might trigger frustration or anxiety more quickly than it would for others. The threshold for emotional arousal is simply lower.

Intense Emotional Responses

Not only do emotionally sensitive individuals react more readily to stimuli, but their reactions are also more intense. When they experience an emotion, they experience it intensely. Sadness becomes despair. Irritation becomes rage. Concern becomes panic. Interest becomes obsession. The exact trigger that might produce a mild emotional response in one person makes a much more intense response in someone with this vulnerability.

This intensity is biological, not chosen. Brain imaging studies have shown differences in the activation of emotion-related brain regions in individuals with emotional dysregulation. Their amygdala, a structure involved in processing emotional information, shows heightened activation in response to emotional stimuli. Other brain regions involved in emotion regulation show patterns consistent with more intense emotional experience.

The subjective experience of intense emotions is overwhelming. It feels as though the emotion has taken over completely. Physical sensations are intense, heart pounding, stomach churning, and muscles tensing. Cognitive processes are affected, making it difficult to think clearly, access other perspectives, and recall skills or information that might be helpful. Urges to act on the emotion are powerful. When emotions reach this intensity, managing them effectively requires considerable skill and self-awareness.

Slow Return to Baseline

Perhaps the most challenging aspect of emotional vulnerability is that emotions, once triggered, take a long time to subside. Whilst someone without this vulnerability might experience a surge of anger that dissipates within minutes, someone with emotional vulnerability might remain intensely angry for hours or even days. The emotion persists, often interfering with sleep, concentration, relationships, and other activities.

This slow return to baseline means that emotionally vulnerable individuals often do not return to a neutral emotional state between events. Before they have fully recovered from one emotional episode, another trigger occurs, producing another intense emotional response. They may spend much of their time in heightened emotional states, rarely experiencing the calm that others take for granted.

The prolonged nature of emotional episodes also means that individuals have more opportunity to engage in behaviours driven by emotion. When anger lasts for minutes, there may not be time to do much damage. When it lasts hours or days, there are many opportunities to say or do things that harm relationships, damage one's reputation, or create other negative consequences. Learning to manage emotions that last this long requires specific skills for distress tolerance and emotion regulation.

The Invalidating Environment

The environmental component of the biosocial theory refers to experiences, particularly in childhood and adolescence, where the individual's internal experiences, emotions, thoughts, and preferences were consistently invalidated. Invalidation means communicating, either explicitly or implicitly, that someone's internal experience is wrong, inappropriate, or should not exist.

Invalidating environments are not necessarily malicious or intentionally harmful. In fact, many invalidating environments occur in families where parents love their children and are trying their best. The invalidation may stem from the parents' own limitations in understanding or managing emotions, from cultural factors that discourage emotional expression, from family circumstances that make attending to emotions seem like a luxury the family cannot afford, or from a mismatch between the child's temperament and the family's style.

Characteristics of Invalidating Environments

Invalidating environments have several defining features. Emotional responses are treated as invalid, inappropriate, or exaggerated. A child who expresses fear is told, "There's nothing to be afraid of, don't be such a baby."

A teenager who expresses sadness about a friendship ending is told, "That's nothing to cry about, you'll make new friends." An adolescent who is angry about perceived unfairness is told, "You're overreacting, calm down." The message is that the emotion itself is wrong.

Communication of internal experience is discouraged or ignored. When the child tries to express what they are feeling or thinking, the response is dismissive or absent. The parent might change the subject, minimise the concern, or not respond. The child learns that their internal world is not of interest to others and that sharing it leads to dismissal rather than connection.

Preferences and beliefs are not respected. The child is told what they should like, what they should want, and what they should believe. Their own inclinations are overridden.

"You will enjoy this activity, everyone does." "You don't really feel that way, you're just tired." The message is that the child cannot trust their own internal experience to guide them; external authorities are thought to know better what is true for them.

Problems are oversimplified, with solutions presented as easy if only the person would make a bit of effort. The complexity of the person's difficulties is not acknowledged. The emotional component of problems is ignored in favour of a purely practical approach.

"Just do your homework and you'll be fine." "If you don't like your job, get a new one." "If you're sad, go out and do something fun." The suggestion is that the person is failing not because the problem is genuinely complex but because they are not trying hard enough.

Extreme emotional displays are occasionally rewarded, whilst more moderate expressions are often ignored. The environment only responds when the person is in crisis or expressing emotions in dramatic ways. This teaches that extreme expression is necessary to be taken seriously. A child whose moderate distress is ignored learns that they must escalate to get help or attention. This pattern can establish problematic ways of communicating needs that persist into adulthood.

Effects of Invalidation

Growing up in an invalidating environment has profound effects. The person fails to develop the ability to accurately understand and label their own emotional experiences. If your emotions were consistently invalidated, you never learned to trust what you feel. You may experience intense emotions but struggle to identify what they are or what triggered them. This makes emotion regulation exceptionally difficult; how can you manage an emotion if you cannot even name it?

Invalidation teaches that emotional experience is unacceptable. The person learns to judge themselves harshly for having emotions. They may believe that feeling sad, angry, or afraid is a sign of weakness or inadequacy. They engage in secondary emotions, feeling ashamed of their fear, angry at themselves for being sad. These secondary emotions exacerbate the difficulty of the primary emotion, making an already challenging situation even more difficult.

The person does not learn how to effectively regulate their emotions. In validating environments, children learn emotion regulation from caregivers who model effective strategies, teach them skills, and help them practice these skills. In invalidating environments, these opportunities are absent. The child is left to figure out emotion regulation on their own, often developing ineffective strategies such as suppression, avoidance, or escalation.

Invalidation also affects expectations in relationships. The person comes to expect that expressing emotions will lead to dismissal or criticism. They may hide their feelings from others, appearing fine on the surface whilst struggling intensely within. Or they may oscillate between suppression and explosive expression, never finding a middle ground of healthy emotional communication.

The Transactional Model

The power of the biosocial theory lies not in either factor alone but in how they interact. This interaction is described as transactional because each factor influences the other in an ongoing cycle, creating and maintaining emotional dysregulation over time.

Consider a child with high emotional sensitivity in a family that handles emotions in a practical, unemotional manner. The child experiences intense emotions frequently and expresses these emotions, seeking comfort and help. The parents, uncomfortable with such intense displays or believing that emotions should be controlled, respond with invalidation.

"You're making too much of this. Calm down. It's not that big of a deal."

The child, whose emotions are biologically intense, experiences this invalidation as confusing and distressing. They feel what they feel powerfully, yet they are being told it is wrong. This creates doubt about their own experience.

The child may respond by escalating emotional expression, hoping that if they show just how bad they feel, the parents will understand and respond more helpfully. However, this escalation is often met with further invalidation or punishment.

"Stop being so dramatic. Go to your room until you can calm down."

The child is sent away precisely when they most need connection and support.

Meanwhile, the parents, faced with a child whose emotional intensity and duration of upset far exceeds what they consider normal or manageable, feel overwhelmed and inadequate. They may become more rigid in their invalidating responses, believing that the child needs to learn to control emotions better. Or they may begin responding inconsistently, sometimes providing comfort when the child is extremely distressed but ignoring moderate distress, inadvertently reinforcing the child's belief that only extreme emotional expression works.

As the child develops, they fail to learn effective emotion regulation because the environment does not teach it. They learn that emotions are problematic and should be hidden or suppressed, but suppression does not work well given their biological intensity. They may develop impulsive or self-destructive behaviours as ways to manage overwhelming emotional states, behaviours that provide temporary relief but create additional problems.

By adolescence or adulthood, the pattern is well established. The person experiences intense emotions that last a long time. They have few effective skills for managing these emotions. They judge themselves harshly for having emotions at all. Their relationships are unstable, characterised by intense connection followed by conflict or withdrawal. They may engage in impulsive behaviours, substance use, self-harm, or other problematic coping strategies. They feel fundamentally different from others, defective, unable to function as others seem to do naturally.

Critically, neither the biological vulnerability alone nor the invalidating environment alone would produce this outcome. A child with emotional sensitivity who grows up in a validating, emotionally attuned environment learns to regulate their emotions. Parents help them label emotions, teach them skills, provide comfort and guidance, and model effective management of intense feelings. The child develops into an adult who, whilst perhaps more emotionally sensitive than average, has good emotion regulation skills.

Similarly, a child without significant emotional vulnerability growing up in an invalidating environment may develop some difficulties with understanding and expressing emotions, but the intensity and pervasiveness of their struggles would be much less. Their emotions are more manageable to begin with, and they can often regulate them even without much external support or skill teaching.

It is the transaction, the ongoing interaction between biological vulnerability and environmental invalidation, which produces severe emotional dysregulation.

Understanding this is crucial for treatment because it explains why comprehensive intervention is necessary.

Case Examples of Biosocial Development

The following case examples illustrate how the biosocial model plays out in real lives. These are composite examples based on common patterns, designed to illustrate the interaction between biology and the environment across various contexts.

Case Example: Sarah

Sarah was a sensitive child from birth. As an infant, she cried more than her siblings did, was easily startled by noise, and took longer to settle when upset. Her parents, both professionals with practical, problem-solving approaches to life, found her intensity challenging. They had raised two older children successfully with minimal fuss and could not understand why Sarah was so difficult.

When Sarah was upset as a young child, her parents' typical response was to tell her she was fine, to distract her, or to send her to her room until she calmed down.

"Big girls don't cry over little things," They would say.

"Look at your brother, he's not crying. Be like him." Sarah learned that her emotional experiences were wrong, that she should be different.

At school, Sarah's sensitivity meant she was deeply affected by peer conflicts. A friend not sitting with her at lunch would send her into hours of distress. A poor mark on a test would devastate her. Her parents, seeing these responses as disproportionate, responded with frustration.

"It's not the end of the world. You need to develop a thicker skin. Life is full of disappointments." Sarah felt increasingly alienated from her family, convinced that something was fundamentally wrong with her.

As a teenager, Sarah discovered that her parents responded differently when she was in crisis. When she broke down sobbing, unable to function, they became concerned and attentive. When she expressed suicidal thoughts during one challenging period, they took her seriously for the first time. Sarah learned, not consciously but through this pattern of reinforcement, that extreme distress was necessary to be heard.

By late adolescence, Sarah had developed several problems. She experienced emotions intensely and frequently, often feeling overwhelmed. She had difficulty trusting her own reactions, constantly second-guessing whether her feelings were valid. She struggled to maintain friendships because her emotional intensity was often perceived as exhausting by her peers. She had discovered that harming herself provided temporary relief from emotional pain, and this had become a regular coping strategy. She felt hopeless about ever feeling better, convinced that she was fundamentally flawed.

Sarah's story illustrates the biosocial transaction. Her biological sensitivity was present from the start, but the invalidating family environment meant she never learned effective emotion regulation. Her intense emotional responses led to invalidation, which increased her distress and confusion, which led to escalating problematic behaviours, which further convinced her parents she was difficult and needed to learn better control. Each factor perpetuated the other.

Case Example: James

James grew up in a home where emotions were rarely discussed. His father was emotionally distant, focused primarily on work and practical matters. His mother managed household affairs efficiently but showed little emotional warmth. There was no overt abuse or neglect; the family appeared to function smoothly on the surface. However, emotional expression was implicitly discouraged through lack of response rather than explicit criticism.

James was a sensitive boy who noticed things others missed. He picked up on the tension between his parents that they never acknowledged. He felt hurt when excluded from peer groups. He worried intensely about performance at school. However, when he tried to discuss these concerns with his parents, their responses were minimal.

"Everything's fine. Don't worry about it."

James learned that bringing up emotional concerns led nowhere, so he stopped trying to address them.

Without guidance, James had no framework for understanding his intense emotional experiences. He did not learn to label emotions or understand what triggered them accurately. He certainly did not acquire the skills necessary for managing them effectively. Instead, he learned to suppress his emotional expression, presenting a capable façade whilst struggling internally.

This pattern continued through adolescence and into young adulthood. James performed well academically and professionally, appearing successful to outsiders. However, he experienced frequent episodes of intense anxiety, particularly around social situations and performance. He avoided relationships because they felt overwhelming; the emotional intensity was something he had no skills to manage. He turned to alcohol as a way to dampen his anxiety and allow himself to relax, a strategy that worked temporarily but created dependence.

By his late twenties, James was functionally impaired despite his apparent success. He avoided social situations that triggered anxiety. He drank most evenings to manage stress. He felt disconnected from others and from himself, going through the motions without experiencing much genuine emotion except during periods of crisis. He had thoughts of ending his life, not because of acute distress, but because he could not imagine continuing to live this way indefinitely.

James's case illustrates that invalidating environments need not be dramatic or overtly harmful. The absence of emotional attunement and teaching, combined with his biological sensitivity, was sufficient to prevent the development of emotion regulation skills. His adaptive response of suppression and avoidance worked in the short term. Still, it prevented him from learning to manage emotions effectively, ultimately creating a fragile system that relied on avoidance and substances rather than genuine coping skills.

Case Example: Rachel

Rachel's early environment was chaotic. Her mother struggled with untreated mental health difficulties and was often unavailable emotionally. Her father worked multiple jobs to support the family and was rarely home. Rachel, being the eldest child, assumed responsibility for her younger siblings from a young age.

Rachel was an emotionally intense child, but her family circumstances meant her needs often went unmet. When she was distressed, there was frequently no one available to help her. When she tried to express her concerns to her mother, she was often told she was adding to her mother's stress.

"I can't deal with your problems right now; I have enough to worry about."

Rachel learned that her emotions were burdensome to others.

At the same time, Rachel had to become emotionally attuned to her mother's moods to navigate the household safely. She learned to suppress her own feelings to avoid triggering her mother's anger or withdrawal. She became hypervigilant to others' emotional states whilst disconnecting from her own. This split between external attunement and internal disconnection would characterise her relationships for years.

As an adolescent, Rachel's emotional intensity manifested in impulsive behaviours. She engaged in risky sexual behaviour, experimented with drugs, and had volatile friendships characterised by intense connection followed by dramatic falling out. These behaviours served multiple functions: they provided temporary escape from overwhelming emotions, they generated excitement that contrasted with the emptiness she often felt, and they sometimes elicited concern from others in ways that her direct expression of distress never had.

Rachel's case illustrates how a chaotic, neglectful environment interacts with emotional sensitivity. The invalidation was not about being told her emotions were wrong, but about her feelings being irrelevant in a family system overwhelmed with other problems. She developed hypervigilance to others' emotions, combined with alexithymia, a difficulty in identifying and describing her own feelings. Her impulsive behaviours served emotion regulation functions but created additional problems. She had learned that extreme behaviours sometimes elicited the response that moderate distress never did, perpetuating a pattern of crisis-driven functioning.

Case Example: David

David grew up in a family with high expectations and little tolerance for failure: his parents, both high achievers, valued academic and professional success above all else. Emotions were viewed as obstacles to achievement.

"Winners don't make excuses,"

His father would say.

"If you're not happy, work harder and success will make you happy."

David was temperamentally sensitive and perfectionistic. He responded to his parents' expectations by driving himself relentlessly. Any grade less than perfect devastated him. Any criticism triggered intense shame. Any perceived failure felt catastrophic. However, expressing these emotions was met with disappointment from his parents. They saw emotional vulnerability as weakness, something to be overcome through willpower and determination.

David learned to hide his emotional struggles behind a façade of competence. He achieved great success, gaining admission to top universities and securing highly competitive positions. Externally, he appeared to be thriving. Internally, he experienced constant anxiety, profound self-doubt, and frequent depressive episodes. The gap between how he appeared and how he felt created a sense of fraudulence, a certainty that if people knew the truth about him, they would be disappointed.

David developed rigid perfectionism as a coping strategy. If he could just be perfect, perhaps the internal turmoil would cease. However, this strategy was exhausting and ultimately unsustainable. He worked excessive hours, sacrificing relationships and health. He could not tolerate any mistake or shortcoming. When a significant setback occurred in his career, David experienced a severe depressive episode. The coping strategy of perfectionistic achievement had failed, and he had no other skills for managing his emotional pain.

David's case illustrates how invalidation in high-achieving environments creates patterns.

The message was not that emotions were wrong per se, but that they were irrelevant to what mattered, which was achievement. This taught David to disconnect from emotions whilst driving himself relentlessly according to external standards. His biological emotional sensitivity, combined with this invalidating achievement-focused environment, created intense internal distress masked by external success. The eventual crisis occurred when the external scaffolding of achievement could no longer contain the internal emotional reality.

Implications for Treatment

Understanding the biosocial theory has direct implications for how treatment is structured and delivered. If emotional dysregulation results from the transaction between biological vulnerability and invalidating environment, then effective treatment must address both components.

The biological component, the emotional sensitivity, cannot be eliminated. Individuals with this vulnerability will likely always experience emotions more intensely and more frequently than others. Attempting to eradicate emotional experience would be futile and invalidating. However, individuals can learn skills for managing intense emotions effectively. This is where skills training becomes essential. The four modules of DBT—mindfulness, interpersonal effectiveness, emotion regulation, and distress tolerance—provide comprehensive strategies for managing emotional experiences.

Equally important is addressing the legacy of invalidation. Individuals need an environment that validates their experiences whilst teaching them new skills and knowledge. This is why validation is so central to DBT. The therapist validates the person's emotions and experiences as understandable given their history and circumstances, whilst also helping them develop more effective responses. This balance of validation and change directly addresses both sides of the biosocial equation.

The theory also explains why DBT is structured as a comprehensive treatment. Skills alone would be insufficient because the person needs validation and support whilst learning. Individual therapy alone would be inadequate because skills are best learned in a structured teaching format. Both components—the validating therapeutic relationship and systematic skills training—are necessary.

The biosocial theory helps individuals understand their difficulties not as personal failings but as understandable outcomes of the interaction between biology and environment. This understanding can reduce shame and self-blame whilst increasing motivation for change. You are not fundamentally defective; you developed difficulties because of factors largely outside your control. At the same time, you now have the opportunity to acquire skills that were not previously learned, creating a different trajectory for your life.

Understanding the theory also helps explain why recovery is a gradual process. The patterns developed over the years cannot be changed overnight. Learning new skills, practising them until they become automatic, changing long-standing relationship patterns, and creating a different relationship with one's emotions, all of this requires sustained effort over time. The biosocial theory provides a framework for patience and persistence.

The Structure of DBT Treatment

DBT is not simply a collection of skills taught in a classroom or workbook. It is a comprehensive treatment system designed to address severe emotional dysregulation from multiple angles simultaneously. Understanding this structure helps clarify why DBT is effective when other approaches may have fallen short and what to expect if you engage in DBT treatment.

Comprehensive DBT, as initially developed and researched, consists of four modes of treatment, each serving distinct functions whilst working together as an integrated system. These modes are individual therapy, skills training group, phone coaching, and therapist consultation team. Whilst adaptations exist that modify this structure for particular settings or populations, understanding the complete model provides essential context.

Individual Therapy

Individual therapy in DBT typically occurs weekly and focuses on helping you apply DBT skills to your particular life circumstances. Unlike traditional psychotherapy, which might concentrate extensively on understanding past experiences or exploring feelings in depth, DBT individual therapy is highly structured and present-focused.

Each session begins with a review of the diary card. The diary card is a tool you complete daily, tracking emotional experiences, use of skills, urges to engage in problematic behaviours, and whether those behaviours occurred. This systematic tracking serves multiple purposes. It increases awareness of patterns in your emotions and behaviours. It helps identify which situations trigger difficulties. It allows monitoring of progress over time. Most importantly, it ensures that the most serious issues are addressed first.

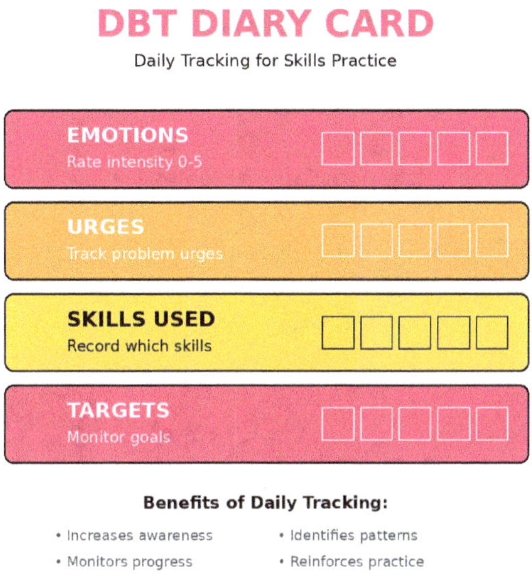

Figure 26: DBT Diary Card

DBT has a clear hierarchy of treatment targets. Behaviours that threaten life come first. If you have engaged in self-harm, had suicidal thoughts, or done anything else life-threatening, this is addressed before anything else. Behaviours that interfere with therapy are addressed second; if you missed sessions, did not complete diary cards, or did not practice skills, these are examined, and problem-solved. Behaviours that interfere with quality of life come third; these might include substance use, disordered eating, relationship conflicts, or anything else that significantly impairs your functioning. Only after addressing these targets does therapy turn to more general life goals.

This hierarchy might seem rigid, but it reflects a fundamental principle: you cannot work on building a satisfying life if you are repeatedly in crisis or at risk. The immediate, serious problems must be stabilised before you can make progress on longer-term goals. Many people initially find this frustrating, wanting to discuss past experiences or relationship concerns when the therapist keeps returning to recent self-harm or substance use. However, this structure is what makes DBT effective for people whose lives have been characterised by repeated crises.

Within each session, after identifying the target behaviour, the therapist conducts a detailed behavioural analysis, often referred to as a chain analysis. This involves examining exactly what happened before, during, and after the target behaviour. What triggered it? What thoughts went through your mind? What emotions did you experience? What physical sensations? What exactly did you do? What were the consequences?

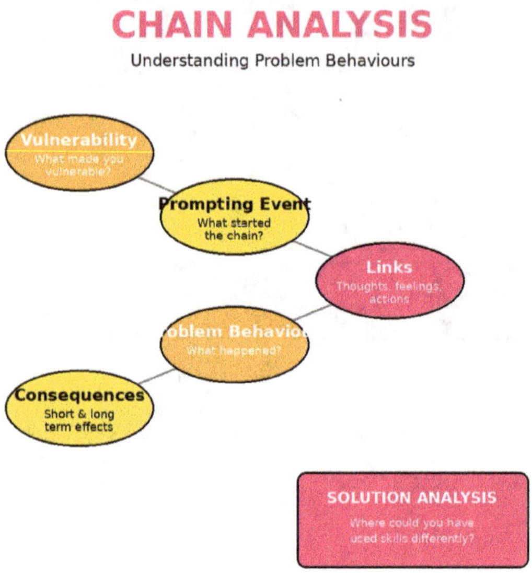

Figure 27: Chain Analysis

The goal of chain analysis is not to assign blame but to understand function. Every behaviour, even problematic ones, serves some purpose. Self-harm might provide relief from overwhelming emotion or communicate distress to others. Substance use might numb painful feelings or facilitate social connection. Therapy dropout may be a way to avoid confronting complex issues or protect against feared failure. Understanding what function, the behaviour serves makes it possible to identify alternative, more effective behaviours that could serve the same function.

Following behavioural analysis, the therapist helps you develop a solution. This typically involves identifying which DBT skills could have been applied at various points in the chain and creating a specific plan for utilising those skills next time a similar situation arises. The therapist might ask you to imagine the problem again, this time using skills, helping you rehearse a different response.

Individual therapy also addresses skill generalisation, helping you apply skills learned in the skills training group to your unique circumstances. Skills are taught in general form in the group, but translating them to your particular relationships, workplace, family, and personal challenges requires individualised attention. Your therapist helps you adapt skills to fit your situation and troubleshoot obstacles to their effective use.

The relationship with your individual therapist is central to DBT. This is a genuine therapeutic relationship characterised by warmth, collaboration, and respect, but clear agreements about treatment goals and expectations also structure it. The dialectical stance, balancing acceptance and change, permeates every interaction. Your therapist validates your experiences and emotions whilst also challenging problematic behaviours and encouraging the use of skills. This balance creates an environment where change becomes possible.

Skills Training Group

Skills training in DBT typically occurs in a group format, usually in weekly sessions lasting 2 to 2.5 hours. The group is psychoeducational rather than process-oriented; the focus is on teaching specific skills systematically rather than on group process or interpersonal dynamics among group members.

The skills training group proceeds through the four modules: Mindfulness, Interpersonal Effectiveness, Emotion Regulation, and Distress Tolerance. Each module is taught over several weeks, with skills within each module covered sequentially. After completing all four modules, the cycle begins again, allowing multiple exposures to each skill. This repetition is intentional; learning skills well enough to use them automatically, particularly in times of high emotion, requires extended practice and multiple teaching exposures.

Each skills training session follows a predictable structure. The session typically begins with a mindfulness exercise, providing practice with these foundational skills and helping group members transition into the learning mindset. The trainers then review homework from the previous week, asking members to share their experiences practising skills. This review serves multiple purposes: it reinforces learning, provides accountability for skills practice, allows members to learn from each other's experiences, and helps trainers identify common obstacles.

The bulk of each session is devoted to teaching new material. Trainers present skills using a variety of methods, including didactic teaching, demonstrations, role-playing, and group discussions. Handouts are provided summarising key points, and worksheets are assigned for homework. The learning is interactive, with trainers regularly checking understanding and encouraging questions.

A key feature of DBT skills training is that it remains focused on skill teaching rather than becoming therapy. If a group member is in crisis or wants to discuss personal problems in depth, the trainers acknowledge the distress and validate the difficulty, whilst redirecting to individual therapy for detailed problem-solving. This boundary keeps the group focused on its primary function of teaching skills systematically. Group members can mention their struggles as they relate to skills practice, but extended discussion of personal issues is reserved for individual therapy.

The group format provides several advantages. It is efficient, allowing multiple people to learn skills simultaneously. It normalises difficulties; members see that others struggle with similar issues, reducing isolation and shame. It provides diverse perspectives; members learn from each other's experiences and creative applications of skills. It can be less intense than individual therapy, providing education in a supportive but structured environment.

However, the group also requires specific commitments. Regular attendance is expected, as each session builds upon previous ones, and missing sessions creates gaps in learning. Completing homework is essential because skills are learned through practice, not just by hearing about them. Respect for other group members is required; whilst detailed personal disclosure is not expected, basic respect and confidentiality are fundamental.

Phone Coaching

Phone coaching, also known as skills coaching, is a distinctive component of DBT that sets it apart from most other treatments. Between sessions, when you encounter situations that require skills, but you are unsure which ones to use or how to apply them, you can contact your individual therapist for brief coaching.

Phone coaching serves a specific purpose: helping you generalise skills from the training environment to real-life situations in the moment. It is not intended for therapy sessions by phone, lengthy emotional processing, or crisis management. Instead, it is a brief consultation about skill use. You might call to ask which skill would be appropriate for a situation you are facing, to get encouragement to use a skill when you are hesitant, or to receive validation after successfully using a skill.

The availability of phone coaching addresses a significant challenge in therapy: what happens between sessions matters more than what happens during them. You live your life between therapy appointments, and it is during this time that skills are needed most. Traditional therapy models leave clients to manage on their own between weekly sessions, hoping they will remember and apply what was discussed. DBT recognises that learning to use skills in vivo, in actual situations as they occur, requires support.

However, phone coaching has clear parameters. It is brief, usually just a few minutes. It focuses on skills, not on extended problem-solving or emotional support. It is used before acting on urges to engage in problematic behaviours, not after. This last point is crucial; if you harm yourself and then call, the therapist might not be available or might keep the call brief, because responding extensively after problematic behaviour would inadvertently reinforce it. The goal is to shape using skills before acting on urges, not to provide comfort after difficulties occur.

Therapists establish specific guidelines for phone coaching, including when calls are appropriate, how long calls typically last, and what happens if the therapist is unavailable. These parameters are discussed at the outset of treatment, so expectations are clear. Most people use phone coaching sparingly, finding that just knowing it is available provides reassurance. Others use it more frequently initially and then taper off as skills become more automatic.

Therapist Consultation Team

The consultation team is the mode of DBT that clients do not directly participate in, but that significantly affects the treatment they receive. DBT therapists meet regularly, usually on a weekly basis, in consultation teams where they support one another, ensure adherence to the DBT model, and address their own challenges in delivering this complex treatment.

Working with individuals who are chronically suicidal, engage in severe self-harm, or show other severe behavioural difficulties is demanding. Therapists can experience burnout, become overly rigid or too lenient in their approach, lose motivation, or develop problematic patterns with clients. The consultation team addresses these therapist difficulties, functioning as a form of therapy for the therapist.

In the consultation team, therapists present challenging cases, receive feedback on their adherence to DBT principles, problem-solve obstacles, and support each other emotionally.

The team helps therapists maintain their dialectical balance, neither becoming purely accepting nor purely change-focused. It helps them troubleshoot difficult clinical situations, identifying creative applications of DBT strategies. It validates the difficulty of the work whilst encouraging continued skill development.

An essential function of the consultation team is maintaining treatment fidelity. DBT is a structured treatment with specific principles and strategies. Without regular consultation, therapists might drift from the model, adding or subtracting elements based on personal preference rather than evidence. The team helps therapists stay true to DBT whilst adapting it appropriately to individual clients.

The consultation team also addresses a common problem in treating severe difficulties: therapists can become personally affected by the intensity of their clients' struggles. They might experience secondary trauma, become excessively worried about clients between sessions, or blur boundaries in attempts to help. The team provides a forum for processing these reactions in healthy ways that protect both therapist and client.

Adapted Models of DBT

Whilst comprehensive DBT includes all four modes, adaptations have been developed for various settings and populations. These adaptations maintain core DBT principles whilst modifying the structure to fit particular contexts or needs.

DBT skills groups are sometimes offered without individual DBT therapy. Individuals may participate in skills training whilst receiving individual therapy from a non-DBT therapist or whilst not in individual therapy at all. This model offers access to valuable skills without requiring a full commitment to DBT. Research suggests that skills training alone can be beneficial, though outcomes are generally better when skills training is combined with DBT individual therapy.

Intensive outpatient programmes sometimes use DBT as their treatment framework, with clients attending multiple group and individual sessions each week. This more intensive format may be suitable for individuals who require more support than standard outpatient treatment offers but do not necessitate hospitalisation.

Inpatient and residential programmes have adapted DBT for their settings. In these environments, where clients are present continuously, multiple opportunities arise for skills teaching and coaching. Staff can prompt skill use throughout the day, provide immediate feedback, and create a therapeutic milieu infused with DBT principles.

Radically Open DBT (RO-DBT) is an adaptation developed for individuals whose difficulties stem from overcontrol rather than under control. These individuals are often rigid, perfectionistic, and emotionally inhibited rather than emotionally dysregulated in the traditional sense. RO-DBT maintains the structure of skills training but teaches different skills focused on increasing openness, flexibility, and social connectedness.

DBT has also been adapted for specific populations, including adolescents, older adults, individuals with developmental disabilities, and people in correctional settings. These adaptations modify language, examples, and specific strategies whilst maintaining core principles.

The Role of Talking Therapies UK

Talking Therapies UK provides comprehensive psychological therapy services, including DBT skills, for individuals experiencing emotional dysregulation and related difficulties, specifically a DBT skills-only program. Talking Therapies UK can give a consultation on whether DBT might be appropriate for you. Talking Therapies UK offers expert, compassionate care delivered by qualified DBT therapists.

Engaging in therapy requires courage. Acknowledging that you need help, committing to regular attendance, and being willing to make changes are significant steps. Talking Therapies UK recognises this and strives to make accessing treatment as straightforward as possible whilst maintaining the rigorous standards that effective DBT requires.

If you are considering DBT or have questions about whether it might be suitable for your circumstances, the clinicians at Talking Therapies UK can provide consultation. They can assess your needs, explain what treatment would involve, and help you make an informed decision about whether to proceed. Information about services and how to access them is available at www.talkingtherapies.co.uk.

The Four Skills Modules: An Overview

DBT teaches four sets of skills, each addressing different aspects of emotional and behavioural regulation. Understanding what each module covers and why these particular skills are included helps you appreciate the comprehensive nature of the treatment. These modules work together synergistically; skills from one module enhance and support skills from others.

Mindfulness Skills: The Foundation

Mindfulness forms the foundation of all other DBT skills. These skills teach you to control your attention, to observe what is happening in the present moment, both within yourself and in your environment, without judgement and without being overwhelmed.

Many people spend little time actually present in the current moment. Instead, they ruminate about the past or worry about the future. They go through daily activities on autopilot, barely noticing what they are doing. They are consumed by judgements about themselves, others, and situations. This lack of presence creates suffering and interferes with effective functioning.

Mindfulness skills teach you to focus your attention intentionally on the present moment. This might sound simple, but maintaining present-moment awareness, particularly when emotions are intense or when situations are complex, requires practice. The skills provide specific strategies for observing thoughts, feelings, and sensations without getting caught up in them, for describing experiences in factual rather than judgemental terms, and for participating fully in activities.

A key concept in mindfulness is Wise Mind, a state that integrates emotional and rational ways of knowing. Many people oscillate between the Emotion Mind, where feelings dictate decisions, and the Reasonable Mind, where emotions are ignored in favour of logic. Wise Mind synthesises both, allowing you to honour your feelings whilst also considering facts and long-term consequences. Learning to access and trust Wise Mind is transformative.

Mindfulness skills are taught first because they underpin all other skills. You cannot effectively regulate emotions if you cannot observe them. You cannot use interpersonal effectiveness skills if you are not present in the interaction. You cannot tolerate distress if you are fighting against the present moment. Mindfulness provides the attentional control necessary for all other skills.

The mindfulness module teaches specific practices that you can incorporate into your daily life, including both formal meditation practices and informal ways of bringing mindfulness to routine activities. Regular practice builds the skill gradually. Initially, maintaining mindful attention for even a few minutes might feel challenging. With practice, mindfulness becomes more natural, a way of being rather than a separate activity.

Interpersonal Effectiveness Skills: Navigating Relationships

Interpersonal effectiveness skills teach you how to manage relationships and interpersonal situations effectively. These skills address three key questions: How do I ask for what I need or say no to requests whilst maintaining the relationship and my self-respect? How do I maintain relationships with people I care about? How do I keep my self-respect in interpersonal situations?

Many people struggle to balance competing priorities in their relationships. They might prioritise getting what they need at the expense of the relationship, becoming demanding or aggressive. Or they might prioritise the relationship so heavily that their own needs go unmet, agreeing to things they do not want or failing to express concerns. Or they might sacrifice self-respect, acting in ways that violate their values to please others or achieve objectives. Interpersonal effectiveness skills teach you to balance these priorities consciously.

The DEAR MAN skill provides a structured approach to asking for what you want or saying no to requests. Each letter represents a specific behaviour: Describe the situation factually, Express feelings and opinions, assert what you want clearly, reinforce by explaining positive consequences, stay Mindful by keeping focus on the objective, appear confident even if you do not feel it, and negotiate if necessary. Using this structure increases the likelihood that requests will be heard and respected.

Figure 11: DEAR MAN - Getting What You Want

GIVE skills focus on maintaining relationships. These involve being Gentle in approach, acting Interested in the other person, validating their perspective, and using an Easy manner. When the priority is maintaining or improving a relationship, perhaps with a family member, close friend, or colleague, GIVE skills guide behaviour towards that goal.

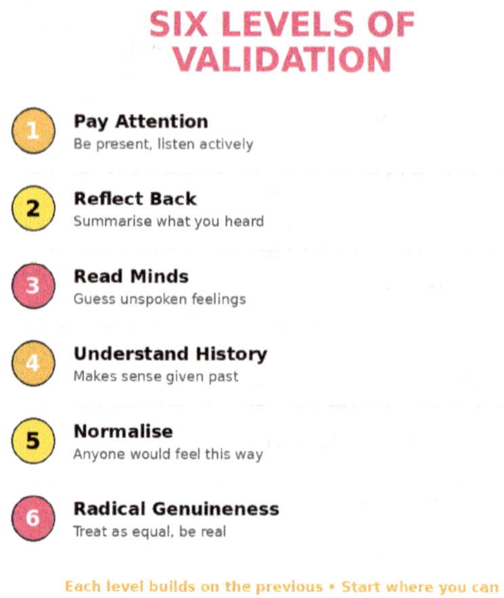

Figure 29: Six Levels of Validation

FAST skills address self-respect. These involve being Fair to yourself and others, not apologising excessively, sticking to your values, and being Truthful. Self-respect is often sacrificed in attempts to please others or avoid conflict, but this creates long-term problems, including resentment, loss of identity, and damaged self-esteem. FAST skills help you maintain self-respect even in difficult interpersonal situations.

Interpersonal effectiveness also encompasses skills for validation and navigating the middle path in relationships. Validation, expressing to others that their experiences and emotions make sense, is fundamental to healthy relationships. Middle path skills address dialectics in relationships, finding balance between extremes.

These skills apply to all types of relationships, including family, friendships, romantic partnerships, and professional work relationships. Learning to express needs clearly, maintain connections with others, and preserve self-respect transforms relationship experiences. Many people find that as their interpersonal effectiveness improves, their relationships become more satisfying and stable, reducing a significant source of distress.

Emotion Regulation Skills: Managing Emotions

Emotion regulation skills address perhaps the core difficulty that brings people to DBT: intense, overwhelming emotions that feel unmanageable. These skills teach you to understand your feelings, reduce emotional suffering, and decrease emotional vulnerability.

The module begins by teaching you about emotions themselves. What are emotions? What functions do they serve? How can you identify and label emotions accurately? Many people struggle with this basic emotional literacy, particularly if they grew up in environments where emotions were not discussed or acknowledged. Understanding emotions as adaptive responses that provide information is the starting point.

A key skill is 'Check the Facts,' which involves examining whether your emotional response aligns with the facts of the situation. Sometimes emotions are entirely appropriate to circumstances; if someone betrays your trust, anger is justified. However, sometimes emotions are based on interpretations rather than facts, or they are more intense than the situation warrants. Checking the facts helps you determine whether the emotion fits and, if not, what needs to change.

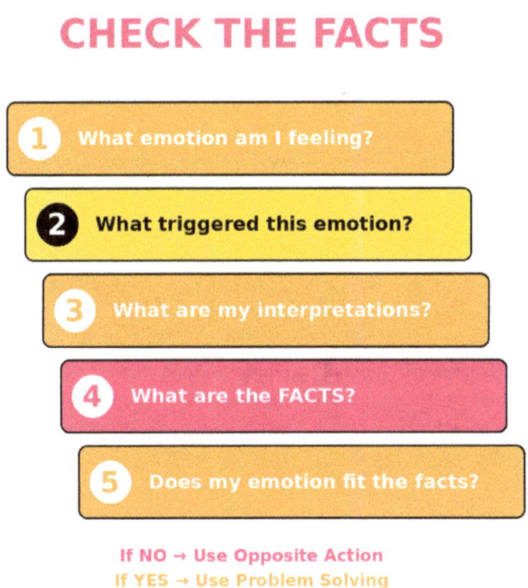

Figure 15: Check the Facts

Opposite Action is one of the most powerful emotion regulation skills. When an emotion does not fit the facts or when acting on the emotion would be ineffective, Opposite Action involves doing the opposite of what the emotion urges you to do. If you feel like isolating when depressed, the opposite action is to reach out and engage. If you feel like attacking someone when angry about something minor, the opposite action is to gently avoid or communicate calmly. Opposite Action, done all the way and repeatedly, changes emotions.

Figure 14: Opposite Action

The module also teaches Problem Solving for situations where emotions do fit the facts. If you are anxious because you have an exam and have not studied, emotion regulation is not the solution; preparing for the exam is. The skill involves identifying the problem clearly and implementing practical solutions.

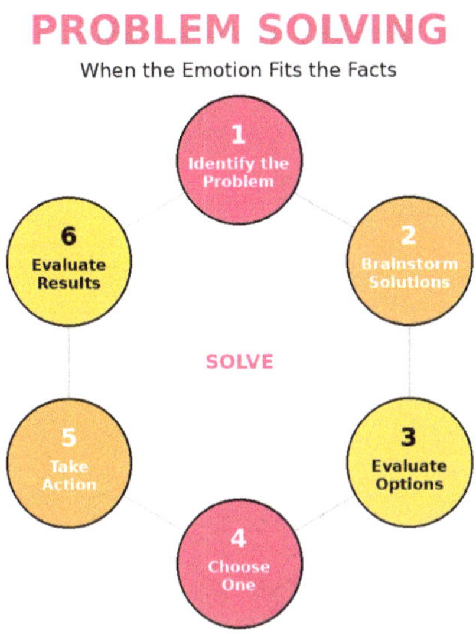

Figure 17: Problem Solving Steps

ABC PLEASE skills address reducing vulnerability to negative emotions. These involve Accumulating positive emotions, building mastery by doing things that create a sense of competence, coping ahead by anticipating difficult situations and planning how to handle them, and treating your body well through balanced eating, avoiding mood-altering substances, getting sufficient sleep, and exercising. When you take care of these basics, you are less vulnerable to emotional overwhelm.

Emotion regulation skills do not eliminate emotions. Rather, they help you experience emotions without being controlled by them, reduce suffering when emotions arise, and prevent emotions from persisting longer than necessary. You learn to surf emotional waves rather than being pulled under by them. For individuals whose emotional intensity has dominated their lives, this increased sense of control is profoundly liberating.

Distress Tolerance Skills: Surviving Crises

Distress tolerance skills are for crisis situations, those moments when emotions feel unbearable and urges to engage in destructive behaviours are intense. These skills do not solve problems or change emotions long-term; rather, they help you survive the immediate crisis without making things worse.

The module is divided into two categories: crisis survival skills and reality acceptance skills. Crisis survival skills are short-term strategies for getting through intense moments. Reality acceptance skills are for accepting painful realities that cannot immediately be changed.

Figure 28: Distress Tolerance Skills Overview

Crisis survival skills include STOP, which involves taking a Step back, taking a breath, Observing the situation, and proceeding mindfully. This simple sequence interrupts impulsive action. TIP skills use biological mechanisms to reduce intense arousal quickly: changing Temperature, engaging in Intense exercise, using Paced breathing, or practising progressive muscle relaxation.

Distraction skills, organised under the acronym ACCEPTS, provide ways to redirect attention away from the crisis temporarily. Activities, contributing to others, Comparisons to worse times or situations, opposite Emotions, pushing away the problem temporarily, different Thoughts, and intense Sensations all can provide brief respite from overwhelming distress. The goal is not avoidance but rather creating a window of time in which intense emotion can diminish to a more manageable level.

Self-soothing skills involve deliberately engaging the five senses in comforting ways. This might include listening to soothing music, looking at calming images, using pleasant scents, tasting favourite foods mindfully, or touching soft textures. These activities work directly on the nervous system to promote calming.

Figure 21: Self-Soothe with Five Senses

IMPROVE the Moment skills provide ways to make a difficult moment better whilst you are in it. These include Imagery of relaxing scenes, finding Meaning in suffering, Prayer or spiritual practice, Relaxation techniques, focusing on One thing at a time, taking a brief Vacation from the situation, and encouraging yourself. Even if the situation itself cannot change immediately, you can change your experience of it.

Reality acceptance skills address longer-term painful realities. Radical Acceptance involves completely accepting reality as it is, without fighting against facts that cannot be changed.

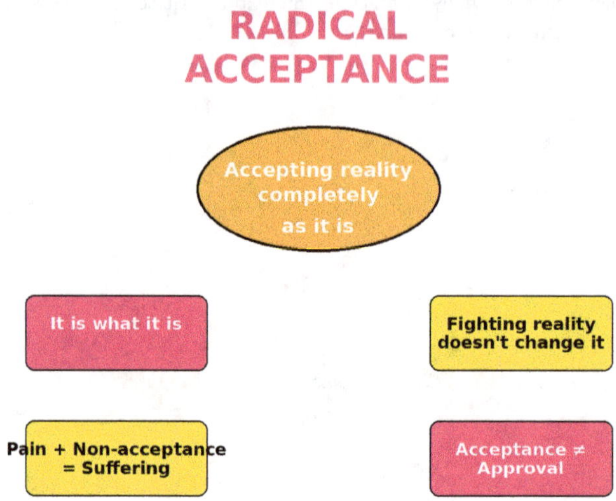

Figure 13: Radical Acceptance

This is distinct from approval; you are not saying the situation is good, only that it is real. Radical Acceptance reduces suffering by eliminating the struggle against unchangeable reality.

Turning the Mind is the skill of repeatedly recommitting to acceptance when you notice you have gone back to fighting reality. Willingness versus Wilfulness addresses the stance you take towards reality: willingness involves participating in reality as it is, whilst wilfulness involves refusing to accept or trying to control what cannot be controlled.

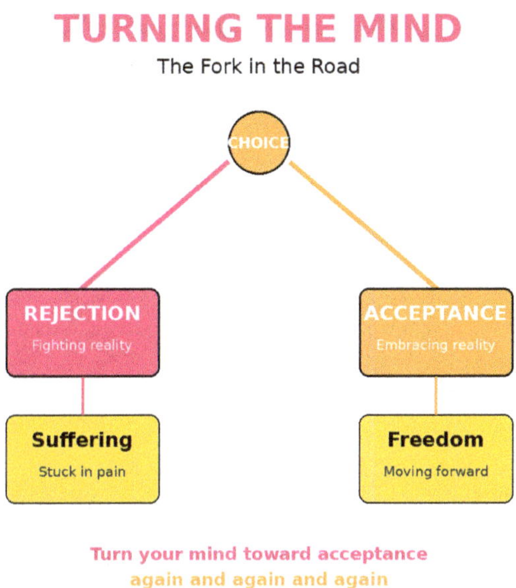

Figure 16: Turning the Mind

Distress tolerance skills acknowledge a fundamental truth: some pain is unavoidable. Life includes loss, disappointment, and suffering. Fighting against this creates additional suffering. Learning to tolerate inevitable pain without making it worse through destructive behaviours is essential for building a life worth living. These skills provide the tools to get through the hardest moments whilst maintaining your commitment to your values and goals.

Principles for Effective Skills Learning

Learning DBT skills is not like learning factual information that you can memorise and recall when needed. These are behavioural skills, more like learning to play a musical instrument or speak a new language than like learning history or mathematics. Becoming skilled requires practice, patience, and a particular approach to the learning process.

Understanding principles for effective skills learning helps you get the most from this manual and from any formal DBT training you undertake.

Skills require practice, not just understanding.

You can understand a skill conceptually without being able to use it when you need it.

Reading about mindfulness does not make you mindful. Knowing that Opposite Action changes emotions does not mean you will remember to use it when you are intensely angry. Skills become effective through repeated practice until they become relatively automatic. Expect to practise each skill many times, in many different situations, before it feels natural.

Start small and build gradually.

When learning a new skill, begin by practising in relatively easy situations. Do not wait for a crisis to try out a skill for the first time. If you are learning distress tolerance skills, practice them when you are mildly uncomfortable, not when you are in the middle of the worst moment of your life. Build competence with simple applications before moving to more challenging situations. This gradual approach builds confidence and competence.

Practise when calm, not just in crisis.

Many people only attempt to use skills when they are in crisis, when emotions are most intense, and thinking is most difficult. This is like trying to learn to swim whilst drowning. Instead, practice skills regularly when you are relatively calm. Practise mindfulness during routine activities. Practise emotion regulation skills when emotions are present but manageable. This regular practice means skills are more accessible when you genuinely need them.

Every attempt is valuable, even imperfect ones.

You will not use skills perfectly, particularly at first. You might remember to use a skill only after the difficult moment has passed. You might use a skill but not execute it quite correctly. You might use skills but still struggle with the situation. All of this is normal and valuable. Each attempt, even unsuccessful ones, provides learning. Trying to use a skill reinforces the behaviour of reaching for skills, making it more likely you will do so next time. Be patient with yourself; skills development takes time.

Adapt skills to your circumstances.

Skills are taught in general form, but you need to adapt them to your particular life. What works as a self-soothing activity for one person might not work for you. The way you apply interpersonal effectiveness skills with your family might differ from how you use them at work. The mindfulness practices that resonate with one person might feel awkward to another. Experiment with variations. Make skills your own rather than rigidly following instructions that do not quite fit.

Use skills in combination.

Whilst individual skills are taught separately for clarity, real-life situations often call for multiple skills used together. You might use mindfulness to observe what you are feeling, emotion regulation to check the facts about the situation, interpersonal effectiveness to communicate with someone involved, and distress tolerance to get through a particularly difficult moment. The skills work synergistically. As you become more skilled, you will naturally begin combining skills in ways that fit the situation.

Expect obstacles and problem-solve them.

You will encounter obstacles to skills practice. You might forget to practise. You might feel too overwhelmed to use skills. You might doubt that skills will help. You might feel self-conscious about using certain skills. These obstacles are normal and predictable. Rather than interpreting them as signs that skills do not work or that you are not capable, treat them as problems to solve. Identify specific obstacles and develop specific solutions. If forgetting is the problem, set reminders. If doubt is the issue, commit to trying skills even when doubtful. Problem-solving obstacles is part of the skills learning process.

Track your practice and progress.

Keeping track of skills practice serves multiple functions. It increases awareness of what skills you are using and when. It provides accountability, making practice more likely. It allows you to see patterns in what works and what does not. It demonstrates progress over time, which can be motivating when change feels slow. Whether you use formal diary cards, a simple notebook, or an app, some form of tracking enhances learning. The act of recording practice reinforces the behaviour.

Be patient with yourself.

Skills development takes time, typically many months of regular practice. Changes might feel gradual and incremental rather than dramatic and immediate. You might experience setbacks where skills that seemed to be working suddenly feel ineffective. This is normal.

Learning complex behavioural skills involves periods of rapid progress, plateaus, and occasional steps backward. Trust the process. Continue practising even when progress feels slow. The cumulative effect of consistent practice is substantial, even if individual practice sessions do not feel transformative.

Remember your 'why.'

Skills practice requires effort, particularly when you are struggling. It is easier to fall back on familiar patterns, even destructive ones, than to try something new. Connecting with your reasons for learning skills helps maintain motivation. Why are you doing this? What kind of life do you want to build? What would be possible if you had better emotion regulation? What relationships could improve? What goals could you pursue? Keeping these larger purposes in mind motivates to persist with practice even when it feels difficult.

Moving Forward

This Introduction has provided a comprehensive context for understanding DBT: its theoretical foundations, evidence base, treatment structure, and the skills you will learn. You now have a framework for making sense of the detailed skills training that comprises the remainder of this manual.

The four modules that follow, Mindfulness, Interpersonal Effectiveness, Emotion Regulation, and Distress Tolerance, will teach you specific skills in depth. Each skill section includes theoretical explanation, step-by-step instructions, multiple examples, case studies, extensive troubleshooting of common problems, practice guidance, and handouts. The level of detail reflects the comprehensive nature of this manual; you should treat it as a complete course in DBT skills rather than a brief overview.

Whether you are learning these skills as part of formal DBT treatment, working through this manual independently, or using it to supplement other therapeutic work, approach it with commitment and patience. The skills work, but only if you practise them. The journey from where you are now to where you want to be requires sustained effort, but it is a journey that thousands of people have successfully made.

You are capable of change. You can learn to manage emotions more effectively. You can build satisfying relationships. You can tolerate distress without destroying what matters to you. You can create a life worth living. The skills in this manual provide the tools. Your practice and persistence give the means. Welcome to your DBT skills journey.

Module 1: Mindfulness Skills

The Foundation of All DBT Skills

Module 1: Introduction to Mindfulness

Mindfulness forms the foundation of all other skills taught in Dialectical Behavioural Therapy. Without the ability to direct attention deliberately, to observe what is happening in the present moment, and to do so without being overwhelmed or immediately reactive, the other skills become significantly more difficult to use. Mindfulness is not merely a pleasant addition to the DBT skills repertoire; it is the bedrock upon which everything else is built.

This chapter provides a comprehensive introduction to mindfulness, clarifying what mindfulness actually is, dispelling common misconceptions, exploring why it matters particularly within the context of DBT, and offering guidance for beginning a mindfulness practice. Understanding mindfulness thoroughly before attempting to practise it increases the likelihood that practice will be sustained and effective.

What Mindfulness Is

Mindfulness, at its most basic, is paying attention to the present moment on purpose and without judgement. This definition, whilst simple, contains several elements worth examining carefully.

Paying attention seems straightforward enough, yet most people pay attention only sporadically to their actual present-moment experience. Instead, attention drifts continuously. You might be washing dishes whilst thinking about a conversation from earlier, planning tomorrow's tasks, worrying about a future event, or replaying a past situation. Your hands are in the water, but your mind is elsewhere. This is the opposite of mindfulness.

The present moment refers to what is happening right now, in this instant. Not what happened five minutes ago, not what might happen later today, but what is occurring in this precise moment. This includes both internal experiences, thoughts, emotions, physical sensations, and external experiences, what you can see, hear, smell, taste, and touch in your environment. Mindfulness anchors attention to this immediate reality rather than allowing it to wander through time.

On purpose indicates that mindfulness is intentional. You deliberately choose to place attention on the present moment rather than arriving there accidentally. This intentionality distinguishes mindfulness from simply being absorbed in an activity. When watching a gripping film, you might be fully present without being mindful, because the film captured your attention rather than you choosing to direct it. Mindfulness involves conscious choice about where attention goes.

Without judgement might be the most challenging aspect of mindfulness. Humans are judgement machines. We constantly evaluate experience as good or bad, right or wrong, pleasant or unpleasant, acceptable or unacceptable. These judgements happen so automatically that we scarcely notice them. Mindfulness asks us to observe experience without adding these evaluative layers, to simply notice what is rather than immediately categorising it.

Consider the difference between these two observations. First: "I notice tightness in my chest and my heart is beating faster." This is mindful observation. Second: "I'm feeling anxious again, this is terrible, I shouldn't feel this way, there's something wrong with me." This is judgemental observation. The first simply notes what is happening. The second adds layers of evaluation, catastrophising, and self-criticism. Mindfulness cultivates the first approach.

Mindfulness is also a way of being, not just a technique. Whilst specific mindfulness practices exist, such as meditation or mindful breathing, mindfulness can be brought to any activity. You can eat mindfully, walk mindfully, listen mindfully, or speak mindfully. Any moment presents an opportunity for mindfulness. It is about how you engage with experience rather than about specific activities.

Another key aspect of mindfulness is acceptance. This does not mean liking everything or resigning yourself to circumstances. Rather, acceptance in mindfulness means acknowledging reality as it is without struggling against unchangeable facts. If you are experiencing an emotion, mindfulness means accepting that the emotion is present rather than fighting against feeling it. You can accept that an emotion is present whilst also choosing how to respond to it.

Mindfulness involves observing rather than controlling. When you try to control experience, you create tension and often paradoxically lose control. When you observe experience with curiosity and acceptance, allowing it to unfold without interference, you often find that difficult experiences become more manageable. This observing stance is central to mindfulness practice.

What Mindfulness Is Not Clarifying what mindfulness is not helps prevent common misunderstandings that can interfere with practice.

Mindfulness Is Not Emptying Your Mind

Many people believe mindfulness means having no thoughts, achieving a blank mental state. This misconception causes considerable frustration. Thoughts arise continuously; this is what minds do. Attempting to stop thinking is like attempting to stop your heart from beating. It is not possible, and trying creates struggle.

Mindfulness does not require stopping thoughts. Instead, it involves observing thoughts without getting caught up in them. You notice thoughts arising and passing without following them down elaborate mental pathways. The goal is not an empty mind but rather a mind that can observe its own contents without being controlled by them.

Mindfulness Is Not Always Relaxing

Another common misconception is that mindfulness is primarily a relaxation technique. Whilst mindfulness practice can certainly be calming, this is not its primary purpose or inevitable result. Sometimes mindfulness practice is quite uncomfortable. When you pay attention to the present moment, you might notice pain you had been avoiding, emotions you had been suppressing, or thoughts you had been escaping.

The value of mindfulness lies not in whether it feels good but in developing the capacity to be present with whatever is happening. This includes being present with discomfort. In fact, learning to tolerate discomfort mindfully is one of mindfulness practice's most valuable outcomes. If you expect mindfulness to always feel pleasant and relaxing, you will be disappointed and may abandon practice precisely when it is most valuable.

Mindfulness Is Not Religious or Spiritual (Though It Can Be)

Mindfulness practices originated in Buddhist contemplative traditions, and many people practice mindfulness as part of their spiritual or religious life. However, mindfulness in DBT is explicitly secular. You do not need to hold any particular religious or spiritual beliefs to practise mindfulness. You do not need to believe in anything beyond the observable benefits of paying attention to present-moment experience.

That said, if you do have spiritual or religious beliefs, mindfulness practice can certainly be integrated with those beliefs. Many people find that mindfulness deepens their spiritual experience. The point is that spirituality is optional; the psychological benefits of mindfulness are available to anyone regardless of belief system.

Mindfulness Is Not Passive Acceptance of Harmful Circumstances

Some people worry that mindfulness, with its emphasis on acceptance and being present with what is, means passively tolerating harmful or unjust situations. This is a serious misunderstanding. Mindfulness involves accepting reality as it is in the present moment, but this does not preclude taking action to change circumstances.

In fact, mindfulness often makes effective action more possible. When you are not fighting against reality, denying what is happening, or being overwhelmed by emotion, you can assess situations more clearly and take wise action. Mindfulness provides the clarity to see what needs to change and the emotional regulation to change it effectively. Acceptance is not resignation; it is the starting point for wise action.

Mindfulness Is Not About Never Thinking About the Past or Future

Mindfulness emphasises present-moment awareness, but this does not mean you should never think about the past or plan for the future. Reflecting on past experiences and planning ahead are valuable human capacities. The issue is not whether you think about past or future but whether you choose to do so or whether it happens automatically and compulsively.

Mindfulness means that when you choose to reflect on the past, you do so deliberately rather than being pulled into rumination. When you plan for the future, you do so consciously rather than being hijacked by worry. The difference is between choosing where your attention goes and having it stolen by automatic mental processes. Mindfulness cultivates choice.

The Importance of Mindfulness in DBT

Mindfulness is taught first in DBT, and mindfulness skills are revisited throughout treatment. This is not arbitrary. Mindfulness is foundational to all other DBT skills for several crucial reasons.

Mindfulness Enables Emotion Awareness

You cannot regulate emotions effectively if you cannot identify what you are feeling. Many people, particularly those who grew up in invalidating environments, have difficulty recognising their emotions accurately. They might feel intensely uncomfortable but cannot name the specific emotion. They might be aware of urges to act, to escape, to attack, to withdraw, without understanding the emotional states driving those urges.

Mindfulness develops the capacity to observe emotional experience. By paying attention to physical sensations, noticing thoughts, and observing urges, you learn to identify emotions as they arise. This awareness is the first step in emotion regulation. If you do not know you are feeling angry until you have already acted on the anger, regulation becomes much more difficult. Mindfulness creates a space between feeling and action, a space in which choice becomes possible.

Moreover, mindfulness helps distinguish between primary emotions, the initial emotional response to a situation, and secondary emotions, your reactions to the primary emotion. You might feel sad (primary emotion) and then feel ashamed of feeling sad (secondary emotion). Mindfulness helps you recognise these layers, which is essential for addressing them effectively.

Mindfulness Creates Space for Choice

Between stimulus and response, there is a space. In that space lies our freedom to choose. Mindfulness expands that space. Without mindfulness, you move from trigger to response almost instantaneously. Someone criticises you, and you immediately snap back. You feel anxious, and you immediately reach for avoidance. The trigger and response are so tightly linked that choice seems impossible.

Mindfulness introduces a pause. You notice the trigger. You observe the emotion arising. You feel the urge to respond in a particular way. This noticing creates distance between what is happening and what you do about it. In that moment of awareness, other options become visible. You can choose a DBT skill. You can choose a different response. You can choose to do nothing and simply observe. The response is no longer automatic; it becomes a choice.

This capacity for choice is transformative. Many people feel that their emotions control them, that they have no option but to act on urges. Mindfulness reveals that whilst you cannot always control what you feel, you can control what you do about it. This realisation is empowering and is central to the entire DBT enterprise of building a life worth living.

Mindfulness Reduces Emotional Suffering

Pain and suffering are not identical. Pain refers to the inevitable discomfort that comes with being human: physical pain, emotional pain, loss, disappointment. Suffering refers to the additional distress we create by fighting against pain, by adding judgements and catastrophic thinking, by trying desperately to avoid or escape inevitable discomfort.

Mindfulness reduces suffering by teaching acceptance of pain. When you experience pain mindfully, observing it without judgement, without resistance, without adding a story about how terrible it is, the pain becomes more bearable. Consider physical pain: if you tense against it, judge it, panic about it, the pain feels worse. If you observe it with curiosity, notice its qualities without judgement, it often becomes more manageable. The same principle applies to emotional pain.

This does not mean that mindfulness eliminates pain; it does not. Difficult emotions still arise, losses still hurt, disappointments still sting. However, by reducing the layers of suffering we add to inevitable pain, mindfulness makes difficult experiences more tolerable. The difference between pain alone and pain plus suffering is substantial.

Mindfulness Supports All Other Skills

Every other DBT skill requires mindfulness. Consider interpersonal effectiveness skills: to use DEAR MAN effectively, you need to be present in the interaction, observing the other person's responses, noticing your own emotional reactions, staying focused on your objective. Without mindfulness, conversations spiral into habitual patterns, and skills cannot be accessed.

Emotion regulation skills require mindfulness to notice what emotion is present, to check facts about whether the emotion fits the situation, to implement opposite action. Distress tolerance skills require mindfulness to recognise that you are in crisis, to notice urges without immediately acting on them, to engage in crisis survival strategies deliberately rather than reacting automatically.

Mindfulness is the attentional control that allows all other skills to function. Without it, skills remain theoretical knowledge that you cannot access when you need them. With mindfulness, skills become available in the moment, precisely when they are most useful.

The Neurobiological Basis of Mindfulness

Understanding the neuroscience of mindfulness helps explain why these practices are effective and motivates sustained practice. Mindfulness is not merely a philosophical stance or psychological technique; it produces measurable changes in brain structure and function.

Neuroplasticity and Practice

The brain is not fixed. Neural connections strengthen with use and weaken with disuse. This capacity for change, called neuroplasticity, continues throughout life. When you repeatedly engage mental activities, the neural networks supporting those activities become stronger and more efficient. This is why physical practice strengthens motor skills; the relevant neural pathways become more robust.

Mindfulness practice exercises specific neural networks. When you deliberately pay attention to the present moment, you are strengthening circuits involved in attention regulation. When you notice when your mind has wandered and bring it back, you are practising cognitive control. When you observe emotions without being overwhelmed, you are developing your capacity for emotion regulation. These are not merely abstract mental states; they are patterns of neural activity that become more accessible with practice.

Research using brain imaging has documented structural changes associated with mindfulness practice. Studies comparing long-term meditators to non-meditators reveal differences in brain regions associated with attention, emotion regulation, and self-awareness. Intervention studies, where people learn mindfulness and researchers scan their brains before and after training, show measurable changes occurring within weeks of regular practice. The brain literally changes in response to mindfulness training.

The Prefrontal Cortex and Emotion Regulation

The prefrontal cortex, particularly regions in the medial and dorsolateral areas, plays crucial roles in emotion regulation, attention control, and decision-making. These are executive functions, higher-order cognitive capacities that allow flexible, goal-directed behaviour. When prefrontal regions function well, you can regulate emotions, control impulses, and make choices aligned with your values. When prefrontal function is compromised, emotional and behavioural dysregulation increases.

Mindfulness practice appears to enhance the function of the prefrontal cortex. Studies have shown increased activation in the prefrontal regions during mindfulness meditation. Structural studies find increased grey matter density in prefrontal areas among experienced meditators. These changes correlate with improvements in emotion regulation and attentional control.

This neurobiological effect helps explain why mindfulness improves emotion regulation. By strengthening prefrontal cortex activity, mindfulness enhances your brain's capacity to modulate emotional responses. The emotional brain, particularly the amygdala, continues to generate emotional reactions; however, the prefrontal cortex becomes more adept at regulating those reactions, enabling measured responses rather than impulsive ones.

The Amygdala and Emotional Reactivity

The amygdala is a small, almond-shaped structure located deep within the brain that plays a central role in processing emotional information, particularly threat-related information.

When the amygdala detects a potential threat, it triggers the fight-or-flight response, preparing the body to deal with danger. This is adaptive when a genuine threat exists, but problematic when the amygdala overreacts to situations that are not truly dangerous.

People with emotional dysregulation often have heightened amygdala reactivity. Their amygdalae respond more intensely to emotional stimuli and recover more slowly. This neurobiological pattern contributes to the emotional sensitivity characteristic of conditions DBT was designed to address.

Remarkably, mindfulness practice appears to affect amygdala function. Studies have shown decreased amygdala activation in response to emotional stimuli following mindfulness training. Long-term meditators show smaller amygdala volume and reduced reactivity compared to non-meditators. These changes correspond to reduced emotional reactivity and improved emotional regulation in daily life.

The mechanism likely involves strengthened connections between the prefrontal cortex and the amygdala. When prefrontal regions are active and strong, they can modulate amygdala reactivity, essentially telling the emotional brain to calm down when threats are not as severe as initially perceived. Mindfulness strengthens this top-down regulation, allowing more measured emotional responses.

The Default Mode Network and Mind-Wandering

When not focused on a specific task, the brain does not rest. Instead, it engages a network of regions called the default mode network. This network is active during mind-wandering, self-referential thinking, rumination, and worry. Whilst some default mode activity is normal and even beneficial, excessive activation is associated with depression, anxiety, and suffering.

Many people spend substantial time caught in default mode activity, ruminating about the past, worrying about the future, or engaging in self-critical thought patterns. This mental wandering often exacerbates suffering, as attention becomes fixated on problems rather than solutions, on fears rather than possibilities.

Mindfulness directly counters default mode activity. When you focus attention on present-moment experience, default mode network activity decreases. Experienced meditators show reduced default mode activity both during meditation and during rest, suggesting that mindfulness practice produces lasting changes in baseline brain function. This reduction in default mode activity corresponds to decreased rumination and worry, contributing to improved mental health.

Implications for Practice

Understanding the neurobiology of mindfulness has several practical implications. First, it reinforces that mindfulness is a genuine skill that develops with practice, not merely a pleasant idea or philosophical concept. The brain changes measurably with mindfulness training, just as muscles change with physical training.

Second, it explains why consistent practice is necessary. Neural changes occur gradually, requiring repeated engagement of particular circuits. Practising mindfulness occasionally produces minimal benefit; regular practice produces substantial change. Just as you cannot get physically fit by exercising once, you cannot develop mindfulness capacity without sustained practice.

Third, it suggests that benefits accumulate over time. The structural changes observed in long-term practitioners take time to develop. Early practice establishes new neural patterns, but substantial reorganisation requires months or years. This knowledge can sustain motivation during periods when benefits feel minimal. Even when you cannot yet feel the changes, your brain is adapting.

Finally, the neuroscience validates effort. If mindfulness were merely sitting quietly, brain changes would not occur. The repeated effort to return attention when it wanders, to observe emotions without being overwhelmed, to notice thoughts without following them, this effort is what drives neural change. The challenge is not an indication that you are doing it wrong; it is the mechanism through which the brain adapts and strengthens.

Common Misconceptions About Mindfulness

Beyond the fundamental misunderstandings already addressed, several other misconceptions commonly arise when people begin mindfulness practice. Addressing these prevents frustration and premature abandonment of practice.

Misconception: Mindfulness Requires Special Equipment or Settings

Some people believe mindfulness requires props, cushions, incense, special clothing, or a dedicated meditation space. Whilst these items can support practice if you find them helpful, they are not necessary. Mindfulness can be practised anywhere, at any time, with nothing except your attention.

You can practise mindfulness whilst washing dishes, walking to work, eating lunch, or sitting in a waiting room. The essential ingredient is intentional attention to present-moment experience, not external circumstances. In fact, practising mindfulness in ordinary settings, without special arrangements, is valuable because it demonstrates that mindfulness is always available regardless of circumstances.

Misconception: You Need Large Amounts of Time

Another barrier people create is believing mindfulness requires extended periods, perhaps thirty minutes or an hour of formal practice daily. Whilst longer practice periods can be beneficial, they are not required for meaningful benefit. Brief practices, even one to five minutes, provide value, particularly when done consistently.

Moreover, informal mindfulness, bringing present-moment awareness to routine activities, requires no additional time at all. You are eating anyway; eat mindfully. You are walking anyway; walk mindfully. You are breathing anyway; notice your breath mindfully. These micro-practices, woven throughout the day, accumulate substantial benefit without requiring dedicated practice time.

The 'I don't have time' excuse rarely withstands examination. Most people can find sixty seconds. If you genuinely cannot find even one minute, your life may need substantial restructuring for reasons beyond mindfulness practice. However, for most people, the time excuse disguises other resistances, perhaps discomfort, doubt, or ambivalence about practice.

Misconception: Mindfulness Is Selfish or Self-Indulgent

Some people, particularly those who habitually prioritise others' needs over their own, worry that taking time for mindfulness practice is selfish. They feel guilty spending time on their own wellbeing when there are so many other demands and responsibilities.

This misconception rests on a false dichotomy between caring for yourself and caring for others. Your capacity to show up effectively for others depends on your own wellbeing. When you are chronically dysregulated, reactive, and overwhelmed, your ability to contribute meaningfully to others' lives diminishes. Mindfulness practice that enhances your emotion regulation and presence ultimately benefits everyone around you.

Moreover, modelling self-care teaches important lessons to others, particularly children. When you demonstrate that attending to your own wellbeing is valuable and necessary, you give others permission to do the same. This is not selfish; it is wise stewardship of your personal resources.

Misconception: You Should Be Good at Mindfulness Quickly

People sometimes expect rapid mastery, believing they should be able to maintain sustained attention, experience deep calm, or achieve profound insights within their first few practice sessions. When this does not occur, they conclude they are not good at mindfulness or that it does not work for them.

Mindfulness is a skill that develops gradually. Early practice is often frustrating. Your mind wanders constantly. You might feel restless, bored, or uncomfortable. This does not mean you are bad at mindfulness; it means you are actually practising. The wandering mind is what you notice and work with, not an indication of failure.

Expecting quick mastery is like expecting to be good at playing an instrument after a few lessons or to speak a new language fluently after studying briefly. Skills development takes time, and mindfulness is no exception. Patience with yourself during the learning process is essential.

Misconception: Mindfulness Means Never Getting Angry or Upset

Some people believe that if they truly became mindful, they would remain perpetually calm and unruffled regardless of circumstances. They imagine mindfulness produces an emotion-free state where nothing bothers them.

This is not mindfulness; this is emotional suppression or disconnection. Mindfulness does not eliminate emotions. You will still feel angry when treated unfairly, sad when experiencing loss, anxious when facing uncertainty, and joyful when good things occur. These emotional responses are part of being human.

What changes with mindfulness are your relationship with emotions. You become less reactive, better able to observe emotions without immediately acting on them, more skilful at choosing responses. Emotions still arise, but you are not controlled by them. You can be angry without attacking, sad without isolating, anxious without avoiding. Mindfulness creates space between feeling and action, not freedom from feeling.

The Benefits of Regular Mindfulness Practice

Understanding the benefits of mindfulness practice motivates sustained engagement.

Research has documented numerous positive outcomes associated with regular mindfulness practice, spanning psychological, physical, interpersonal, and neurobiological domains.

Psychological Benefits

The psychological benefits of mindfulness are substantial and well-documented. Regular practice is associated with reduced symptoms of depression and anxiety. This occurs through multiple mechanisms, including decreased rumination, improved emotion regulation, and reduced identification with negative thoughts.

Emotional regulation improves significantly with mindfulness practice. You become better at identifying emotions as they arise, at tolerating uncomfortable emotions without immediately acting to escape them, and at modulating emotional intensity. This does not mean emotions become less intense overall, though some people experience this, but rather that your capacity to manage intense emotions increases. You develop confidence that you can handle emotional experiences without being destroyed by them.

Attention and concentration improve with regular mindfulness practice. The ability to sustain focus on chosen targets, to notice when attention has wandered, and to redirect attention strengthens. This enhanced attention control benefits virtually every area of life, from work performance to interpersonal interactions to enjoying leisure activities more fully.

Self-awareness deepens through mindfulness. You develop a clearer understanding of your patterns, triggers, habitual reactions, values, and needs. This enhanced self-knowledge allows more intentional, values-aligned living. When you understand yourself better, you can make choices that genuinely fit who you are rather than automatically following scripts learned long ago.

Cognitive flexibility, the capacity to shift perspective and adapt thinking to changing circumstances, increases with mindfulness practice. Rather than being rigidly attached to viewpoints or ways of doing things, you develop ability to consider alternatives, to see situations from multiple angles, to adjust approaches when needed. This flexibility is associated with better problem-solving and more satisfying relationships.

Many people report increased overall life satisfaction with regular mindfulness practice. This likely results from the combination of benefits already mentioned, improved emotion regulation, better relationships, enhanced self-awareness, plus an increased capacity to appreciate positive experiences when they occur. Mindfulness helps you notice and savour good moments rather than rushing past them toward the next thing.

Physical Health Benefits

Whilst mindfulness is often pursued for psychological reasons, physical health benefits also occur. Regular mindfulness practice is associated with improved immune function, with studies showing enhanced antibody response to vaccines and better resistance to illness among regular practitioners.

Chronic pain can become more manageable through mindfulness. This does not mean pain disappears, but the relationship with pain changes. Rather than fighting against pain, creating tension and suffering, mindfulness allows observing pain without adding layers of distress. Many people with chronic pain conditions find that mindfulness substantially improves quality of life even when pain levels remain unchanged.

Cardiovascular health may benefit from mindfulness practice. Studies show reductions in blood pressure among regular practitioners, decreased inflammation markers, and improved heart rate variability—a key indicator of cardiovascular health. These effects likely result from both direct stress reduction and indirect impact through improved health behaviours.

Sleep often improves with regular mindfulness practice. The enhanced ability to observe racing thoughts without getting caught up in them, combined with better emotion regulation and reduced rumination, allows more restful sleep for many people. Mindfulness offers tools for managing the anxious thoughts and worries that often disrupt sleep.

Interpersonal Benefits

Mindfulness enhances relationship quality in multiple ways. Being more present during interactions means you hear what others are saying rather than planning your response or thinking about other matters. Others feel this presence and deepens connection.

Emotional reactivity in relationships tends to decrease with mindfulness practice. Rather than immediately snapping back when someone says something hurtful, you notice your reaction arising and can choose your response. This reduced reactivity prevents escalation of conflicts and allows more constructive communication.

Empathy, the capacity to understand others' experiences and emotions, appears to increase with mindfulness practice. As you become more aware of your own internal experience, you become better at recognising others' experiences as well. This enhanced empathy fosters more satisfying and connected relationships.

Communication improves when you are mindful. You choose words more carefully, notice the impact of your communication on others, and adjust accordingly. You listen more effectively rather than waiting for your turn to speak. These improvements make interactions more productive and satisfying for everyone involved.

Workplace and Academic Benefits

In work and academic settings, mindfulness practice is associated with numerous positive outcomes. Performance improves as attention and concentration strengthen. You make fewer careless errors, process information more efficiently, and maintain focus on tasks for longer periods.

Stress management improves significantly, which is particularly valuable in high-pressure work environments. Rather than becoming overwhelmed by demands, mindfulness allows you to approach challenges more calmly, prioritise effectively, and maintain perspective. Burnout rates decrease among people who practice mindfulness regularly.

Creativity may be enhanced through mindfulness. By quieting the critical internal voice and allowing present-moment awareness, you create space for creative insights to emerge. Many people report that solutions to problems appear during or after mindfulness practice, seemingly arising from nowhere but actually resulting from the mind's capacity to work on the issues in the background when not being forced.

Decision-making improves as mindfulness develops. You become better at recognising when emotions are unduly influencing choices, at considering multiple perspectives, and at choosing options aligned with long-term values rather than short-term urges. These improved decision-making capacities benefit all areas of life but are particularly valuable in professional contexts.

Cumulative and Long-Term Benefits

Many benefits of mindfulness practice are cumulative, building over time with sustained practice. Initial benefits might be subtle, perhaps slightly improved sleep or moments of greater calm. As practice continues, benefits become more pronounced and pervasive. Long-term practitioners often describe fundamental shifts in how they experience life, including greater overall peace, less identification with thoughts and emotions, and more consistent access to a wise perspective.

Importantly, benefits do not require perfect practice. Even irregular practice provides value, though consistent practice yields greater benefits. Starting and stopping practice does not eliminate gains; you can always begin again. This is crucial to remember during periods when practice lapses, which happens to virtually everyone. Rather than abandoning mindfulness entirely when you miss days or weeks, restart practice.

Research on long-term practitioners, people who have practised mindfulness for years or decades, reveals substantial benefits. These individuals show remarkable emotional resilience, stable wellbeing across changing circumstances, and often report living with greater meaning and satisfaction. Whilst most people will not become long-term intensive practitioners, these findings suggest that mindfulness is a practice worth sustaining throughout life, continuing to offer benefits the longer you engage with it.

Beginning Your Mindfulness Journey

Starting a mindfulness practice can feel daunting, particularly if you are new to deliberately working with attention and awareness. The following guidance provides a foundation for beginning practice in ways that promote sustainability and prevent common pitfalls.

Start Where You Are

You do not need to be calm to begin mindfulness practice. You do not need to have your life sorted out. You do not need to feel particularly motivated. You simply need to be willing to try. Whatever your current state, stressed, depressed, anxious, scattered, angry, this is where practice begins.

People sometimes believe they need to achieve certain conditions before starting mindfulness, perhaps resolving current crises or feeling more stable. This is backwards. Mindfulness is not a reward for having your life together; it is a tool for building the capacity to handle whatever life brings. Start where you are, because where you are is the only place you can start.

Your first practice sessions might be quite uncomfortable. Your mind might race with thoughts. You might feel restless, bored, or irritated. You might notice how much pain you carry that you usually distract yourself from. This discomfort does not mean you are doing it wrong; it means you are actually doing it. Mindfulness brings you face-to-face with your experience, which is sometimes uncomfortable. This is the practice.

Set Realistic Expectations. Mindfulness is a skill that develops gradually through repeated practice. Do not expect immediate transformation. Some people experience noticeable shifts quickly, whilst others practice for weeks or months before recognising clear benefits. Both patterns are normal. Your timeline is your own.

Set intentions for practice rather than goals. An intention might be.

"I will practise mindfulness for five minutes each morning." or "I will bring mindful awareness to one routine activity daily." These are process-focused and within your control. A goal like "I will become calm and peaceful" is outcome-focused and not entirely under your control. Intentions keep you grounded in what you can actually do, which is practice, rather than what you hope will result, which is not guaranteed.

Expect your mind to wander. This is not failure; this is what minds do. The practice is not preventing mind-wandering, but noticing when it has occurred and gently returning attention. Each time you notice wandering and return, you are strengthening attention control. The wandering itself is not the problem; staying lost in wandering without noticing is the problem mindfulness addresses.

Create Supportive Conditions Whilst mindfulness does not require special equipment or settings, certain conditions support practice, particularly when starting. Finding a relatively quiet location where you will not be interrupted helps. This might be a corner of a room, a spot in a park, anywhere you can be relatively undisturbed for a few minutes.

Choose a time when you are not exhausted. Practising mindfulness when you are so tired you can barely keep your eyes open often results in falling asleep rather than developing awareness. Morning practice, after you have woken sufficiently but before the day's demands begin, works well for many people. Others prefer evening practice. Experiment to find what fits your life.

Start with brief practices. Five minutes is sufficient initially. One minute is better than nothing. Brief practices are easier to fit into busy schedules, feel less daunting, and allow you to establish the habit before attempting longer sessions. You can extend duration as practice becomes more comfortable, but there is no requirement to do so. Brief regular practice is more valuable than long irregular practice.

Consider using guided practices initially. Many apps, websites, and recordings offer guided mindfulness practices. Having someone's voice guiding you through the process provides structure and prevents your mind from wandering quite as readily. As you become more comfortable, you can transition to unguided practice if you prefer, though many long-term practitioners continue using guidance.

Develop Consistency

Consistency matters more than duration. Practising five minutes daily produces more benefit than practising thirty minutes occasionally. Establishing a regular time for practice helps; routines reduce the decision fatigue of constantly choosing when to practise.

Linking mindfulness practice to existing habits creates natural reminders. You might practise immediately after brushing your teeth, before your morning coffee, during your lunch break, or before bed. This habit-stacking approach leverages routines you already have rather than requiring you to remember something entirely new.

Track your practice somehow, whether through a simple journal notation, an app, or marking a calendar. Tracking increases accountability and allows you to see patterns. When life becomes busy and practice slips, tracking helps you recognise the lapse and recommit rather than losing touch with practice entirely.

When you miss days, as you will, simply begin again without self-recrimination. Missing practice is not moral failure. Everyone's practice lapses sometimes. The skill is not maintaining perfect consistency from the start but rather beginning again after lapses. Each time you restart practice after it has lapsed, you strengthen your commitment and demonstrate that practice is sustainable even when imperfect.

Work With Obstacles

You will encounter obstacles to practise. Rather than being surprised or discouraged when obstacles arise, expect them and approach them as part of learning. Common obstacles include forgetting to practise, feeling too busy, doubting whether practice is worthwhile, experiencing discomfort during practice, and feeling too distressed to sit still.

For forgetting, use reminders: alarms, notes, linking to established habits. For feeling too busy, start with extremely brief practices that require minimal time. For doubting whether it is worthwhile, commit to practising for a set period, perhaps two weeks or a month, before evaluating. For discomfort during practice, remember that discomfort is not an indication of failure but rather evidence that you are present with actual experience. For feeling too distressed to sit still, try movement-based mindfulness like walking or gentle yoga.

Resistance to practise often increases when practice would be most beneficial. When you find yourself thinking you do not have time, are too tired, or cannot be bothered, pause and examine this resistance. Often, it signals that you are struggling and could use the support that practice provides. Rather than accepting resistance at face value, gently challenge it and practice anyway, even briefly.

Cultivate Patience and Self-Compassion

Approach mindfulness practice with patience toward yourself. You are learning a new skill, and skills take time to develop. Judging yourself harshly for finding practice difficult, for having a wandering mind, or for missing practice days creates additional suffering without improving performance.

Self-compassion, treating yourself with the same kindness you might offer a good friend, supports sustained practice. When practice feels difficult, rather than criticising yourself, acknowledge the difficulty with understanding. When you miss days, rather than berating yourself, gently recommit. When your mind wanders constantly, rather than becoming frustrated, remind yourself that noticing wandering is the practice.

Remember that everyone who has ever practised mindfulness has faced the same challenges. The wandering mind, the resistance, the doubt, these are universal experiences, not personal failures. You are not uniquely bad at mindfulness; you are experiencing what everyone experiences when learning this skill. This normalisation can reduce the sense of isolation and inadequacy that sometimes accompanies early practice.

Seek Support When Helpful

Whilst mindfulness can certainly be practised independently using this manual, support can be valuable, particularly when starting. If you are engaged in DBT treatment, your skills training group provides structured mindfulness teaching and group support for practice. Your individual therapist can help troubleshoot obstacles to practise and adapt mindfulness to your circumstances.

Mindfulness courses and groups exist in many communities, both in-person and online. Practising with others provides accountability, normalises common struggles, and offers the opportunity to learn from others' experiences. Many people find that group practice supports their individual practice.

Books, apps, and online resources offer additional support. However, beware of overwhelming yourself with too many resources simultaneously. Choose one or two approaches and work with those consistently rather than constantly seeking new methods. Sustained engagement with basic practices produces more benefit than superficial engagement with numerous advanced techniques.

Conclusion

This chapter has provided a comprehensive introduction to mindfulness, clarifying what it is and is not, explaining why it matters within DBT, exploring its neurobiological basis, addressing common misconceptions, outlining benefits, and offering guidance for beginning practice.

Mindfulness is simultaneously simple and profound. At its essence, it is merely paying attention to the present moment without judgement. Yet this simple practice produces far-reaching changes in how you experience life, how you relate to emotions, how you interact with others, and even how your brain functions.

As you move into the following chapters, which teach specific mindfulness skills in detail, remember the foundations established here. Mindfulness is not about achieving particular states but about being present with whatever is. It is not about perfection but about repeatedly returning attention when it wanders. It is not a quick fix but a lifelong practice that offers cumulative benefits.

You are beginning a journey that has been travelled by countless others before you, each finding their own way, encountering their own obstacles, and discovering their own insights. Trust the process. Be patient with yourself. Practice consistently, even imperfectly. The skills taught in the following chapters provide specific techniques, but the foundation is what you carry forward from this introduction: the willingness to be present, to observe without judgement, to work with your mind rather than against it.

Mindfulness is the foundation upon which all other DBT skills rest. As you develop mindfulness capacity, every other skill becomes more accessible and effective. Welcome to your mindfulness practice.

The Three States of Mind

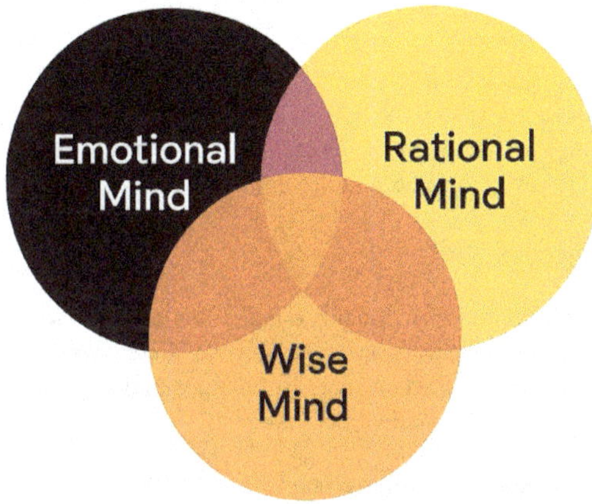

Figure 1: The Three States of Mind

One of the most fundamental and practical concepts in DBT is the identification of three states of mind: Reasonable Mind, Emotion Mind, and Wise Mind. Understanding these states allows you to recognise which mode you are operating in at any given moment and, crucially, to shift between states intentionally rather than being at the mercy of whichever state has seized control.

These are not discrete, separate entities but rather ways of describing how attention, thinking, and decision-making are influenced by different aspects of experience. At times, logical analysis dominates, and emotions are minimised or ignored; this is Reasonable Mind. At other times, emotions overwhelm, and rational thinking becomes inaccessible; this is the Emotion Mind. Ideally, you can access Wise Mind, where both emotion and reason are integrated, allowing decisions that honour feelings whilst considering facts and consequences.

Most people spend time in all three states, moving between them depending on circumstances and internal state. The goal is not to eliminate Reasonable Mind or Emotion

Mind; both have value in appropriate contexts. Rather, the goal is to develop awareness of which state you are in, to recognise when your current state is serving you and when it is not, and to cultivate the capacity to access Wise Mind, particularly for important decisions and challenging situations.

Figure 1: The Three States of Mind

This chapter explores each state in detail, providing theoretical understanding, practical examples, case studies, and guidance for recognising and working with each state. We begin with Reasonable Mind, examining both its strengths and its limitations.

Reasonable Mind /Rational mind

Reasonable Mind is the state where thinking is logical, rational, and focused on facts, data, and objective information. When you are in Reasonable Mind, emotions are minimised or set aside. Decisions are made based on analysis, evidence, and logical reasoning. This is the mind of science, mathematics, planning, and systematic problem-solving.

Characteristics of a Reasonable / Rational Mind

Reasonable Mind has several defining features. First, it is analytical and logical. When in this state, you approach situations by breaking them down into parts, examining evidence, considering cause and effect, and drawing conclusions based on data rather than feelings. Your thinking follows rational principles; if A leads to B, and B leads to C, then A leads to C. This logical processing dominates.

Second, Reasonable Mind is emotionally cool. Feelings are present but muted, placed in the background, treated as largely irrelevant to the task at hand. You might notice emotions peripherally, but they do not influence thinking or decision-making significantly. This emotional distance allows clear-headed analysis uncoloured by feeling states.

Third, Reasonable Mind values objectivity. The focus is on facts, evidence, and what can be demonstrated or proven. Subjective experience, intuition, and gut feelings are discounted as unreliable. What matters is what can be verified, measured, or logically deduced. This commitment to objectivity can be a strength, preventing decisions based purely on transient emotional states.

Fourth, Reasonable Mind is planful and organised. When operating from this state, you create systematic approaches to problems, develop step-by-step plans, consider consequences methodically, and implement solutions in an orderly fashion. This structured approach is valuable for complex challenges requiring careful analysis.

Fifth, language in Reasonable Mind tends to be precise and technical. You might use formal vocabulary, speak in measured tones, and structure communication logically with clear points supported by evidence. The style is more like writing an academic paper than having an intimate conversation.

When Reasonable / Rational Mind Is Helpful

Reasonable Mind serves important functions and is valuable in many contexts. Understanding when this state is helpful allows you to access it deliberately when appropriate.

Problem-Solving and Planning

When facing complex practical problems, Reasonable Mind's analytical capacity is invaluable. Planning a budget, organising a project, troubleshooting technical difficulties, or developing a step-by-step approach to a challenge all benefit from the logical, systematic thinking that Reasonable Mind provides.

Consider financial planning. Determining how much to save, comparing investment options, calculating costs, these tasks require rational analysis. Emotion might tell you to spend money on something appealing right now, whilst Reasonable Mind calculates long-term consequences and suggests saving instead. For financial decisions, particularly complex ones, Reasonable Mind's detached analysis prevents impulsive choices driven purely by immediate emotional states.

Professional and Academic Contexts

Many work and academic tasks require Reasonable Mind. Writing reports, analysing data, conducting research, troubleshooting systems, following procedures, these activities demand logical thinking relatively free from emotional influence. The scientist analysing experimental results, the accountant reviewing financial statements, the programmer debugging code, all rely heavily on Reasonable Mind.

This does not mean emotions should never inform professional decisions; passion for work, concern for clients, and values certainly matter. However, many specific tasks within professional contexts benefit from the cool analysis that Reasonable Mind provides. You would not want your surgeon making decisions during your operation based primarily on how they feel in the moment; you want them accessing Reasonable Mind, applying their knowledge and training systematically.

When Emotions Are Overwhelming

Paradoxically, Reasonable Mind can be valuable precisely when emotions are very intense. When you are overwhelmed emotionally, temporarily shifting to Reasonable Mind can provide relief and allow you to function until emotions become more manageable.

Imagine receiving devastating news. In the immediate aftermath, shifting to Reasonable Mind allows you to handle practical necessities: making necessary phone calls, arranging logistics, and informing others. You set emotions aside temporarily, not because they are unimportant but because managing immediate practical demands requires functioning.

Later, when circumstances allow, you can attend to your emotional response more fully. This use of Reasonable Mind is adaptive when temporary and when you return to emotional processing once circumstances permit. It becomes problematic when extended indefinitely, becoming emotional avoidance rather than temporary coping.

Learning New Information Learning, particularly of technical or complex information, often benefits from Reasonable Mind. When studying scientific concepts, learning a new language, mastering software, or understanding legal principles, the logical, systematic approach of Reasonable Mind helps process and organise information effectively.

Students who can access Reasonable Mind whilst studying often learn more efficiently. They break material into manageable chunks, identify key concepts, make logical connections between ideas, and test understanding systematically. Whilst interest and motivation, which have emotional components, certainly support learning, the actual cognitive processing benefits from Reasonable Mind's analytical clarity.

When Reasonable Mind Is Problematic Despite its value in many contexts, the Reasonable Mind becomes problematic when overused or applied to situations that require emotional awareness and integration. Understanding these limitations is as important as recognising strengths.

In Intimate Relationships A Reasonable Mind struggles in intimate relationships, which require emotional attunement, vulnerability, and genuine connection. When your partner is upset and needs emotional support, responding with logical analysis rather than empathy creates disconnection. Imagine your partner comes home distressed about a conflict with a friend. If you respond from a pure Reasonable Mind, you might say, "Let's analyse the situation logically. What were the specific events? What evidence do you have for your interpretation? What alternative explanations exist?" Whilst this might be intellectually helpful, it misses what your partner actually needs, emotional validation and support. They need you to recognise their feelings, not debate whether those feelings are logically justified.

People who spend excessive time in Reasonable Mind in relationships often find their partners complaining that they are cold, distant, or robotic. Their partners feel unheard and invalidated. Intimacy requires emotional presence, which Reasonable Mind alone cannot provide.

When Making Values-Based Decisions

Decisions involving values, meaning, and personal significance cannot be made by Reasonable Mind alone. These decisions require knowing what matters to you, what you care about deeply, and what kind of person you want to be. This knowledge lives in feelings and intuitions, not in logical analysis.

Consider choosing a career. You might create a spreadsheet listing various options with columns for salary, benefits, prestige, job security, and advancement potential. You might assign numerical ratings to each factor and calculate totals. However, this analysis cannot tell you what kind of work would feel meaningful, where your passions lie, or what would make you excited to start your day. Those answers require accessing something beyond pure logic.

Many people make major life decisions, careers, relationships, where to live, purely from Reasonable Mind, only to find themselves unhappy despite having made the 'logical' choice. The decision looked right on paper but feels wrong in lived experience. This disconnect reveals Reasonable Mind's limitation: it cannot access the emotional and intuitive knowing essential to satisfying life choices.

When Emotions Provide Important Information

Emotions evolved because they serve functions, communicating important information about us and our circumstances. When you override or ignore emotions entirely, staying exclusively in Reasonable Mind, you lose access to this valuable information.

Fear alerts you to potential danger. Anger signals that boundaries have been violated. Sadness indicates loss. Guilt suggests behaviour inconsistent with values. Joy points toward what enhances wellbeing. When you dismiss these signals because they are not 'logical,' you navigate life without crucial guidance.

Someone who stays perpetually in Reasonable Mind might ignore mounting anxiety about a job situation, reasoning that objectively the job is fine, and anxiety is irrational. However, the anxiety might be communicating something important: perhaps the work environment is toxic in ways not immediately obvious, perhaps the work conflicts with core values, perhaps burnout is approaching. Dismissing emotions as illogical prevents attending to their messages.

As Avoidance of Emotional Pain

Some people use Reasonable Mind as a defence against emotional pain. By staying in their heads, analysing and intellectualising, they avoid feeling. This might work temporarily, but emotions do not disappear when ignored; they simply go underground, often emerging in problematic ways.

After a loss, you might throw yourself into work, staying busy and focused on practical tasks, never allowing yourself to grieve. This extended residence in Reasonable Mind postpones healing rather than facilitating it. Eventually, the unprocessed grief will likely surface, perhaps as depression, physical illness, or sudden emotional breakdown.

Reasonable Mind used this way becomes a prison rather than a tool. You remain safe from emotional pain but also cut off from emotional joy, connection, and aliveness. Life becomes flat, manageable, but not meaningful.

Examples of Reasonable Mind Across Contexts: Understanding a Reasonable Mind becomes clearer through concrete examples across various life situations. The following examples illustrate both appropriate and problematic uses of this state.

Example 1: Making a Purchase Decision Alex needs a new car. From Reasonable Mind, Alex researches reliability ratings, compares fuel efficiency across models, calculates total cost of ownership including insurance and maintenance, reads expert reviews, and makes a spreadsheet comparing top options. Alex selects the car that scores highest on practical criteria.

This is Reasonable Mind functioning appropriately. For a major financial decision with clear practical criteria, logical analysis serves well. However, if Alex never considers which car he actually enjoys driving, what feels comfortable, or what suits his lifestyle emotionally, he might end up with a sensible car that he does not enjoy. Complete integration would involve Reasonable Mind's analysis plus attention to emotional responses during test drives.

Example 2: Responding to a Friend's Distress Sarah's friend calls, upset about a relationship ending. From pure Reasonable Mind, Sarah responds: "Let's think about this rationally. The relationship had several incompatibilities that we discussed. Statistically, relationships with those incompatibilities have low success rates.

This outcome was predictable and probably for the best. You'll be fine." This is Reasonable Mind functioning inappropriately. The friend needs emotional support, not statistical analysis. A more helpful response would acknowledge the emotional reality: "I know this hurts so much right now. Breakups are painful even when they make sense logically. What do you need from me?" This honours both the reality that the breakup might be for the best and the emotional pain of loss.

Example 3: At Work

James is a project manager facing a complex deadline challenge. From Reasonable Mind, he breaks the project into tasks, estimates time for each, identifies dependencies, allocates resources, builds in buffers, and creates a detailed timeline. He communicates the plan to his team with clear expectations and checkpoints.

This demonstrates Reasonable Mind's strengths in professional contexts. The analytical, systematic approach is exactly what the situation requires. However, if James never considers team morale, never checks in about how people are feeling about the workload and treats his team purely as resources to be allocated rather than people with emotions and needs, he might encounter problems. Wise leadership integrates Reasonable Mind's planning with awareness of the human dimension.

Example 4: Managing Grief

After her mother's death, Emma throws herself into work. She makes arrangements, handles the estate, responds to condolences, but never actually allows herself to feel the loss. She stays in Reasonable Mind, managing tasks efficiently but avoiding emotional processing.

Initially, this might be adaptive, allowing Emma to handle necessary practical matters. However, six months later, Emma is still avoiding grief, staying busy, refusing to talk about her mother, dismissing her feelings as unproductive. She develops physical symptoms, insomnia, headaches, digestive problems, and finds herself irritable and numb.

This illustrates Reasonable Mind used as prolonged avoidance. Emma needs to move beyond practical management and actually grieve, allowing herself to feel sadness, anger, longing, and whatever else arises. Healing requires emotional processing, which cannot occur whilst staying exclusively in Reasonable Mind.

Example 5: Health Decisions

Maria is diagnosed with a health condition requiring treatment. From Reasonable Mind, she researches treatment options thoroughly, reads medical studies, compares success rates and side effects, consults multiple specialists, and evaluates options systematically. She creates a comparison chart and selects the treatment with the best evidence base.

This is an excellent use of Reasonable Mind. Medical decisions benefit enormously from rational analysis of evidence. However, Maria also needs to consider her emotional responses to different treatments. One option might be statistically superior but require lifestyle changes that Maria finds intolerable. Another might be slightly less effective but fit better with her values and life circumstances. Complete decision-making integrates data analysis with self-knowledge about what matters emotionally.

Case Studies: Reasonable Mind in Practice

The following case studies illustrate how Reasonable Mind operates in real lives, showing both adaptive and problematic patterns.

Case Study 1: Thomas - The Engineer

Thomas, aged thirty-four, is a software engineer who prides himself on logical thinking. At work, his Reasonable Mind serves him exceptionally well. He debugs complex code systematically, breaking problems into component parts and testing hypotheses methodically. His colleagues appreciate his clear, analytical communication and structured approach to projects.

However, Thomas's relationship with his partner, Lisa, is struggling. Lisa frequently complains that Thomas is cold and unresponsive. When she shares concerns or upsets, Thomas immediately shifts into problem-solving mode, offering logical solutions rather than emotional support. Last week, Lisa was distressed about a conflict with her sister. Thomas responded by outlining a five-step plan for resolving the conflict, complete with anticipated outcomes for each approach. Lisa became more upset, saying Thomas did not care about her feelings.

Thomas felt confused and frustrated. He had tried to help by applying rational analysis to the problem. How was this uncaring? From his perspective, emotions were clouding Lisa's judgement, preventing her from seeing obvious solutions. He reasoned that if she would just think logically about the situation, she would feel better.

In therapy, Thomas began recognising his overreliance on Reasonable Mind. He learned that whilst analytical thinking served him well professionally, intimate relationships required emotional presence that Reasonable Mind alone could not provide. Lisa did not need his problems solved; she needed him to understand and validate her emotional experience.

Thomas practised noticing when Lisa shared emotions and consciously choosing to stay emotionally present rather than immediately shifting to analysis. He learned to say things like "That sounds really hurtful."

or "I can see why you're upset."

before offering any practical suggestions. He discovered that often, Lisa did not want solutions at all; she simply wanted to be heard and understood. This shift required Thomas to access something beyond Reasonable Mind; to connect with his own emotional experience so he could resonate with Lisa's.

Over time, Thomas found that balancing Reasonable Mind with emotional awareness improved not just his relationship but his life overall. He felt more connected to himself and others. His default mode remained Reasonable Mind, which continued to serve him well in many contexts, but he developed the flexibility to access emotions when situations called for it.

Case Study 2: Dr. Chen - The Academic

Dr. Chen is a university professor who has spent her adult life in academic environments where Reasonable Mind is highly valued. She excels at research, teaching, and scholarly debate. Her ability to analyse complex theoretical issues, construct logical arguments, and evaluate evidence critically has earned her professional success and respect.

When Dr. Chen's father became terminally ill, she approached the situation as she approached everything: through analysis and planning. She researched his condition thoroughly, evaluated treatment options systematically, organised practical arrangements efficiently, and managed all logistics with characteristic competence.

However, after her father's death, Dr. Chen found herself struggling unexpectedly. She experienced insomnia, difficulty concentrating, and a pervasive sense of emptiness. She had handled everything 'properly,' so why did she feel so bad? She reasoned that grief was a normal process that would resolve with time and tried to push through her discomfort by staying busy with work.

Months later, Dr Chen's difficulties intensified. She developed physical symptoms, migraines and digestive problems. Her work performance declined. She found herself irritable with colleagues and students. When a friend suggested she might be experiencing complicated grief, Dr Chen initially dismissed this as unscientific.

Eventually, Dr Chen sought therapy. Her therapist helped her recognise that she had never actually grieved her father's death. She had managed it, organised it, analysed it, but never allowed herself to feel it. By staying exclusively in Reasonable Mind, she had avoided emotional pain but also prevented healing.

Learning to access her emotions felt foreign and uncomfortable to Dr Chen. She had spent decades privileging rational thought over feeling. However, as she began allowing grief to surface, sitting with sadness rather than immediately analysing or dismissing it, she experienced gradual relief. The physical symptoms began resolving. Her concentration improved. She felt more present in her life.

Dr. Chen came to understand that emotions are not irrational distractions from clear thinking but rather essential aspects of human experience that provide important information. She remained an analytical person; this was core to her identity and profession, but she developed a greater capacity to access and honour emotional experience alongside rational thought.

Case Study 3: Michael - The Manager

Michael manages a team of fifteen people in a fast-paced business environment. His strength lies in strategic thinking and operational efficiency. He excels at analysing market trends, developing business plans, and optimising processes. From Reasonable Mind, Michael has successfully grown his department and consistently meets targets. However, Michael's team has high turnover. Exit interviews reveal a consistent theme: whilst employees respect Michael's intelligence and strategic vision, they feel he does not care about them as people. They describe him as cold, unapproachable, and focused only on results. Several departing employees mention feeling like interchangeable resources rather than valued team members.

Michael's supervisor points this out during his performance review. Michael feels frustrated; he treats everyone fairly, provides clear expectations, and rewards good performance with bonuses. What more do people want? His supervisor suggests leadership coaching to address this pattern.

Through coaching, Michael begins to recognise that whilst his Reasonable Mind approach works well for strategic planning and operational decisions, managing people requires emotional intelligence. His team members are not machines that simply require clear instructions to produce results; they are humans with emotional needs for recognition, appreciation, and connection.

Michael learns to check in with team members about how they are doing, not just about project status. He practises noticing and acknowledging emotions in workplace interactions. When someone seems stressed, rather than immediately problem-solving, he might say, "This project timeline seems overwhelming. How are you holding up?"

He learns to celebrate team successes with genuine enthusiasm rather than immediately moving to the next task. He begins holding regular one-on-one meetings focused on employee development and wellbeing, not just performance metrics.

These changes feel awkward initially. Michael's natural inclination remains analytical and task-focused. However, he notices improvements. Team morale increases. Turnover decreases. Interestingly, productivity improves when people feel valued and supported. Michael discovers that integrating emotional awareness with his analytical strengths makes him a more effective leader overall.

Case Study 4: Rachel - The Medical Student

Rachel is a third-year medical student known for her excellent academic performance. She approaches her studies with meticulous organisation, creates detailed revision schedules, analyses practice questions systematically, and excels in exams. Her ability to master complex information through disciplined study serves her well in medical school's demanding environment.

However, Rachel struggles during clinical placements. Whilst she knows the material perfectly, she finds interacting with actual patients' anxiety-provoking. Patients seem to sense her discomfort and sometimes complain that she seems distant or uncaring. Her supervising physicians note that whilst Rachel's medical knowledge is exceptional, her bedside manner needs development.

Rachel recognises this problem but feels confused about how to address it. She approaches patient interactions the same way she approaches everything: analytically. She takes thorough histories, following the standard format precisely. She performs examinations correctly. She generates appropriate differential diagnoses. Why do patients perceive her as uncaring when she is being professionally thorough?

A mentor helps Rachel understand that effective patient care requires more than technical competence. Patients need to feel heard, understood, and cared for as whole people, not just as collections of symptoms. Rachel's pure Reasonable Mind approach, whilst medically sound, lacks the human connection that is central to healing relationships.

Rachel begins practising presence with patients. Rather than mentally running through her checklist whilst patients speak, she focuses on actually listening. She notices emotions in patients' faces and voices. She learns to acknowledge feelings:

"I can see this diagnosis is frightening for you."

or "It sounds like these symptoms have been really disruptive to your life."

She discovers that taking thirty extra seconds to connect emotionally does not significantly slow her down, but it dramatically improves patient satisfaction and trust.

Rachel continues to rely heavily on Reasonable Mind for diagnosis, treatment planning, and medical decision-making, as she should. However, she develops a greater capacity to temporarily set aside the analytical focus when an emotional connection is needed. This balance makes her not just a knowledgeable doctor, but a good doctor—one who treats the whole person.

Common Problems and Solutions: Working with a Reasonable Mind

Developing balanced use of Reasonable Mind involves recognising common difficulties and having strategies to address them. The following section addresses frequent challenges people encounter.

Problem 1: Difficulty Recognising When You Are in a Reasonable Mind

Many people, particularly those who naturally gravitate toward analytical thinking, do not recognise when they are operating exclusively from Reasonable Mind. They experience this state as simply 'normal thinking' rather than as one particular mode among several.

Solution:

Learn cues that indicate Reasonable Mind. Notice when you are: analysing situations logically, planning systematically, focused on facts and data, feeling emotionally cool or detached, speaking in precise or technical language, creating lists or spreadsheets, evaluating options objectively. These are all signals of Reasonable Mind. Practice labelling "I'm in Reasonable Mind right now."

when you notice these cues. Initially, this labelling might happen in retrospect, but with practice, you can recognise the state as it occurs.

Problem 2: Believing Reasonable Mind Is Always Superior

Our culture often privileges rationality over emotion, leading many people to believe Reasonable Mind is inherently better than other states. They view emotions as weaknesses to be overcome and see their identity as particularly rational people as a source of pride.

Solution:

Recognise that different situations require different states of mind. Reasonable Mind is not superior; it is appropriate for particular contexts. Emotions provide essential information and are necessary for values-based decisions, intimate relationships, and meaning-making.

Challenge the belief that emotions are irrational or signs of weakness. Emotions are adaptive responses that evolved because they serve important functions. A life lived exclusively in Reasonable Mind might be orderly and logical, but lacks richness, connection, and meaning.

Problem 3: Using Reasonable Mind to Avoid Emotional Pain

When emotions are painful, staying in Reasonable Mind provides escape. You intellectualise rather than feel, analyse rather than grieve, plan rather than be present with loss. This avoidance might work temporarily but prevents healing.

Solution:

Notice if you are using Reasonable Mind defensively. Ask yourself:

"Am I analysing this situation to understand it better, or am I analysing to avoid feeling something painful?"

If avoidance is the function, gently challenge yourself to allow some emotional experience. You do not need to dive into overwhelming emotion, but creating small spaces to feel rather than analyse moves you toward healing. Remember that emotions, even painful ones, are time-limited; they peak and then subside. By allowing yourself to feel, you discover emotions are survivable.

Problem 4: Dismissing Others' Emotions as Illogical

People who spend significant time in Reasonable Mind sometimes struggle to understand why others are upset about situations that seem objectively manageable. They respond to others' distress with logical analysis rather than empathy, creating interpersonal conflict.

Solution:

Remember that emotions are valid even when they do not seem logically justified. Someone's emotional response makes sense from their perspective, given their history, temperament, and current state. Rather than evaluating whether their emotions are reasonable, focus on understanding and validating their experience. Practice saying "I can see this is really difficult for you."

before offering any analysis or solutions. Notice the difference in how people respond when their feelings are acknowledged first.

Problem 5: Difficulty Accessing Reasonable Mind When Needed

Whilst some people overuse Reasonable Mind, others struggle to access it when needed. When overwhelmed by emotion, they cannot think clearly or evaluate situations objectively. Reasonable Mind feels unavailable.

Solution:

Recognise that intense emotion interferes with analytical thinking. When very upset, trying to force Reasonable Mind often fails. Instead, use distress tolerance skills first to reduce emotional intensity to a more manageable level. Once somewhat calmer, Reasonable Mind becomes more accessible. You might also engage deliberately in activities that promote Reasonable Mind: working on puzzles, organising physical spaces, balancing your accounts, reading analytical material. These activities can help shift you into Reasonable Mind when you need access to this state.

Problem 6: Making Life Decisions Purely from Reasonable Mind

Major life decisions, careers, relationships, where to live, require integration of multiple factors including values, meaning, and what matters emotionally. Approaching these decisions purely from Reasonable Mind, perhaps by creating pro-con lists or ranking criteria numerically, often leads to choices that look right on paper but feel wrong in lived experience.

Solution:

For major decisions, gather information and analyse options from Reasonable Mind, but also check in with your emotional responses. How do you feel when you imagine choosing each option? What excites you? What creates dread or heaviness? These emotional responses provide important information. The goal is not to choose based purely on emotion but to integrate emotional information with rational analysis. Wise Mind, which we will explore later, is ideal for major life decisions precisely because it synthesises both sources of knowing.

Problem 7: Intellectualising in Therapy Some people approach therapy from a pure Reasonable Mind, analysing their problems intellectually, discussing theories about their difficulties, but never actually accessing the emotions involved. They can explain their childhood experiences brilliantly but never allow themselves to feel the pain those experiences caused.

Solution: Notice when you are intellectualising rather than experiencing. Your therapist might point this out: "I notice you're analysing this situation rather than telling me how it feels." When this occurs, pause and ask yourself what you are feeling. You might need help identifying emotions if you habitually disconnect from them. Remember that insight alone, understanding why you are the way you are, does not produce change. Healing requires emotional processing alongside intellectual understanding.

Practice Exercises: Developing Awareness of Reasonable Mind The following exercises help develop awareness of Reasonable Mind and flexibility in accessing or moving beyond this state as circumstances require.

Exercise 1: Reasonable Mind Log For one week, notice and record times when you are clearly in Reasonable Mind. Note the situation, what indicated you were in this state, whether this state was helpful or problematic in that context, and what the outcome was. This builds awareness of how frequently you access Reasonable Mind and in what contexts.

Example entry: "Saturday morning, planning next week's schedule. I was creating a detailed timetable, blocking out time for specific tasks, very organised and systematic. This was Reasonable Mind, and it was helpful; I felt prepared for the week. Later, my partner wanted to discuss weekend plans, and I launched into logistical analysis instead of asking what he wanted to do. This was Reasonable Mind being problematic; he felt like I wasn't considering his preferences." Exercise 2: Deliberate Practice Choose a problem in your life that requires logical analysis. Set aside dedicated time to work on it from pure Reasonable Mind. Set emotions aside deliberately, focus on facts and data, create systematic plans or analyses. This practice strengthens your ability to access Reasonable Mind when needed.

Then, on a different day, choose an experience that invites emotional engagement, perhaps listening to music you love, spending time in nature, or watching a film that moves you.

Practice staying with the emotional experience rather than analysing or intellectualising. Notice if you drift into Reasonable Mind and gently redirect to emotional experiencing. This builds capacity to move beyond Reasonable Mind.

Exercise 3: Check-In Questions

When making decisions, ask yourself:

"Am I considering only logical factors, or am I also checking in with how I feel about each option? If I'm only using Reasonable Mind, what happens if I also attend to my emotional response? If I'm dismissing emotional information as irrelevant, might I be missing something important?"

These questioning builds awareness of whether you are over-reliant on Reasonable Mind and invite integration of other ways of knowing.

Notes for Therapists and Skills Trainers

When teaching Reasonable Mind, several points merit particular attention.

First, validate that Reasonable Mind has genuine value. Clients who naturally gravitate toward analytical thinking should not feel pathologised for this tendency. The issue is not that Reasonable Mind is problematic but that exclusive reliance on any single state limits flexibility and effectiveness.

Second, be aware that discussing states of mind intellectually can itself become Reasonable Mind. Ensure teaching includes experiential elements: have clients identify times they have been in each state, practice noticing states in real time, and discussing emotional impacts alongside theoretical understanding.

Third, some clients use Reasonable Mind defensively to avoid painful emotions. Gently point this out when observed, whilst validating the understandable human tendency to avoid pain. Help these clients recognise that whilst avoidance works short-term, emotional processing is necessary for healing.

Fourth, other clients struggle with over-emotionality and need explicit permission to access Reasonable Mind. They might believe that rational thinking is cold or means dismissing feelings. Help them understand that temporarily setting emotions aside to think clearly, particularly in crisis, is adaptive, not avoidant, as long as they return to emotional processing when appropriate.

Finally, use examples relevant to clients' lives. The examples in this manual provide starting points, but tailoring illustrations to clients' specific circumstances increases relevance and understanding.

Emotion Mind is the state where feelings dominate thinking and behaviour. When in Emotion Mind, you experience emotions intensely, and these emotions colour perception, drive decisions, and dictate actions. Facts become less relevant than feelings. Logic takes a back seat to emotional urgency. This is the mind of passion, intensity, and feeling-driven action.

Characteristics of Emotion Mind: Emotion Mind has several defining features. First, emotions are intense and consuming. When in this state, feelings seem true and overwhelmingly important. If you feel angry, the situation seems genuinely outrageous and the other person clearly at fault. If you feel anxious, danger seems imminent, and catastrophe is inevitable. The emotion provides a lens through which everything is interpreted.

Second, thinking becomes emotion-congruent. Your thoughts match and reinforce your emotional state. When anxious, you notice threats and imagine worst-case scenarios. When depressed, you recall failures and anticipate continued disappointment. When angry, you remember all past wrongs and interpret ambiguous situations negatively. This selective attention and interpretation strengthen the emotional state in a self-perpetuating cycle.

Third, urges to act on emotions are powerful. Anger creates urges to attack verbally or physically. Fear generates urges to escape or avoid. Sadness produces urges to withdraw and isolate. Love creates urges toward closeness and connection. These action urges feel compelling, as though you must act on them immediately. Resisting urges whilst in Emotion Mind requires considerable effort.

Fourth, facts and logic seem irrelevant or irritating. When someone in Emotion Mind is presented with rational analysis that contradicts their emotional reality, they often become more upset rather than reassured. If you are terrified and someone says "Statistically, the risk is very low," this does not typically reduce fear. The emotional experience feels more real than statistics.

Fifth, communication in the Emotion Mind tends to be expressive and intense. You might speak loudly, use dramatic language, express yourself through tears or yelling, or communicate non-verbally through body language and facial expressions. The priority is expressing how you feel rather than transmitting information clearly.

When Emotion Mind Is Helpful

Despite its challenges, Emotion Mind serves important functions and is valuable in certain contexts. Understanding when emotional intensity is adaptive allows you to honour these experiences rather than judging them as universally problematic.

When Emotions Provide Crucial Information

Emotions communicate important information about us and our circumstances. Fear alerts you to danger. Anger signals boundary violations. Sadness indicates loss. Guilt suggests value violations. These signals are essential for navigating life effectively.

When you are in a situation that triggers intense emotion, that intensity often indicates something important. Perhaps a boundary has been crossed that you need to address. Perhaps danger exists that requires action. Perhaps something matters deeply and deserves attention. Emotion Mind, by amplifying emotional signals, ensures you pay attention to these important messages.

Consider walking alone at night and suddenly feeling intense fear. This fear might be responding to subtle cues you have not consciously noticed, someone following you, an unusual sound, or something wrong about the situation. In this moment, Emotion Mind's fear might literally keep you safe by prompting you to change course, find other people, or call for help. Overriding this fear through pure rational analysis could be dangerous.

In Creative and Artistic Expression

Art, music, writing, and other creative endeavours often flow from the Emotion Mind. The passion and intensity of this state fuel creative expression. When creating art, you often need to access deep feeling, to let emotions guide the process rather than analysing every choice logically.

Musicians playing with genuine feeling rather than technical precision alone create more moving performances. Writers who access emotional truth rather than merely constructing logical plots create resonant stories. Artist's channelling emotion into visual form creates powerful work. Pure Reasonable Mind can produce technically correct but emotionally flat art; Emotion Mind provides the passion that makes art come alive.

When Responding to Injustice

Anger in response to genuine injustice, whether personal or social, can be adaptive and necessary. Throughout history, significant social change has been driven by people who felt angry about injustice and channelled that anger into action. Civil rights movements, labour protections, and environmental activism all emerged from emotional responses to wrongs that rational analysis alone might not have motivated people to address.

If you witness genuine mistreatment and respond with intense anger, this is Emotion Mind being appropriate. The key is channelling that anger effectively rather than acting destructively. Pure Reasonable Mind might analyse injustice objectively but lack the motivational force to drive sustained action for change. Emotion Mind provides the fuel for passionate engagement with important causes.

In Moments of Joy and Connection

Positive emotions, joy, love, excitement, and passion are experienced most fully in the Emotion Mind. When you fall in love, celebrate an achievement, play with children, or experience awe in nature, Emotion Mind allows full immersion in these positive experiences.

Someone who stays perpetually in Reasonable Mind misses the richness of positive emotional experience. They might appreciate achievements intellectually but never feel truly excited. They might care about loved ones but never experience the full depth of connection that comes from emotional openness. Emotion Mind allows the highs of human experience, the moments of transcendence, joy, and love that make life worth living.

When Emotion Mind Is Problematic

Whilst Emotion Mind serves important functions, it becomes problematic when emotions overwhelm reason, when feeling-driven actions create negative consequences, or when emotional intensity prevents effective functioning.

When Emotions Do Not Fit Facts

Sometimes emotions arise that do not match the actual situation. You might feel intensely angry about a minor slight, terrified of a situation that poses no real danger, or devastated by a disappointment that is quite manageable. When emotions are disproportionate to circumstances, acting from the Emotion Mind creates problems.

Imagine feeling furious because a friend cancels plans. In Emotion Mind, you might send an angry text, end the friendship, or say hurtful things you later regret. However, if you stepped back, you might recognise that the cancellation, whilst disappointing, does not justify relationship-ending actions. The emotion is real, but acting on it as though it provides accurate information about the situation creates unnecessary damage.

When Actions Driven by Emotion Create Harm

Acting directly on emotional urges often creates adverse consequences. Anger fuels aggressive communication, which can damage relationships. Anxiety produces avoidance that restricts life. Impulsive joy might lead to overspending or commitments you cannot maintain. Acting from the Emotion Mind without considering consequences frequently creates problems you must address later.

Consider someone who quits their job in anger after a difficult day, posts rude comments on social media whilst upset, makes major purchases impulsively when feeling good, or reaches out to an ex-partner when lonely. These Emotion Mind actions often provide immediate relief or gratification but create longer-term difficulties: financial problems, damaged reputations, complicated relationships, and regretted communications.

When Emotions Prevent Problem-Solving. Some problems require clear thinking to resolve. When overwhelmed by emotion, you cannot think systematically about solutions. Emotion Mind might lead you to see problems as insurmountable when practical solutions exist, or to respond reactively when strategic action is needed.

If you receive a concerning medical test result, panic (Emotion Mind) might prevent you from gathering information, asking clarifying questions, or developing a plan. The emotional response is understandable, but functioning effectively in this situation requires accessing some Reasonable Mind capacity to think clearly about next steps.

In Professional Contexts Requiring Objectivity, Certain professional situations require emotional regulation and objectivity. A surgeon cannot perform effectively while overwhelmed with anxiety. A judge cannot make fair decisions while consumed by anger. A therapist cannot help clients effectively while caught in their own intense emotional reactions.

This does not mean professionals should never have emotions; they absolutely do, but rather that certain professional tasks require sufficient emotional regulation to think clearly and act skilfully. Pure Emotion Mind interferes with professional effectiveness in many contexts.

When Emotions Lead to Values Violations. When in Emotion Mind, you might act in ways that violate your own values. Anger might drive you to say cruel things to people you love.

Fear might cause you to miss important opportunities. Jealousy might lead to controlling behaviours you later recognise as wrong.

Acting from emotion alone, without considering your values and long-term goals, often creates actions you regret.

Someone who values kindness might be verbally aggressive when angry. Someone who values courage might avoid challenges when anxious. Someone who values integrity might lie to avoid uncomfortable emotions. These discrepancies between values and behaviour create guilt and erode self-respect. Emotion Mind, whilst providing authentic feelings, does not automatically align actions with values.

Examples of Emotion Mind Across Contexts The following examples illustrate Emotion Mind in various situations, showing both when it serves us and when it creates difficulties.

Example 1: Relationship Conflict Sophie's partner forgets their anniversary. From the Emotional Mind, Sophie feels devastated and furious. She thinks:
"He doesn't care about me at all. This relationship means nothing to him. I should just leave." She sends an angry text threatening to end the relationship and refuses to speak to him for days.

This is Emotion Mind driving perception and action. The hurt and anger feel absolutely true and overwhelming. However, one forgotten anniversary does not actually mean the relationship is meaningless. Sophie's partner might be stressed, forgetful, or simply made a mistake. Acting purely from the Emotion Mind, Sophie creates relationship damage that might be difficult to repair.

Example 2: Job Interview Marcus has an important job interview. As the day approaches, anxiety builds. From Emotion Mind, Marcus becomes convinced he will fail. He imagines stumbling over questions, appearing incompetent, embarrassing himself. The anxiety feels like truth: he is going to fail, so why even try?

On the morning of the interview, Marcus calls in sick and cancels. The immediate relief from anxiety reinforces that cancelling was the right choice. However, Marcus lost an opportunity that might have been excellent. His emotional mind anxiety predicted a disaster that might never have occurred, and by acting on the emotion, he ensured he would never find out.

Example 3: Creative Expression Aisha is a painter working on a piece about loss. She allows herself to fully feel grief whilst painting, accessing Emotional Mind deliberately. The painting that emerges is raw, powerful, deeply moving. Critics and viewers respond strongly to its emotional authenticity.

This demonstrates Emotion Mind functioning adaptively in creative work. By accessing deep feeling rather than overthinking, Aisha creates art that resonates. Pure Reasonable

Mind might have produced technically correct but emotionally flat work. Emotion Mind provides the passion and authenticity that make the art powerful.

Example 4: Medical Emergency David's child falls and hits her head. She is crying, there is blood, and David feels intense panic. From Emotion Mind, he imagines the worst, catastrophic brain injury, permanent damage. He freezes, unable to think clearly about what to do.

This is the Emotion Mind interfering with effective action. The situation requires calm assessment and appropriate response. The panic is understandable, but acting from panic prevents David from helping effectively. He needs to access enough Reasonable Mind to assess the injury, provide first aid, and get appropriate medical care.

Example 5: Social Activism

Maya witnesses injustice in her community. She feels intense anger about the unfair treatment of vulnerable people. From the Emotion Mind, this anger motivates her to organise, advocate, and push for change. She channels the emotional energy into sustained activism, founding a community organisation that creates real impact.

This shows Emotion Mind providing fuel for important action. Pure Reasonable Mind might analyse injustice objectively but lacks the passionate commitment necessary for sustained advocacy. Maya's anger, whilst intense, drives meaningful positive change when channelled effectively.

Case Studies: Emotion Mind in Practice Case Study 1: Elena - The Impulsive Spender Elena, aged twenty-nine, has significant credit card debt from impulsive purchases made during emotional states. When she feels sad, she shops online; the excitement of purchasing and the anticipation of packages provides temporary relief from her low mood. When angry after conflicts, she treats herself to expensive items to feel better. When anxious, buying things creates a sense of control.

Each purchase made from Emotion Mind feels justified in the moment. Elena thinks, "I deserve this," or "I need this to feel better." The emotional relief is real but temporary. Within days, guilt and stress about debt intensify her distress, often triggering more emotional spending in a destructive cycle.

In therapy, Elena learns to recognise Emotion Mind. When she feels urges to shop, she identifies which emotion is driving the urge. She practises pausing rather than immediately acting, using distress tolerance skills to manage uncomfortable feelings without spending.

She learns that emotions are temporary; if she can tolerate them without acting impulsively, they pass without creating financial consequences.

Elena also explores what functions shopping serves. The temporary mood boost suggests she needs healthier ways to manage emotions. She develops a list of non-spending activities that provide similar relief: walking in nature, calling a friend, and engaging in hobbies. When shopping urges arise, she commits to trying three alternative activities first. Often, by the time she has done these, the urge has passed.

Over time, Elena's impulsive spending decreases substantially. She still occasionally shops from Emotion Mind, but now recognises it happening and can often choose differently. Her debt begins to reduce, which itself improves her mood and reduces the stress that had been triggering emotional spending.

Case Study 2: James - The Angry Driver

James experiences intense road rage. When other drivers cut him off, drive slowly, or make mistakes, James becomes furious. From the Emotion Mind, these incidents feel like personal attacks. He tailgates, honks aggressively, yells, and sometimes makes rude gestures. Several times, he has nearly caused accidents whilst reacting angrily.

James's partner refuses to drive with him anymore, saying his anger is frightening. A near-miss accident where James almost crashed whilst pursuing someone who had cut him off finally motivates him to seek help.

In therapy, James explores what happens when he is driving. He recognises that he is often already stressed when incidents occur, making Emotion Mind more easily triggered. Work stress, rushing, or feeling disrespected creates a baseline of irritability. Minor driving incidents then ignite intense anger.

James learns that his angry thoughts in the Emotion Mind are distorted. Someone cutting him off is not a personal attack; it is a mistake or inattention. The other driver does not even know James. His Emotion Mind interpretation, that people are deliberately disrespecting him, makes situations feel more serious than they are.

James practises noticing early signs of anger whilst driving. When irritation begins building, he deliberately shifts attention to his breath, relaxes his grip on the steering wheel, and reminds himself that arriving a minute later matters less than arriving safely. He challenges his Emotion Mind thoughts: is this driver really attacking me, or did they simply make a mistake?

He also addresses baseline stress. Rather than rushing to work, already stressed, James leaves earlier, reducing pressure. He uses the drive as an opportunity to listen to calming music or podcasts rather than news that increases agitation. These changes reduce how easily Emotion Mind is triggered.

James's road rage does not disappear entirely, but it decreases dramatically. He catches himself earlier in the anger cycle and can often shift to a more balanced state. His partner agrees to drive with him again, noticing real change.

Case Study 3: Priya - The Anxious Avoider

Priya, aged thirty-five, struggles with anxiety that has progressively restricted her life. From the Emotion Mind, situations that trigger anxiety feel genuinely dangerous. Social gatherings feel threatening, public speaking seems impossible, and unfamiliar situations appear risky. Acting on these feelings, Priya avoids more situations.

Initially, Priya declined invitations to large gatherings. Then she stopped attending smaller events. Eventually, she stopped meeting friends one-on-one unless they came to her home. She turned down a promotion that required presentations. She ordered groceries online to avoid the shops. Her world became smaller and smaller, whilst ironically her anxiety grew stronger.

When Priya sought therapy, she felt trapped. The anxiety felt so real, so overwhelming, that she could not imagine facing feared situations. Her Emotional Mind insisted that avoiding was necessary for survival.

Therapy helped Priya understand that whilst anxiety feels like the truth, it often lies. Emotion Mind anxiety predicts catastrophes that rarely occur. Her avoidance, whilst reducing anxiety temporarily, strengthened it long-term by preventing her from discovering that feared situations were manageable.

Priya began exposure gradually, starting with situations that triggered mild anxiety. She practised noticing Emotion Mind thoughts: "Something terrible will happen." "I can't handle this." "Everyone will judge me." She learned to recognise these as Emotion Mind predictions rather than facts, and to test them by facing situations.

Each successful exposure, even when uncomfortable, provided evidence that Emotion Mind was wrong. The catastrophes did not occur. She did cope. People were not judging harshly. Gradually, Priya's confidence in her ability to handle anxiety-provoking situations increased, whilst her actual anxiety decreased.

Recovery was not linear. Priya had setbacks where Emotion Mind reasserted control and avoidance felt necessary. However, she learned to recognise these patterns and could usually redirect back to an approach rather than avoidance. Her world gradually expanded again.

Case Study 4: Marcus - The Passionate Advocate Marcus works in community advocacy. His passion for social justice comes from his Emotional Mind; he feels deeply about inequality and injustice. This emotional intensity fuels his commitment to difficult, often frustrating work. When facing bureaucratic obstacles or resistance, his anger at injustice keeps him persisting rather than giving up. However, Marcus's Emotion Mind also creates problems. In meetings, when he feels others are not taking issues seriously enough, he becomes angry and aggressive. His passionate intensity, whilst demonstrating genuine commitment, sometimes alienates potential allies.

He dismisses more moderate approaches as inadequate, insisting on immediate, dramatic change.

Marcus's supervisor suggests he needs to develop more flexibility. Change requires building coalitions, compromising sometimes, and persuading people rather than attacking them. Pure Emotion Mind, whilst providing fuel, does not provide strategy.

Marcus learns to distinguish between the anger that motivates his work, which remains valuable, and the anger-driven behaviour that undermines his effectiveness. He can feel passionate whilst communicating strategically. He practises noticing when Emotion Mind is driving him to attack rather than persuade and deliberately shifting to a more balanced approach.

Marcus discovers that integrating some Reasonable Mind actually makes him more effective. He can analyse situations strategically, identify realistic next steps, and communicate persuasively, all whilst maintaining the passion that drives his commitment. His anger remains, fuelling persistence, but he gains more control over how that anger is expressed.

Common Problems and Solutions: Working with the Emotion Mind Problem 1: Not Recognising You Are in Emotion Mind When emotions are intense, they feel like reality rather than one way of experiencing reality. You do not recognise that you are in Emotion Mind; you simply believe your thoughts and perceptions are accurate.

Solution: Learn cues that indicate Emotion Mind. Notice when: emotions feel overwhelming and all-consuming, urges to act are very strong, you are thinking in extremes, your thinking matches your emotional state, facts seem irrelevant, you communicate intensely or dramatically. When you notice these cues, pause and label: "I'm in Emotion Mind right now." This simple labelling creates some distance from the emotional state.

Problem 2: Acting Impulsively on Emotions. The emotional mind creates powerful urges to act immediately. You send the angry text, make the impulsive purchase, quit the job, end the relationship, all whilst emotions are intense. Later, when emotions subside, you regret these actions.

Solution: Build in a delay between feeling and acting. Commit to waiting (ten minutes, an hour, overnight) before acting on strong emotions. Use this time to engage in distress tolerance skills. Often, waiting allows emotions to decrease in intensity, making more balanced decisions possible. If, after waiting, you still want to take the action, at least you have chosen rather than reacted automatically.

Problem 3: Believing Emotions Are Facts Emotion Mind treats feelings as truth. If you feel guilty, you must be guilty. If you feel anxious, danger must be present. If you feel unlovable, you must be unlovable. Emotions become evidence rather than experiences.

Solution: Practise distinguishing between emotions and facts. Just because you feel something does not make it true. Anxiety does not mean danger is present. Guilt does not mean you have done wrong. Remind yourself: "Feelings are not facts. My emotion is telling me something, but it might not be accurate." Then check facts separately from checking feelings.

Problem 4: Getting Stuck in the Emotion Mind Sometimes Emotion Mind persists, with intense feelings continuing for extended periods. You want to shift to a more balanced state, but cannot seem to.

Solution: Use the opposite action. If the Emotion Mind urges you toward a particular behaviour, do the opposite. If anger urges attack, practice gentleness. If sadness urges withdrawal, reach out to others. If anxiety urges avoidance, approach feared situations. Opposite action, done completely and repeatedly, shifts emotional states. Also try activities that engage Reasonable Mind: puzzles, organising, planning, and reading analytical material. These can help shift out of pure Emotion Mind.

Problem 5: Judging Yourself for Having Emotions You might judge yourself harshly for being in the Emotion Mind, believing you should be more rational or controlled. This judgement creates shame, which is itself an emotion, creating a cycle of Emotion Mind about being in Emotion Mind.

Solution: Accept that the Emotion Mind is a normal human state. Everyone experiences it. Having intense emotions does not mean you are weak or irrational. The goal is not to eliminate the Emotion Mind but to recognise it and not be controlled by it. Treat yourself with the same compassion you would offer a friend experiencing intense emotions.

Wise Mind Wise Mind is the synthesis of Reasonable Mind and Emotion Mind, integrating both logic and emotion, facts and feelings, reason and intuition. This is the state where you make decisions that honour feelings whilst considering consequences, where you can think clearly whilst remaining emotionally connected, where both head and heart inform your choices. Wise Mind is your inner knowing, the deep sense of what is proper for you.

Everyone has a Wise Mind, though accessing it consistently requires practice. Some people naturally access Wise Mind more readily than others, but it is always available. Learning to recognise and deliberately access this state is one of the most valuable skills you can develop. Wise Mind is not something you achieve and then possess permanently; it is a state you move in and out of, sometimes easily accessible and sometimes requiring deliberate cultivation.

Characteristics of Wise Mind

Wise Mind has several defining features that distinguish it from Reasonable or Emotion Mind. First, it integrates thinking and feeling. You can think clearly whilst remaining emotionally present. Facts and feelings both inform decisions. Neither is ignored or overridden; both contribute to understanding. This integration creates a completeness that pure thinking or pure feeling cannot provide.

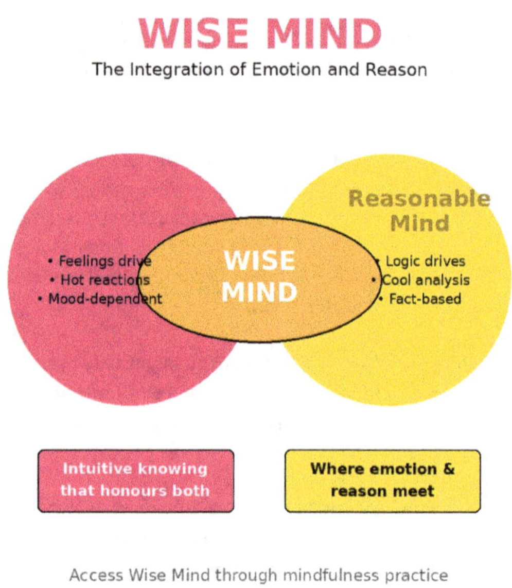

Figure 19: Wise Mind - The Integration of Emotion and Reason

Second, Wise Mind brings a sense of rightness or truth. When in Wise Mind, decisions feel aligned with your deepest values and knowing. There is often a calm certainty, not arrogant certainty, but quiet confidence that you are choosing rightly. This differs from the urgency of Emotion Mind or the cool detachment of Reasonable Mind. Wise Mind decisions feel solid, grounded, and true to who you are.

Third, Wise Mind is balanced and measured. It avoids extremes. Rather than pure logic or pure emotion, it finds a middle ground that honours both. Rather than rigid thinking or chaotic feeling, it holds complexity and nuance. This balance allows flexibility and wisdom rather than dogmatic adherence to either thinking or feeling alone.

Fourth, Wise Mind often has an intuitive quality. You might just know something is right or wrong without being able to explain exactly why. This intuition is not mere feeling; it is the integration of all your knowledge, experience, values, and emotional information, synthesised below conscious awareness. Wise Mind knows things before your conscious mind can articulate them fully. This intuitive knowing deserves respect and attention.

Fifth, Wise Mind is calm even when emotions are present. You might feel deeply whilst maintaining perspective. Strong emotions do not overwhelm thinking, and clear thinking does not disconnect you from feeling. Both coexist, informing each other. This calm quality differs from the emotional intensity of Emotion Mind and the detachment of Reasonable Mind. It is present in equilibrium.

Sixth, Wise Mind considers the bigger picture. Rather than focusing narrowly on immediate circumstances, it holds long-term consequences, multiple perspectives, and a broader context. Decisions from Wise Mind account for how you will feel about choices later, how actions affect others, and whether choices align with the person you want to become.

When Wise Mind Is Most Important

Whilst Wise Mind is valuable in all situations, certain contexts particularly benefit from accessing this integrated state.

Making Important Life Decisions

Major decisions, choosing careers, partners, where to live, whether to have children, demand Wise Mind. These decisions involve both practical considerations that Reasonable Mind can analyse and personal meaning that Emotion Mind provides. Choosing from pure Reasonable Mind might lead to logically sound but emotionally unsatisfying choices.

Choosing from pure Emotion Mind might create immediate satisfaction but long-term regret.

Wise Mind integrates analysis of practical factors with awareness of what matters deeply to you. It considers logical consequences whilst honouring emotional truth. Decisions from Wise Mind feel right both intellectually and emotionally. They align with values, account for realities, and create the foundation for a life worth living.

Navigating Difficult Relationships

Relationships often trigger intense emotions whilst requiring thoughtful responses. Pure Emotion Mind in relationships creates reactivity, with hurt or anger driving destructive communication. Pure Reasonable Mind creates coldness, with logical analysis replacing empathy. Wise Mind allows emotional connection whilst maintaining perspective, enabling authentic yet skilful interaction.

When your partner upsets you, Wise Mind helps you recognise your hurt feelings (Emotion Mind's contribution) whilst considering their perspective and choosing a constructive response (Reasonable Mind's contribution). The synthesis allows you to express feelings honestly whilst preserving the relationship connection. You can be authentic without being destructive.

During Crisis

In crisis, the Emotion Mind threatens to overwhelm, whilst the Reasonable Mind alone might disconnect you from the emotional truth of the situation. Wise Mind provides calm within intensity, allowing you to acknowledge the crisis's seriousness whilst thinking clearly about responses. You can feel afraid whilst assessing actual danger. You can grieve whilst making necessary practical arrangements.

Wise Mind in crisis prevents both emotional overwhelm that creates paralysis and emotional disconnection that creates poor judgement. It allows an appropriate emotional response whilst maintaining function. This balance is precisely what crisis demands.

When Values Are at Stake

Situations involving values, questions of right and wrong, and choices about integrity require Wise Mind. Reasonable Mind alone might calculate advantage without considering ethics. Emotion Mind alone might create righteous anger without strategic thinking. Wise Mind integrates moral knowing with practical wisdom, allowing choices that honour values whilst navigating reality effectively.

When facing ethical dilemmas at work, in relationships, or in community life, Wise Mind provides access to your deepest values whilst considering consequences. You can stand for what matters without naive disregard for practical realities. You can navigate complexity without abandoning principle.

Recognising When You Are in Wise Mind

Learning to recognise Wise Mind when you are in it helps you access this state more deliberately. Several cues indicate Wise Mind's presence.

First, decisions feel right. Not just logical or emotionally satisfying but deeply aligned with who you are. There is a sense of truth, of congruence, of wholeness. This feeling differs from the urgency or intensity of Emotion Mind and the detached calculation of Reasonable Mind.

Second, you can access both thoughts and feelings simultaneously. You are not cut off from emotions, but neither are you overwhelmed by them. You can think whilst feeling, feel whilst thinking. This simultaneity creates completeness.

Third, there is calm even when emotions are strong. Wise Mind does not require the absence of feeling, but it brings perspective that prevents emotional overwhelm. You might feel intensely whilst maintaining awareness that feelings are not the whole truth.

Fourth, you consider multiple perspectives naturally. Rather than being locked into one viewpoint, Wise Mind holds complexity. You can see your perspective and others', short-term and long-term, immediate feelings and future consequences. This capacity for holding multiple truths simultaneously characterises Wise Mind.

Fifth, there is often a physical quality to Wise Mind. Many people describe feeling it in their body, a sense of centredness, groundedness, or presence. Some feel it as warmth in the chest, a settled quality in the belly, or simply as physical calm. Paying attention to physical sensations can help identify Wise Mind.

Examples of Wise Mind Across Contexts

Example 1: Career Decision

James receives two job offers. One pays significantly more but requires long hours and frequent travel, leaving little time for family. The other pays less but offers better work-life balance and aligns with his values around environmental sustainability.

From Reasonable Mind alone, James might calculate: the higher salary allows financial security, career advancement, and greater future options. The logical choice seems clear.

From the Emotion Mind alone, James might focus on his passion for environmental work and his desire to be present with family. The lower-paying job feels right emotionally.

From Wise Mind, James considers both factors. He acknowledges that financial security matters (Reasonable Mind) whilst recognising that money alone does not create satisfaction

(Emotion Mind). He reflects on his deepest values: whilst financial security is important, being present for his children and contributing to work he finds meaningful matter more. The Wise Mind decision honours both practical realities and emotional truth. James chooses the lower-paying job, accepting reduced income in exchange for greater alignment with values. This decision integrates logic and feeling and feels deeply right.

Example 2: Relationship Conflict

Maria's partner repeatedly breaks promises. From Emotion Mind, Maria feels furious and hurt. She wants to end the relationship immediately or to attack verbally, punishing her partner for the pain caused.

From Reasonable Mind, Maria might analyse: the relationship has many strengths, ending it would create practical complications, and perhaps better communication could resolve the problem. The emotional pain seems like an overreaction.

From Wise Mind, Maria acknowledges both her pain (Emotion Mind) and the relationship's strengths (Reasonable Mind). She recognises that whilst the relationship has value, repeated broken promises violate her needs for reliability and trust. Wise Mind tells her that this pattern matters deeply and requires addressing. She chooses to communicate her needs clearly and set a boundary: if promises continue being broken, the relationship cannot continue. This honours both her feelings and the relationship's reality. She neither attacks destructively nor dismisses her legitimate needs.

Problem 3: Thinking Wise Mind Should Always Be Easy to Access

Some days, Wise Mind is readily accessible; other days, it feels impossible to find. This is normal.

Solution: Accept that access to Wise Mind varies. When stressed, tired, or emotionally intense, Wise Mind is harder to reach. Use distress tolerance skills first to reduce intensity, then access Wise Mind. Also, remember that with practice, Wise Mind becomes more accessible over time.

Problem 4: Doubting Whether You Are Actually in Wise Mind

You might second-guess yourself, wondering if this is really Wise Mind or just Emotion Mind or Reasonable Mind disguised.

Solution: If you are integrating both thinking and feeling, considering multiple perspectives, and the decision feels right in a balanced way, you are likely in Wise Mind. Over time, you will develop trust in recognising this state. Also, the proof is often in outcomes: decisions from Wise Mind tend to feel right both immediately and over time.

PRACTICE EXERCISES

Exercise 1: Daily Wise Mind Moments - Each day, identify one moment when you accessed Wise Mind, even briefly. What were you doing? What did it feel like? Building awareness of natural Wise Mind moments helps recognise this state more readily.

Exercise 2: Wise Mind Log - Keep a log of decisions made from Wise Mind. Note the situation, how you accessed Wise Mind, what the decision was, and how it felt. Over time, patterns emerge that help you recognise and trust Wise Mind.

Exercise 3: States of Mind Awareness - Throughout your day, periodically pause and identify which state you are in. Am I in Reasonable Mind? Emotion Mind? Wise Mind? Simply noticing builds awareness and flexibility.

The 'What' Skills of Mindfulness

The 'What' skills answer the question: What do I do when practising mindfulness? These three skills—Observe, Describe, and Participate—form the core actions of mindfulness practice. They are called 'What' skills because they describe what you actually do with your attention. Understanding and practising these skills systematically builds mindfulness capacity.

Figure 9: The What Skills - Observe, Describe, Participate

Whilst the three States of Mind (Reasonable, Emotion, and Wise Mind) describe different states of being, the 'What' skills describe different ways of engaging with experience. You can practise these skills in any state of mind, though they are particularly helpful for accessing Wise Mind and developing present-moment awareness.

Each 'What' skill has particular strengths and applications. Observing develops awareness and reduces reactivity. Describing creates distance from experience and enhances clarity. Participating allows full engagement and connection. Together, these skills create a comprehensive mindfulness practice that enhances well-being across all life domains.

Observe

Observing means paying attention to what is happening in the present moment without reacting to it, describing it, or trying to change it. You simply notice—sensations, thoughts, emotions, sounds, sights, smells—allowing experience to unfold without interference. Observe is the foundational mindfulness skill, the bedrock upon which all other skills rest.

What Observing Is

Observing is pure noticing. When you observe, attention rests on experience itself rather than on thoughts about experience. You watch thoughts arise and pass without following them. You feel emotions without being overwhelmed by them. You notice sensations without immediately reacting. This creates a witnessing stance, a position from which you can see experience unfolding without being entirely caught up in it.

Consider the difference between being caught in anger and observing anger. When caught in anger, you are the anger—fused with it, acting from it automatically. When observing anger, you notice anger as an experience you are having—you can feel the heat in your chest, the tension in your jaw, the thoughts about injustice, but you are not entirely identified with these experiences. You are the observer, not just the anger itself.

Observing requires suspending reaction. Normally, experience triggers immediate response. You see something and immediately think about it. You feel something and immediately act on it. Observing interrupts this automaticity. You notice without immediately doing anything about what you notice. This creates space—a pause between stimulus and response where choice becomes possible.

Observing also means allowing experience without trying to change it. When you observe pain, you do not immediately try to make it go away. When you observe pleasant sensations, you do not grasp at them. You simply notice what is, allowing reality to be as it is in this moment. This acceptance does not mean liking everything or resigning yourself to circumstances; it means acknowledging what is real right now.

The observing skill applies to both internal and external experience. Externally, you might observe sounds, sights, smells, temperatures, textures—the sensory information from your environment. Internally, you observe thoughts, emotions, urges, body sensations—the stream of internal experience. Both domains provide rich material for observation.

Why Observing Matters

Creates Distance from Experience

Observing creates psychological distance from experience, allowing you to see thoughts as thoughts rather than truth, emotions as emotions rather than identity, and urges as urges rather than commands. This distance is transformative. When completely fused with experience, you have no choice—the thought seems like reality, the emotion seems like who you are, the urge seems like what you must do. Observing creates enough space to recognise that these are experiences you are having, not the totality of who you are.

Consider someone experiencing intense anxiety. Without observing skills, they experience anxiety, are entirely consumed by fear, unable to function. With observing skills, they can notice: 'I am feeling anxiety. My heart is racing. I am having thoughts about danger.' This noticing does not eliminate anxiety, but it creates enough distance to function despite anxiety, to recognise that the anxiety will pass, and to choose responses other than panic or avoidance.

Reduces Reactivity

When you observe experience rather than immediately reacting to it, reactivity decreases. The pause that observing creates allows responses to be chosen rather than automatic. You notice anger arising and, rather than immediately attacking, you observe the anger, feel it in your body, notice the urges, and then decide how to respond. This does not mean suppressing anger or pretending it is not there; it means seeing it clearly enough to choose what to do about it.

Research demonstrates that regular observing practice changes brain structure, strengthening regions involved in emotion regulation and reducing activity in areas associated with reactivity. The more you practise observing, the more your brain develops the capacity to notice experience without immediately being hijacked by it. This neural change underlies the reduced reactivity that regular practitioners experience.

Enhances Awareness

Most people live mainly on autopilot, barely aware of moment-to-moment experience. Observing develops awareness, helping you notice what is actually happening rather than moving through life semi-consciously. This enhanced awareness is valuable in multiple ways. You become better at recognising emotions as they arise, identifying needs before they become overwhelming, noticing patterns in your thoughts and behaviours, and recognising when you are moving out of Wise Mind.

Enhanced awareness also allows you to notice positive experiences more fully. When eating, observing helps you taste your food rather than consuming it automatically. When with loved ones, observing enables you to be present rather than being lost in thoughts. This capacity to notice and savour positive experience contributes significantly to wellbeing.

Supports Other Skills

Observing is foundational to all other DBT skills. To use emotion regulation skills, you must first observe what emotion is present. To use distress tolerance skills, you must observe that you are in crisis. To use interpersonal effectiveness skills, you must observe the interaction and your own responses. Without observing, other skills remain theoretical; you cannot use what you do not notice.

Observing also supports the development of Wise Mind. By observing both thoughts (Reasonable Mind) and feelings (Emotional Mind), you create the possibility of integrating them. The witnessing stance that observing cultivates is itself an aspect of Wise Mind—that part of you that can hold all experience with acceptance and perspective.

How to Practise Observing

Observing can be practised both formally through structured exercises and informally throughout daily life. Both approaches develop the skill, and regular practice in both contexts creates the strongest foundation.

Formal Observing Practices

Formal practice involves setting aside dedicated time to practise observing. This might be five minutes or thirty minutes. The key is deliberate, focused practice of paying attention without reacting or interfering.

Observing the breath: Sit comfortably with your back relatively straight but not rigid. Close your eyes or lower your gaze. Focus attention on your breath. Notice the sensation of air moving in and out of your nostrils or feel your chest or belly rising and falling. You are not trying to change the breath or breathe in any particular way; you are simply observing it as it is. When your mind wanders, as it inevitably will, gently return attention to the breath without judging yourself for wandering. The practice is noticing when attention has drifted and bringing it back, repeatedly, with patience.

Observing sounds: Sit comfortably and close your eyes. Simply listen to whatever sounds are present. Notice sounds near and far, loud and soft, pleasant and unpleasant. Do not label them or think about what is making the sounds; simply hear them as pure sensation. Let sounds come and go without trying to hold onto pleasant ones or push away unpleasant ones. If you find yourself thinking about sounds rather than hearing them, gently return to listening. Notice the space between sounds as well as the sounds themselves.

Observing body sensations: Begin at the top of your head and slowly scan down through your body, noticing sensations wherever you find them. Warmth or coolness. Tension or relaxation. Tingling, pressure, lightness, heaviness. Areas that feel tight and areas that feel loose. Do not try to change anything; simply notice what is. If you notice areas of tension, do not immediately try to relax them; just observe the tension itself. Move slowly through your entire body from head to toes. This practice develops awareness of physical experience and reveals how much sensation you typically ignore.

Observing thoughts: Imagine sitting beside a stream watching leaves float past. Each thought is a leaf. Watch thoughts appear in your awareness, float by, and disappear downstream. Do not grab the leaves or push them away. Do not judge the thoughts as good or bad. Simply observe them passing. Some thoughts will be sticky, trying to pull you into thinking rather than observing. When you notice you have been pulled into thinking, gently return to the bank of the stream and continue watching. This practice creates distance from thoughts, helping you see them as mental events rather than truths.

Observing emotions: Sit quietly and notice what emotions are present. You might feel calm, irritated, sad, content, anxious, or multiple emotions simultaneously. Where do you feel each emotion in your body? What physical sensations accompany it? What thoughts arise with the emotion? What urges does the emotion create? Observe all of this without judging the emotion as good or bad, without trying to make it go away or hold onto it. Simply notice this is what I am feeling right now. Emotions are experiences, not truths about reality. This practice cultivates the ability to experience emotions without being overwhelmed or dominated by them.

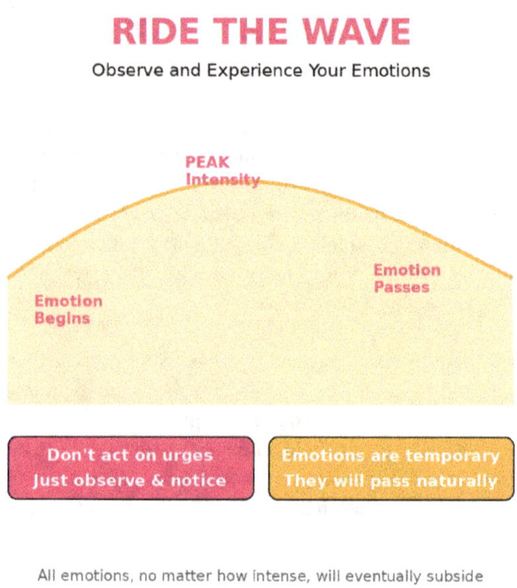

Figure 25: Ride the Wave - Observing Emotions

Informal Observing Practices

Informal practice involves bringing observing awareness to routine activities throughout your day. These micro-practices, woven into daily life, build observing capacity without requiring dedicated time.

Observing whilst eating: Before eating, pause and look at your food. Notice colours, shapes, and arrangement. Smell the food. Take a bite and notice tastes and textures. Chew slowly, observing the experience of eating rather than eating automatically whilst thinking about other things. Notice when your mind wanders to thoughts and gently return to tasting, chewing, and swallowing. Eating becomes an opportunity to practise observing rather than just a way to fuel your body.

Observing whilst walking: Feel your feet touching the ground with each step. Notice the movement of your legs, the swing of your arms, the sensations in your body as you walk. See the environment around you, rather than walking on autopilot, lost in thought. Walking becomes meditation in motion, an opportunity to practise observing rather than just a way to get from one place to another.

Observing during routine tasks: Washing dishes, brushing teeth, and showering, these mundane activities provide perfect opportunities for observing practice. Feel the warm water on your hands. Notice the sensation of the toothbrush on your teeth. Smell the soap. These moments, usually performed automatically, become opportunities to strengthen observing capacity.

Observing in conversation: Notice your reactions as someone speaks. Observe urges to interrupt, to plan your response whilst they are still talking, to agree or disagree. Simply notice these urges without immediately acting on them. This creates space to actually listen rather than waiting for your turn to talk. Conversations become richer when you observe your own reactions without being entirely controlled by them.

Observing difficult emotions: When upset, pause for even just thirty seconds and observe. Notice where you feel the emotion in your body. Notice what thoughts are arising, notice urges to act. This brief observation creates distance from the emotion without suppressing it. You are feeling angry, sad, or anxious, but you are not only those emotions. You are also the one who can observe them.

Case Studies: Observing in Practice

The following case studies illustrate how people use observing skills in real-life situations.

Case Study 1: Sarah - Managing Panic Attacks

Sarah, aged thirty-two, experiences frequent panic attacks. When panic begins, she typically fights against it desperately, which intensifies the panic into a full attack. She describes feeling like she is dying or going mad during attacks. The panic controls her life; she avoids situations where attacks might occur, which increasingly restricts her world.

In DBT, Sarah learns to observe panic rather than fighting it. Initially, this seems impossible. How can she simply observe when panic feels so overwhelming? Her therapist explains that fighting panic adds fear on top of fear—panic about panic—which intensifies the experience. Observing does not mean liking panic or wanting it; it means acknowledging what is happening without adding layers of struggle.

Sarah begins practising observing during formal practice when not panicking. She observes her breath, body sensations, and thoughts. She learns what observing feels like. Then, when early signs of panic appear, she practises observing: 'Heart racing. Notice that. Chest tight. Notice that. Thought that I am dying. Notice that thought. Urge to run. Notice that urge.'

This observing creates distance. The panic sensations are still present, but Sarah is not entirely fused with them. She recognises them as sensations and thoughts rather than as truth. The sensations feel like danger, but observing helps her remember they are not actually dangerous. They are uncomfortable but temporary.

Over weeks of practice, Sarah's panic attacks decrease in both frequency and intensity. When panic arises, she can often observe it without it escalating into a full attack. She stops avoiding situations, and her world expands again. Sarah still feels anxious sometimes, but anxiety no longer controls her life. The observing skill made this transformation possible.

Case Study 2: Michael - Breaking Rumination Cycles

Michael, aged forty-five, struggles with persistent rumination. His mind loops endlessly over problems, past mistakes, and worries about the future. This rumination creates significant distress and interferes with sleep, concentration, and relationships. He describes feeling trapped in his head, unable to stop the constant thinking.

Michael's rumination follows predictable patterns. He replays conversations, analysing what he said and imagining better responses. He worries about work situations that might go wrong. He ruminates about past failures. The rumination feels productive—surely all this thinking will solve something—but it never does. Instead, it creates anxiety and depression.

Learning to observe thoughts transforms Michael's experience. His therapist introduces the leaves-on-stream exercise. Michael imagines sitting beside a stream, watching thoughts float past like leaves. Each thought appears, floats by, disappears. He does not grab the leaves or follow them downstream. He simply watches.

Initially, Michael finds this nearly impossible. Thoughts grab him immediately. He intends to observe but gets caught in thinking within seconds. However, with practice, he develops the capacity to see thoughts as events in awareness rather than being entirely caught in thinking. When rumination begins, Michael practises observing: 'Thought about work situation. Another thought about the work situation. Thought about what I should have said. Worry thought about tomorrow's meeting.'

This simple labelling creates distance. Michael is not the thoughts; he is the one observing thoughts. The thoughts still arise, minds think, that is what they do, but Michael is not entirely identified with them. He develops the capacity to let thoughts pass without following them endlessly down ruminative pathways. His rumination decreases significantly, and he sleeps better. He still thinks about problems, but now he can choose when to think analytically rather than being hijacked by compulsive rumination.

Case Study 3: Aisha - Managing Chronic Pain

Aisha lives with chronic pain from a car accident three years ago. The physical pain is constant, but her suffering intensifies through fighting against the pain. She tenses against it, gets angry about it, catastrophises about the future. Pain plus struggle against pain creates overwhelming suffering.

Aisha's physiotherapist refers her to DBT specifically for learning to manage pain differently. Her therapist explains that whilst DBT cannot eliminate physical pain, it can reduce the suffering that is added to pain through resistance and catastrophic thinking. Aisha is sceptical—how can simply observing pain help when pain is so overwhelming?

Aisha begins by observing sensations in areas of her body without pain. She notices warmth, coolness, tingling, and pressure. She learns what observing feels like. Then, carefully, she begins observing pain itself. Rather than experiencing pain as one massive overwhelming sensation, she begins noticing details: 'Burning sensation in lower back. Aching in the right hip. Sharp sensation when I move this way. Dull throb that intensifies and then subsides slightly.'

This observation reveals something unexpected: pain is not constant. It fluctuates. Some moments are more intense, others slightly less so. There are different qualities of pain. By observing rather than tensing against pain, Aisha also notices that tension itself intensifies pain. When she observes pain without tensing, pain becomes somewhat more bearable.

Observing also helps Aisha notice catastrophic thoughts: 'This will never get better,' 'I cannot stand this,' 'My life is ruined.' Rather than believing these thoughts automatically, she observes them as thoughts. They might be true or might not be. Observing creates enough distance to recognise that these thoughts are not facts, just mental events that arise when she is in pain.

Aisha's pain levels do not change dramatically, but her suffering decreases substantially. She can function more effectively because she is not constantly fighting pain. She still has difficult days, but observing gives her a tool for working with pain rather than being entirely overwhelmed by it. Quality of life improves significantly despite ongoing pain.

Case Study 4: James - Reducing Reactive Anger

James has trouble with anger. Small frustrations escalate quickly into rage. He snaps at his partner, yells at drivers, and becomes furious over minor inconveniences. His anger damages relationships and creates problems at work. James describes feeling like anger goes from zero to one hundred in seconds, giving him no opportunity to respond differently.

In DBT, James learns that whilst anger feels instantaneous, it actually builds through stages. Early signs appear before full rage. His therapist teaches observing as a tool for catching anger early. James begins noticing tension in his jaw, heat rising in his chest, critical thoughts about others, and urges to attack verbally. These are early signs that anger is building.

James practises observing these early signs without immediately acting on them. When frustration begins, he pauses and observes: 'Feeling tension. Heart rate increasing. Thought that this person was inconsiderate. Urge to say something harsh.' This observation creates a pause between trigger and response. In that pause, James can choose a different response rather than automatically exploding.

Initially, James often catches his anger too late, after he has already reacted. However, even then, observing helps. He can observe what happened: 'I got angry quickly. My jaw was tense, but I did not notice. I was thinking critical thoughts. Next time, I might catch these signs earlier.' This reflection, itself a form of observing, helps him develop earlier awareness.

Over months, James gets better at catching anger early. He still feels angry, certain situations genuinely are frustrating—but he is not controlled by anger. He can feel angry whilst choosing how to respond. His relationships improve dramatically. His partner notices he is easier to live with. James himself feels more in control of his life rather than being constantly hijacked by rage.

Common Problems When Practising Observing

Problem 1: Mind Constantly Wanders

When practising observing, your mind will wander repeatedly. You intend to observe your breath, but within seconds find yourself thinking about your shopping list, work problems, or past conversations. This feels like failure.

Solution: Wandering is not failure; it is what minds do. The practice is not preventing wandering but noticing when it has occurred and gently returning attention. Each time you notice wandering and return, you are strengthening attention control. The wandering itself is an opportunity to practise, not an indication of doing it wrong. Be patient with yourself. Everyone's mind wanders constantly when beginning observing practice.

Problem 2: Trying Too Hard Some people approach observing with intense effort, straining to maintain focus. This creates tension, headaches, and frustration rather than awareness.

Solution: Observing should be effortful but not strained. Think of it as gentle attention rather than fierce concentration. When you notice straining, soften your approach. Let attention rest lightly on experience rather than gripping it tightly. Observing is more like allowing experience to come to you than like forcing yourself to focus intensely.

Problem 3: Getting Caught in Thoughts Rather than observing thoughts, you get lost in thinking. You intend to observe your thoughts, but instead follow them down elaborate mental pathways, lost in the content rather than observing the process.

Solution: When you notice you are thinking rather than observing, label it gently: 'thinking.' Then return to observing. Do not judge yourself harshly for getting caught in thoughts; this happens to everyone. Over time, you develop the capacity to see thoughts as objects of awareness rather than being entirely caught up in them. The noticing itself is the practice.

Problem 4: Judging Experience Whilst attempting to observe, you judge what you notice: 'This sensation is bad,' 'I should not be thinking this,' 'This emotion is wrong.' Judging interferes with pure observing. Solution: Notice judging as another experience to observe. When you catch yourself judging, note 'judging' and return to observing without judgement. The goal is to observe what is, not to evaluate whether it should be. All experiences are acceptable objects of observation. Nothing you observe is wrong to notice.

Problem 5: Expecting Particular Outcomes You approach observing with expectations: you should feel calm, peaceful, and relaxed. When you do not feel these states, you conclude that observing is not working.

Solution: The goal of observing is not producing particular states but developing awareness and attention control. Some sessions feel calm, others do not. Both are valuable. Sometimes observing reveals agitation, discomfort, or difficult emotions. This is still successful observing. You are building the skill regardless of whether the content feels pleasant.

Problem 6: Forgetting to Practise You intend to practise observing, but consistently forget, days passing without practice.

Solution: Build reminders into your day. Set phone alarms. Link practice to existing habits (after brushing teeth, before meals, during lunch break). Start with very brief practices that feel manageable, rather than committing to long sessions you never complete. One minute of actual practice is more valuable than thirty minutes of intended practice that never happens.

Problem 7: Becoming Discouraged You feel like you are bad at observing, that it is not working, and that you should be better at it by now.

Solution: Remember that observing is a skill that develops gradually. Early practice is often frustrating. Your mind will wander constantly, you will get caught in thoughts, and you will judge yourself. This is normal. With consistent practice over weeks and months, observing becomes easier and more natural. Trust the process. Every session contributes to development even when progress feels invisible.

Practice Exercises

Exercise 1: Five-Minute Daily Observation, Choose one formal observing practice (breath, sounds, or body sensations) and practice for five minutes daily for two weeks. Build consistency before extending duration. Track your practice to maintain accountability.

Exercise 2: Informal Observing Log, each day, bring observing awareness to one routine activity (eating, walking, washing dishes). Notice what you observe. Log your experience to build awareness of how observing affects daily life.

Exercise 3: Observing Emotions. When you notice a strong emotion, pause and observe it for one minute. Notice physical sensations, thoughts, and urges. This builds the capacity to observe emotions without being overwhelmed. Do this at least once daily.

Exercise 4: Noting Practice, throughout your day, periodically pause and note what you are experiencing. Simply label: 'thinking,' 'feeling,' 'hearing,' 'seeing.' This builds continuous observing awareness outside formal practice.

Describe

Describing means putting words to what you observe. After noticing experience through observing, describing involves labelling or narrating what you have noticed. You might describe out loud, write descriptions, or describe silently to yourself. The key is using words that stick to observable facts rather than interpretations, judgements, or assumptions.

Describing works hand, -in- hand with observing. First, you notice (observe), then you put words to what you noticed (describe). This two-step process, observe then describe, creates clarity and distance from experience that neither skill alone can provide. You stick to what is verifiably present rather than adding layers of interpretation.

Consider the difference between these statements. First: 'She is angry with me.' This is an interpretation, not a description. You cannot observe someone else's emotion directly; you observe behaviours and interpret them. Second: 'Her voice is raised, and her face is flushed.' This is a description. You can observe these facts. The first statement assumes you know what she feels and why. The second sticks to observable data.

Describing your own internal experience follows the same principle. Rather than 'I am a terrible person,' which is judgement, you might describe: 'I am having the thought that I am a terrible person.' Rather than 'This situation is unbearable,' you might describe: 'I am feeling intense distress. My chest feels tight, and I am having thoughts that I cannot cope.' These descriptions stick to observable internal experience.

A good description is specific and concrete rather than vague and abstract. 'I feel bad' is vague. 'I feel sad. My energy is low. I have been crying. I am having thoughts about loss, which is specific. The specificity allows a clearer understanding of the experience. You know what you are actually dealing with rather than having a fuzzy sense of general badness.

Describing can be done out loud, in writing, or silently to yourself. Speaking descriptions aloud or writing them down often provides the most clarity, but silent describing, whilst in situations where you cannot speak or write, still provides value. The key is the act of putting experience into words.

Why Describing Matters

Creates Distance from Experience

When you describe an experience, you create psychological distance from it. The act of putting words to experience places you in an observing, reporting stance rather than being completely fused with experience. When feeling intense emotion, you are the emotion—entirely identified with it. When describing emotion, you become the observer of emotion: 'I am feeling intense anger. My jaw is clenched. I am having aggressive thoughts.' This shift, subtle as it sounds, is profound.

Describing thoughts creates a particularly powerful distance. When caught in a thought, it seems like reality. When you describe it as a thought, you recognise it as a mental event. 'Everyone hates me' feels like the truth. 'I am having the thought that everyone hates me' is recognised as a thought, which might or might not be accurate. This distinction allows checking facts, questioning accuracy, and choosing responses rather than automatically believing every thought.

Reduces Emotional Intensity

Research demonstrates that labelling emotions reduces their intensity. When you put words to what you are feeling, brain regions involved in emotion regulation become more active, whilst areas generating emotional arousal become less active. The neuroscience confirms what practitioners report: describing feelings makes them more manageable.

This does not mean suppressing emotion. You are not pushing feelings away or pretending they are not there. You are acknowledging them explicitly, giving them names. This acknowledgement paradoxically reduces intensity. Emotions intensify when fought against or avoided. They become more manageable when clearly acknowledged through description.

Enhances Communication

Describing skills dramatically improve interpersonal communication. When you describe observable facts rather than interpretations, misunderstandings decrease. Saying 'You are being thoughtless' is judgement that invites defensiveness. Saying 'When you cancelled our plans without calling, I felt hurt' describes observable behaviour and your response. The second statement communicates more clearly and invites dialogue rather than conflict.

In relationships, much conflict arises from assumptions presented as facts. 'You don't care about me' is an assumption. 'When you arrived home late without texting, I had the thought that you don't care' describes your experience without claiming to know the other person's motivations. This creates space for them to explain rather than having to defend against accusations.

Supports Problem-Solving

Vague descriptions of problems make solving them difficult. 'Everything is terrible' provides no actionable information. A specific description clarifies what the actual problem is. 'I have been sleeping poorly for two weeks. I am having difficulty concentrating at work. I have been more irritable than usual. It identifies specific difficulties that can be addressed. The description itself often reveals solutions that vague distress obscures.

Describing also helps distinguish between different types of problems. 'I feel awful' might describe physical illness, emotional distress, or both. Specific describing reveals: 'I have a headache and feel nauseated' (physical) versus 'I feel sad and have been crying' (emotional) versus both. This clarity determines appropriate responses.

How to Practise Describing

Describing can be practised formally and informally. Both build the skill and make describing available when you need it.

Formal Describing Practices

Describing objects: Choose an object in your environment. Describe it using only observable facts. Stick to shape, colour, size, texture, and temperature. Notice when you drift into interpretation or association and return to observable description. This builds the skill of distinguishing facts from interpretations.

Describing sensory experience: Observe your sensory experience for a minute, then describe it. What do you see, hear, smell, and feel physically? Use specific sensory words rather than evaluative words. Not 'nice' but 'smooth' or 'warm.' Not 'annoying' but 'high-pitched' or 'repetitive.' Describing thoughts: Sit quietly and notice thoughts. Describe them: 'Thought about dinner.

Planning thought. Memory of this morning. Worry thought about tomorrow.' Simply label thoughts as they arise. This builds awareness of thoughts as events and reduces fusion with thought content.

Describing emotions: When you notice an emotion, describe it thoroughly. Name the emotion. Describe physical sensations accompanying it. Describe thoughts arising with it.

Describe urges. This comprehensive description enhances emotional awareness and regulation.

Writing descriptions: Keep a describing journal. Write descriptions of your day, sticking to observable facts. These builds describing skill and reveals patterns you might not notice otherwise.

Informal Describing Practices Informal describing involves bringing describing awareness to daily activities and interactions.

Describing in conversations: Notice when you make interpretations ('He is angry at me') and practice describing facts instead ('He spoke loudly and left the room'). This builds communication skills.

Describing emotions as they arise: Throughout your day, when you notice emotions, practice naming them. 'Feeling frustrated. Feeling content. Feeling anxious.' This builds emotional awareness.

Describing difficult moments: When distressed, pause and describe what is happening. This creates distance and reduces intensity.

Case Studies: Describing in Practice

Case Study 1: Emma, Improving Communication

Emma's relationships were damaged by her communication style. She made frequent accusations based on interpretations rather than facts. 'You don't care about me,' 'You never listen,' 'You're always thoughtless.' These statements, whilst expressing genuine feelings, created defensiveness and conflict.

Learning to describe transformed Emma's communication. Instead of 'You don't care,' she learned to say: 'When you cancelled our plans without calling, I felt hurt.' Instead of 'You never listen,' she said: 'I notice when I'm talking, you're often looking at your phone, and I have the thought that you're not interested in what I'm saying.' These descriptions stuck to observable facts whilst expressing her experience.

Her partner responded very differently to descriptions than to accusations. Descriptions invited dialogue rather than defence. Emma's relationships improved dramatically once she could describe her experience without claiming to know others' motivations.

Case Study 2: David, Managing Depression

David experienced severe depression. His thinking was globally negative: 'Everything is terrible. I'm worthless. Nothing will ever get better.' These vague, catastrophic thoughts intensified his depression and blocked problem-solving.

His therapist taught describing as a tool for working with depressive thinking. David learned to describe specific experiences rather than making global statements. Instead of 'Everything is terrible,' he described: 'I have been sleeping poorly. Work has been stressful. I cancelled plans with friends twice this week.' This specific description revealed actionable problems.

Describing also helped David recognise depressive thoughts as thoughts rather than truths. 'I am having the thought that I'm worthless' creates distance that 'I'm worthless' does not. The description helped David see depression as something he was experiencing rather than who he was. This shift was transformative.

Common Problems with Describing

Problem 1: Confusing Interpretation with Description

You believe you are describing facts when making interpretations. 'She was being rude' feels like a description but is an interpretation. Observable facts would be: 'She spoke in a sharp tone and walked away whilst I was mid-sentence.'

Solution: Check whether what you are describing could be observed by a video camera. If a camera could record it, it is observable. If it requires mind-reading or interpretation, it is not pure description. Practise distinguishing the two.

Problem 2: Over-Describing

You describe in such elaborate detail that the point is lost. Describing becomes a verbose analysis rather than clear labelling.

Solution: Aim for specific but concise descriptions. Include enough detail for clarity but not so much that describing becomes overwhelming. Practise one-sentence descriptions initially.

Problem 3: Difficulty Finding Words

You struggle to find words to describe an experience, particularly emotions. Your vocabulary for internal experience is limited.

Solution: Build your descriptive vocabulary deliberately. Keep lists of emotion words, sensation words, and thought words. When you notice experience, consult your lists to find accurate words. Vocabulary expands with use.

Practice Exercises

Exercise 1: Fact versus Interpretation Practice, Write ten statements about your day. Mark each as fact or interpretation. Rewrite interpretations as observable facts. This builds skill at distinguishing the two.

Exercise 2: Emotion Describing Log, each time you notice a clear emotion today, describe it completely: name the emotion, describe physical sensations, describe thoughts, describe urges. Do this for at least three emotions daily for a week.

Exercise 3: Describing Difficult Situations. When something difficult occurs, write a factual description of what happened, sticking to observable facts. Notice how this differs from your initial interpretation of events.

Participate

Participating means entering completely into an activity, becoming one with what you are doing. When participating, you are not observing from the outside or describing what is happening. You are fully engaged, immersed in the moment, acting intuitively without self-consciousness. This is the experience of flow, of being completely present in action.

What Participating Is

Participating is throwing yourself completely into the present moment's activity. When you participate, awareness and action merge. You are not thinking about what you are doing; you are simply doing it. You are not watching yourself from the outside; you are inside the experience fully.

Consider a skilled musician performing. They are not thinking about each note; they have become the music. A skilled athlete is not thinking about technique; they have become the movement. This is participating. You lose self-consciousness and become one with the activity.

Participating is often described as being in the zone or experiencing flow. Time feels different—it might seem to slow down or speed up. Effort feels effortless. You are completely absorbed, fully present, utterly engaged. Nothing exists except this moment, this activity.

Participating differs from observing and describing. Those skills create distance from experience; participating eliminates distance. All three skills are valuable, but they serve different purposes. Sometimes you need distance (observe and describe); sometimes you need full immersion (participate).

Why Participating Matters

Breaks Self-Consciousness

Many people live with persistent self-consciousness, constantly watching themselves from the outside, judging their performance, worrying about how they appear to others. This self-consciousness creates anxiety and prevents full engagement with life. Participating breaks this pattern. When truly participating, self-consciousness disappears. You are not thinking about how you look or whether you're doing it right; you are simply doing it.

Enhances Enjoyment

Full participation dramatically enhances enjoyment. When eating whilst distracted, you barely taste food. When eating whilst participating, flavours are vivid and satisfying. When spending time with loved ones whilst preoccupied, the connection feels thin. When participating fully in interactions, connection deepens and satisfaction increases. Life is richer when you participate rather than merely going through the motions.

Improves Performance

Peak performance in any domain requires participation. Athletes perform best when in flow. Artists create best when fully absorbed. Even routine tasks are done more effectively when you participate rather than operating on autopilot. Participating harnesses intuitive knowledge and skill that conscious thinking cannot access.

Reduces Rumination

When fully participating in an activity, rumination stops. You cannot think repetitively about problems whilst completely absorbed in what you are doing. This provides valuable relief from chronic rumination and worry. Participating is not avoidance; it is engagement with life that naturally displaces unproductive thinking.

How to Practise Participating

Participating is practised by deliberately engaging fully in activities throughout your day. Start with activities you already enjoy, where participating comes more naturally, then extend to other activities.

Participating in movement: Engage in physical activity, walking, dancing, yoga, sports, and throw yourself into it completely. Feel your body moving. Let movement happen intuitively rather than thinking about each action. Become the movement.

Participating in conversation: Be completely present when someone speaks. Let go of planning your response. Simply be there, absorbed in listening and responding authentically. Let conversation flow naturally rather than controlling it.

Participating in creative activities: When drawing, writing, playing music, cooking, or any creative endeavour, let yourself become absorbed. Stop judging whether you're doing it well. Simply create.

Participating in routine tasks: Even mundane activities offer opportunities for participating. When washing dishes, become the washing. When walking, become the walking. Full engagement transforms routine tasks.

Case Studies: Participating in Practice

Case Study 1: Lisa, Overcoming Performance Anxiety Lisa suffered from severe performance anxiety. As a professional violinist, she could practise beautifully at home but froze during performances.

To deepen your ability to participate, it helps to notice when your attention drifts and gently bring it back to the present moment. Mindfulness practices, such as focusing on your breath or sensations, can support your capacity to stay engaged. Over time, these habits strengthen your skill in participating in varied activities.

Her self-consciousness was crippling. She watched herself from outside, judging every note, terrified of making mistakes. Watching prevented playing.

Learning to participate transformed Lisa's performance. Her teacher helped her understand that her problem was not insufficient skill but too much thinking. During performances, she needed to participate—to become the music—rather than observing herself play. Lisa practised deliberately letting go of self-consciousness, throwing herself into playing, trusting her extensive training.

This shift took time and practice. Lisa had to repeatedly choose participating over self-monitoring. Gradually, she developed the capacity to lose herself in the music during performances. Her anxiety decreased dramatically. Her playing improved. She rediscovered the joy that had brought her to music initially.

Case Study 2: Marcus, Finding Flow in Work. Marcus felt constantly distracted and dissatisfied at work. He went through motions but never felt engaged. Time dragged. Work felt tedious. He was productive enough, but found no satisfaction in what he produced. He wondered whether he was in the wrong career. His therapist explored how Marcus worked. Marcus realised he never participated fully. He multitasked constantly, checked email whilst on calls, and thought about other things whilst in meetings. He was physically present but not genuinely engaged. He had forgotten how to participate.

Marcus experimented with participating. He chose one task and committed to doing only that task, fully, for one hour. No email. No phone. Just the task. Initially, this felt difficult. His mind pulled toward distractions. However, after fifteen minutes of deliberate participation, something shifted. He entered flow. Time passed quickly. The work was engaging rather than tedious.

Marcus began structuring his days around periods of full participation rather than constant fragmented attention. His satisfaction with work increased dramatically. He realised his job was fine; his relationship with it was the problem. Participating restored meaning.

Common Problems with Participating

Problem 1: Too Much Self-Consciousness

You cannot participate because self-consciousness intrudes constantly. You watch yourself rather than losing yourself in activity.

Solution: Practise deliberately letting go of self-observation. When you notice self-consciousness arising ('How do I look? Am I doing this right?'), gently redirect attention to the activity itself. Participating requires a willingness to temporarily abandon self-monitoring. This becomes easier with practice.

Problem 2: Difficulty Stopping Thinking.

You remain caught in thinking rather than participating. Your mind analyses, plans, judges, rather than simply experiencing.

Solution: Choose activities that demand full attention and naturally interrupt thinking—physical activities, creative activities, activities requiring skill. These make participating easier because thinking interferes with performance. Build participating capacity here, then extend to quieter activities.

Problem 3: Feeling Like Participating Is Dangerous You fear letting go of control, of losing yourself in experience. Participating feels risky.

Solution: Start with safe activities where losing control has no negative consequences—dancing alone in your room, drawing, walking in nature. Build trust that participating is safe. You can always return to observing and describing when needed.

Practice Exercises

Exercise 1: Flow Activity Practice - Choose an activity you enjoy. Dedicate thirty minutes to participating fully in it. Notice when self-consciousness or thinking intrudes and gently return to participating. Do this three times this week.

Exercise 2: Mindful Movement - Engage in movement (walking, yoga, dancing) with the intention to participate fully. Let your body move intuitively. Become the movement rather than controlling it.

Exercise 3: Conversation Practice - In one conversation today, practice participating completely. Let go of planning responses. Be genuinely present. Notice how this changes the interaction.

The 'How' Skills

The 'what' skills teach us what to do in mindfulness practice: observe, describe, and participate. The 'how' skills teach us the manner in which we practise these skills. They describe the quality of attention we bring to our experience. If the 'what' skills are the actions of mindfulness, the 'how' skills are the attitudes that make those actions truly mindful.

There are three 'how' skills: non-judgementally, one-mindfully, and effectively. Each represents a way of engaging with experience that reduces suffering and increases awareness. Together, they create the conditions for genuine mindfulness practice and support all other DBT skills.

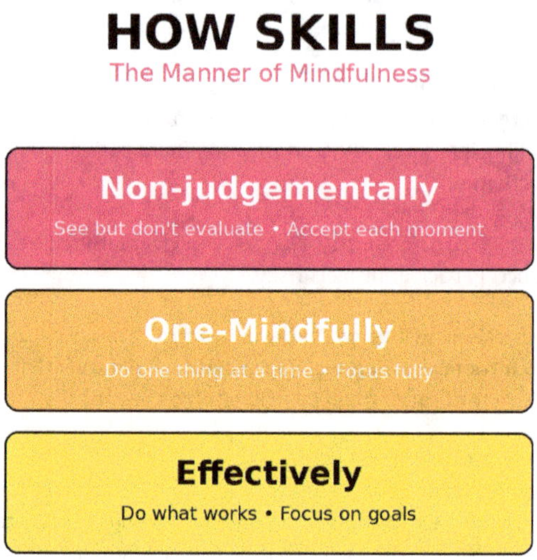

Figure 10: The How Skills

Non-judgementally means observing and describing without adding evaluations of good or bad, right or wrong, fair or unfair. It means seeing facts as they are, without the overlay of judgement that creates much of our emotional suffering.

One-mindfully means doing one thing at a time with full attention. It means bringing our awareness completely to whatever we are doing in this moment, rather than scattering our attention across multiple tasks or allowing our mind to wander to the past or future.

Effectively means doing what works, focusing on outcomes rather than being right or proving a point. It means being willing to let go of our attachment to how things should be and instead doing what the situation requires.

These three skills work together to create a mindful approach to life. Non-judgementally reduces the emotional reactivity that clouds our awareness. One-mindfully deepens our concentration and presence. Effectively keeps us focused on our goals and values rather than becoming lost in unproductive struggles. Practised together, they transform how we engage with ourselves, others, and the world.

The Relationship Between 'What' and 'How' Skills

Understanding the relationship between the 'what' skills and the 'how' skills help us practice mindfulness more effectively. The 'what' skills are incomplete without the 'how' skills, and vice versa.

When we observe judgementally, we do not see clearly. Our observations are coloured by our evaluations, and we miss important aspects of our experience. When we observe one-mindfully, we notice more detail and nuance. When we observe effectively, we focus our observations on information that helps us move towards our goals.

When we describe judgementally, our descriptions are distorted by our evaluations. We use loaded language that triggers emotional reactions rather than neutral language that promotes understanding. When we describe one-mindfully, we pay full attention to finding accurate words. When we describe effectively, we communicate in ways that work rather than ways that make us feel right.

When we participate judgementally, we cannot throw ourselves fully into experience because we are simultaneously evaluating it. When we participate one-mindfully, we become absorbed in our activity. When we participate effectively, we engage in ways that serve our long-term interests rather than our immediate urges.

The 'how' skills, then, are not separate from the 'what' skills. They are qualities we bring to observing, describing, and participating. Every moment of mindfulness practice involves both 'what' and 'how'. We are always doing something (observing, describing, or participating) in some manner (judgementally or non-judgementally, one-mindfully or not, effectively or ineffectively). Skilled mindfulness means choosing both what we do and how we do it.

Nonjudgementally

Non-judgemental observation is perhaps the most challenging and most transformative of all mindfulness skills. Most of us spend our lives adding judgements to our experience. We label events as good or bad, right or wrong, fair or unfair. We judge ourselves harshly when we make mistakes. We judge others constantly. These judgements feel automatic and true, but they are learned habits that create much of our emotional suffering.

to practise non-judgementally means to observe facts without adding evaluations. It means seeing what is, rather than judging what is as good or bad. This does not mean we cannot prefer some experiences over others, or that we should not work to change difficult situations. It means we acknowledge preferences without adding layers of judgemental evaluation that increase suffering.

Understanding Judgement

Judgement in DBT refers to evaluations that go beyond objective facts. When we judge, we add words like good, bad, right, wrong, should, shouldn't, fair, unfair, stupid, terrible, wonderful, perfect. These words express our evaluations, not facts about reality.

Consider the difference between these statements:

Factual: It is raining today.

Judgemental: This weather is terrible.

Factual: I made a mistake in my report. Judgemental: I am stupid and incompetent.

Factual: My friend did not respond to my message. Judgemental: She is selfish and doesn't care about me.

Factual: I feel anxious before presentations.

Judgemental: I should not feel anxious. Something is wrong with me.

The factual statements simply describe what happened or what is. The judgemental statements add evaluations that trigger emotional reactions. The rain itself is neutral; calling it terrible creates negative emotions. Making a mistake is an event; calling oneself stupid creates shame and damages self-worth. A friend not responding is an action; deciding she is selfish creates anger and relationship damage. Feeling anxious is an experience; judging it as wrong adds shame to the anxiety.

Judgements often masquerade as facts. We believe our evaluations are observations of reality rather than interpretations we have added to reality. Learning to distinguish facts from judgements is essential for practising non-judgementally.

Why We Judge

If judgements create suffering, why do we judge so habitually? Judgement serves several functions, and understanding these functions helps us recognise when we are judging and choose non-judgemental alternatives.

Firstly, we use judgement to communicate quickly. Saying the weather is terrible conveys not just the fact that it is raining but also our preference against rain. This shorthand can be efficient in casual conversation. However, in our internal experience and in important communications, judgemental shorthand often creates problems.

Secondly, we use judgement to process our emotions. When we feel strong emotions, judgement provides an outlet. Calling traffic terrible gives voice to our frustration. Calling ourselves stupid expresses our disappointment. However, whilst judgement may provide temporary emotional release, it usually intensifies negative emotions rather than resolving them.

Thirdly, we use judgement to protect ourselves. Judging others as wrong or bad can help us feel right or good by comparison. Judging situations as unfair protects us from accepting our own responsibility. These protective judgements may shield our self-esteem in the short term but prevent us from learning and growing.

Fourthly, we judge because we have learned to judge. From childhood, we are taught to evaluate everything. Schools grade us. Parents praise and criticise. Society constantly communicates what is good and bad, right and wrong. We internalise these evaluative patterns and apply them automatically to our own experience.

Finally, we judge because our emotions drive judgemental thoughts. Emotions have inherent action urges and interpretive tendencies. Anger makes us see others as wrong. Fear makes us see situations as dangerous. Disgust makes us judge things as contaminated or bad. These emotion-driven judgements feel like facts but are interpretations shaped by our emotional state.

The Consequences of Judgement

Understanding the consequences of habitual judgement motivates us to practise non-judgementally. Judgement creates suffering in multiple ways.

Judgement intensifies negative emotions. When we judge a situation as terrible, unfair, or awful, we feel worse than if we simply acknowledge the difficult facts. When we judge ourselves as stupid, worthless, or failures, we add shame to whatever mistake or difficulty we are facing. The original pain of a situation is often bearable; the judgemental evaluation makes it unbearable.

Judgement distorts our perception. When we judge, we stop seeing clearly. Our observations become shaped by our evaluations. We notice evidence that confirms our judgement and miss evidence that contradicts it. This distorted perception prevents us from responding effectively to situations because we are responding to our judgemental interpretation rather than to reality.

Judgement damages relationships. When we judge others, we communicate disrespect and disapproval. Others feel criticised and respond defensively. This creates conflict and damages trust. Even when we do not express our judgements aloud, they affect how we interact with others, creating subtle tension and distance.

Judgement reduces self-compassion. Self-judgement is particularly damaging. When we judge ourselves harshly, we relate to ourselves as an enemy rather than an ally. This harsh self-criticism does not motivate positive change. Instead, it demoralises us, reduces our confidence, and often leads to avoidance and giving up. We cannot learn and grow effectively whilst simultaneously attacking ourselves.

Judgement interferes with acceptance. Much of what we must accept in life becomes unacceptable when we add judgemental evaluation. A difficult fact may be bearable, but a terrible, unfair, unbearable fact creates ongoing struggle. Judgement keeps us fighting against reality rather than accepting what is and moving forward.

Judgement traps us in suffering. When we judge situations as intolerable, we tell ourselves we cannot bear what we are experiencing. This creates desperation and impulsive action. When we judge ourselves as defective, we believe we cannot change or improve. These judgemental beliefs trap us in patterns of suffering.

Practising nonjudgementally

Practising non-judgementally means developing the skill of observing and describing without adding evaluations. This skill develops through deliberate practice.

The first step is noticing when you are judging. Throughout your day, observe your thoughts and language. Notice words like good, bad, right, wrong, should, shouldn't, fair, unfair, terrible, wonderful, stupid, brilliant. These words signal judgement. Simply notice them without judging yourself for judging. Awareness is the foundation of change.

The second step is separating facts from judgements. When you notice a judgement, ask yourself: What is the actual fact here? What happened or is happening? Can I describe this without evaluative words? Practise translating judgemental statements into factual descriptions.

For example:

Judgement: This traffic is terrible.

Fact: Traffic is moving slowly. I will arrive later than planned.

Judgement: I am so stupid for making that mistake. Fact: I made an error in my calculations. I can correct it.

Judgement: He is being selfish and inconsiderate. Fact: He did not do what I asked him to do.

The factual descriptions are neither optimistic nor pessimistic. They simply state what is. This neutral stance allows us to see clearly and respond effectively.

The third step is acknowledging consequences without judgement. Non-judgementally does not mean we ignore whether outcomes are helpful or harmful, pleasant or painful. It means we describe consequences factually rather than judging them evaluatively.

We can say: This behaviour tends to result in negative consequences for me, or This action moves me towards my goals. These statements acknowledge reality without adding unnecessary judgement. We can prefer positive consequences without judging negative consequences as terrible or unfair.

The fourth step is practising self-compassion instead of self-judgement. When you notice yourself judging yourself, pause. Acknowledge the judgement. Then deliberately choose a non-judgemental, compassionate alternative. Instead of I am stupid, try I made a mistake, which is part of being human. I can learn from this. Instead of I should be better at this, try I am learning and developing this skill. Progress takes time.

The fifth step is accepting preferences without demanding a change in reality. We can acknowledge that I prefer sunny weather without judging rain as terrible. We can admit I wanted things to go differently without judging what happened as unfair or wrong. Preferences are natural; demanding that reality match our preferences creates suffering.

The sixth step is using non-judgemental language consistently. Our language shapes our thoughts and emotions. Practise replacing judgemental words with neutral, descriptive words. Practise describing your experience, others' behaviour, and situations using factual language. This discipline gradually rewires habitual judgemental thinking.

Common Challenges Many people encounter specific challenges when learning to practise non-judgementally.

Understanding these challenges and their solutions helps us persist in practising this skill.

Challenge 1: Confusing Nonjudgementally with Passivity or Approval Some people fear that practising non-judgementally means they must accept harmful behaviour, give up their values, or stop working to change difficult situations. This misunderstanding can create resistance to the skill.

Non-judgementally does not mean passivity or approval. We can work to change situations, set boundaries, and uphold our values without adding unnecessary judgement. We can say: This behaviour violates my boundaries, and I will not tolerate it, without judging the person as evil or terrible. We can work for social justice without judging all who disagree as immoral. We can protect ourselves from harm without judging ourselves as weak for being harmed.

Non-judgementally means seeing facts clearly and responding effectively. Often, judgement interferes with effective action because it triggers intense emotion that clouds our thinking. Non-judgemental observation allows us to see situations clearly and take appropriate action from Wise Mind.

Challenge 2: Believing Judgements Are Facts

We often experience our judgements as observations of reality. The weather seems objectively terrible. We seem objectively stupid. These judgements feel like truth rather than interpretation. This makes it difficult to recognise and let go of judgements.

The solution is practising the distinction between facts and judgements. Facts can be verified by observation and agreed upon by different observers. Judgements are evaluations that vary between observers. Different people have different opinions about whether weather is terrible, whether a mistake makes someone stupid, whether a situation is fair. These differences reveal that judgements are interpretations, not facts.

Practise asking: Is this a fact or my judgement? Could someone else observe this situation differently? What are the actual observable facts here? This practice gradually helps us recognise judgements as judgements rather than truth.

Challenge 3: Judging Oneself for Judging

When people learn about non-judgementally, they often begin judging themselves for judging. They notice a judgement and think I should not be judging. I am doing this wrong. This creates layers of judgement about judgement, increasing rather than decreasing suffering.

The solution is applying non-judgemental observation to the process of noticing judgement. When you notice yourself judging, simply note: Judging is occurring, or There is a judgemental thought. This neutral observation acknowledges what is happening without adding evaluation. You might even say: Judging is natural and habitual. I am learning to judge less. This is a process.

Remember that learning non-judgemental observation is a skill that develops gradually. You will judge. You will judge yourself for judging. You will judge yourself for judging yourself for judging. Each time you notice this process, you are building awareness. Awareness is the first step towards change.

Challenge 4: Difficulty Distinguishing Between Judgement and Discernment

Some people worry that non-judgemental observation means they cannot make necessary decisions or distinctions. They confuse judgement with discernment, evaluation, or decision-making.

Discernment and decision-making differ from judgement. Discernment means recognising differences and making choices based on our values and goals. We can discern that one option serves our goals better than another without judging the other option as bad or wrong. We can decide not to continue a friendship without judging the person as terrible. We can recognise that a behaviour has harmful consequences without judging ourselves as defective for engaging in that behaviour.

The key difference is that judgement adds evaluative labels that trigger emotional reactions and distort perception. Discernment involves neutral assessment that supports effective decision-making. Practise making decisions without judgement by focusing on consequences and values rather than evaluative labels.

Case Studies: Nonjudgementally in Practice

Case Study 1: Rachel and Self-Judgement

Rachel struggled with severe self-judgement. Following any mistake, however small, she would berate herself internally: You are so stupid. You cannot do anything right. Everyone else is more competent than you. These self-attacks would spiral into hours of rumination and self-loathing, often triggering depression that lasted days.

Her therapist helped Rachel recognise that these judgements, not the mistakes themselves, created her intense suffering. A small error was simply that - a small error. The judgement was stupid, making it feel catastrophic. Rachel began practising catching judgemental self-talk and replacing it with factual descriptions.

When she made a mistake in a presentation at work, her automatic thought was I am incompetent, and everyone now knows it. She caught this judgement and replaced it with facts: I lost my place in my presentation and needed a moment to find it again. The people in the audience looked confused briefly, then became attentive again. The presentation continued successfully. I received positive feedback afterwards.

This factual description was accurate and verifiable. It allowed Rachel to acknowledge her momentary difficulty without adding catastrophic judgement. She felt brief embarrassment, which passed naturally, rather than lasting shame. Over time, this practice reduced the frequency and intensity of her depressive episodes. She could make mistakes without falling into self-judgement spirals. Her self-compassion increased, and paradoxically, her actual competence improved because she was no longer paralysed by fear of judgement.

Case Study 2: James and Judging Others

James experienced chronic anger and relationship difficulties. He found fault with others constantly. His colleagues were incompetent. His wife was unreasonable. Other drivers were idiots. These judgements triggered frequent anger and created conflict in nearly all his relationships. James believed he was seeing the truth about others' flaws.

His therapist asked James to distinguish between facts and judgements for one week. James was surprised to discover how many of his thoughts were judgemental. When his wife suggested they visit her family, his immediate thought was: She is so selfish, always putting her family first. His therapist asked him to identify the fact. The fact was: She suggested we visit her family this weekend.

This factual description was neutral. James could acknowledge he preferred to spend the weekend differently without judging his wife as selfish. He practised communicating factually: I would prefer to stay home this weekend as I need rest. Can we schedule a visit for next month? This communication was received quite differently than his usual judgemental criticisms.

As James practised non-judgementally, he noticed his anger decreased significantly. He still encountered behaviour he disliked, but without the overlay of judgement labelling others as terrible, incompetent, or selfish, he felt frustration rather than rage. He could address problems without attacking people. His relationships gradually improved as others felt respected rather than constantly criticised.

Case Study 3: Amira and Accepting Difficult Emotions

Amira judged her own emotions harshly. When she felt anxious, she thought I should not feel this way. I am weak. Something is wrong with me. When she felt sad, she judged herself as pathetic. These judgements made her emotions unbearable. She would avoid situations that might trigger anxiety, which increasingly limited her life.

Her therapist introduced non-judgemental observation of emotions. When anxiety arose, Amira practised simply noting: Anxiety is present. My heart is beating faster. My thoughts are moving to worst-case scenarios. These factual observations acknowledged her experience without adding judgement that the anxiety meant something was wrong with her.

At first, this felt strange. Amira was so habituated to judging her emotions that simply observing them neutrally seemed almost impossible. But she persisted. Gradually, she noticed that anxiety without self-judgement was more tolerable. The physical sensations were uncomfortable but not unbearable. The thoughts were unpleasant but passed. When she did not add judgement about being weak or defective, the anxiety episode was shorter and less intense.

This practice extended to all emotions. Sadness was acknowledged as sadness, not judged as weakness. Anger was acknowledged as anger, not judged as bad. This non-judgemental stance towards her emotional experience transformed Amira's relationship with herself.

She became more accepting of her full range of human emotions. She could experience difficult feelings without those feelings meaning anything catastrophic about her character or mental health.

Practice Exercises for Nonjudgementally

Exercise 1: Judgement Journal - For one week, keep a journal of judgements. Each day, write down three judgemental thoughts you noticed. For each judgement, write the underlying fact without evaluation. For example: Judgement - This traffic is awful. Fact - Traffic is moving slowly and I will be late. Notice how translating judgements into facts changes your emotional response.

Exercise 2: Non-Judgemental Descriptions - Choose an object in your environment. Describe it non-judgementally for two minutes, using only factual observations. Notice any judgements that arise (beautiful, ugly, useful, annoying) and return to pure description. Extend this practice to describing your activities, other people's behaviour, and your own thoughts and emotions.

Exercise 3: Self-Compassion Practice - Each time you notice yourself engaging in self-judgement this week, pause. Acknowledge the judgement, then deliberately choose a non-judgemental, compassionate alternative. Practise speaking to yourself as you would speak to a good friend who made the same mistake or faced the same difficulty.

Exercise 4: Non-Judgemental Communication - In one conversation this week, practice speaking entirely non-judgementally. Describe your observations, preferences, and feelings using factual language rather than evaluative language. Notice how this affects the conversation and the other person's response.

Exercise 5: Accepting Reality as It Is - Choose one situation in your life that you have been judging as unfair, wrong, or terrible. Practise describing this situation entirely factually, without judgemental language. Acknowledge any consequences without evaluative words. Notice whether this non-judgemental description changes your relationship to the situation.

One-Mindfully

One-mindfully means focusing your attention completely on one thing in the present moment. It means doing one thing at a time with your full awareness, rather than dividing your attention across multiple activities or allowing your mind to wander to the past, future, or irrelevant present concerns.

In our modern world, multitasking has become a badge of honour. We eat whilst checking email, listen to podcasts whilst exercising, plan tomorrow whilst washing dishes, and scroll through our phones whilst watching television. We rarely give anything our full attention. This scattered attention creates stress, reduces effectiveness, and prevents us from being truly present in our lives.

One-mindfully is the antidote to this fragmented way of living. When we practise one-mindfully, we bring ourselves fully to whatever we are doing. If we are washing dishes, we wash dishes. If we are listening to someone, we listen. If we are working on a task, we work on that task. Our attention is gathered, focused, and present.

The Cost of Divided Attention

Understanding what we lose when we divide our attention helps motivate the practice of one-mindfulness. Research and experience reveal multiple costs of habitual multitasking and divided attention.

Divided attention reduces effectiveness. Despite our belief that we can successfully do multiple things at once; research consistently shows that multitasking decreases performance on all tasks. We make more errors, take longer to complete tasks, and miss important details. Our brains cannot truly attend to multiple things simultaneously; instead, we rapidly switch attention between tasks, and each switch carries a cognitive cost.

Divided attention increases stress. When we attempt to do several things at once, our stress hormones increase. We feel pressured, overwhelmed, and scattered. Even when we successfully complete our multitasking, we feel exhausted rather than satisfied. The chronic stress of divided attention takes a toll on our physical and mental health.

Divided attention reduces enjoyment and satisfaction. When we do not fully attend to pleasant experiences, we miss much of the pleasure they offer. Food tastes less interesting when we eat whilst working. Conversations feel less connecting when we check our phones.

Accomplishments feel less satisfying when we move immediately to the next task without pausing to acknowledge what we have done. We live our lives without truly experiencing them.

Divided attention interferes with learning and memory. We remember experiences we attend to fully and forget experiences we only half-notice. When we are distracted whilst learning, the information does not consolidate properly. When we are scattered whilst experiencing something, we later struggle to recall details. Our lives become a blur of forgotten moments.

Divided attention prevents depth and absorption. Many of life's most meaningful experiences require sustained attention. Creative work, intimate conversation, appreciating beauty, physical flow states, and spiritual experiences—all require gathering our attention and focusing it entirely. When we habitually divide attention, we lose access to these deeper dimensions of human knowledge.

Divided attention fuels anxiety. When our mind constantly jumps from past regrets to future worries, from current tasks to unrelated concerns, we create and maintain anxiety. We cannot worry about the future whilst fully absorbed in the present. Mindfulness naturally reduces anxiety by anchoring us in the now.

The Practice of One-Mindfully

Practising one-mindfully means intentionally gathering your scattered attention and directing it fully to one object, activity, or experience. This practice has several key elements.

The first element is choosing what to attend to. One mindfully requires a deliberate decision about where to place your attention. Rather than allowing your attention to be pulled by whatever is loudest, brightest, or most urgent, you consciously choose: Right now, I am doing this.

The second element is bringing your full attention to your chosen focus. All of your awareness is directed towards this one thing. When washing dishes, you attend to the temperature of the water, the texture of the plates, the movement of your hands, and the sound of the water. If you are listening to someone, you attend to their words, tone, facial expressions, and the meaning they are conveying. Your attention is gathered, not scattered.

The third element is noticing when your attention wanders. The human mind naturally wanders. Thoughts about other things will arise. Urges to check your phone or start another task will appear. This is normal. One-mindfully does not mean your attention never strays. It means you notice when it wanders.

The fourth element is gently returning attention to your chosen focus. When you notice your mind has wandered, you bring it back—no judgement, no frustration—just a gentle return. You are training your attention like training a puppy: with patience, consistency, and kindness. Each time you notice and return, you strengthen your ability to maintain sustained attention.

The fifth element is accepting that this is a practice, not a perfect state. You will not maintain one-pointed focus indefinitely, especially at first. Your mind will wander. You will get distracted. This is not failure; this is the practice. The practice involves the repeated return, or the continuous gentle guidance of attention back to its chosen focus.

One-Mindfully in Daily Life

One-mindfulness can be practised with any activity. Every moment offers an opportunity to gather scattered attention and be fully present. Here are practices for bringing one-mindfulness to everyday daily activities.

One-mindful eating means giving full attention to the experience of eating. Put away your phone, turn off the television, and close your computer. Look at your food. Notice colours, textures, and arrangement. Bring the food to your mouth slowly. Notice the smell. Take a bite and pay attention to taste, texture, and temperature. Chew slowly, noticing how flavours change. Swallow and notice the sensation. This simple practice transforms eating from mindless fuel consumption to a rich sensory experience. It also improves digestion and helps with healthy eating patterns.

Figure 24: Mindful Eating Exercise

One-mindful listening means bringing your full attention to the task of hearing another person. When someone speaks to you, put down what you are holding. Turn to face them. Make eye contact. Listen to their words without planning your response. Notice their tone, their body language, their emotions. When your mind starts composing your reply or wandering to other thoughts, gently return to listening. This quality of attention is rare and precious. People feel truly heard when someone listens one-mindfully, and relationships deepen significantly.

One-mindful working means focusing entirely on the task at hand—close unnecessary tabs on your computer. Put your phone out of sight. If you are writing, write. If you are analysing data, analyse data. If you are creating something, create. When urges to check email or news arise, acknowledge them and return to your task at hand. Work in focused blocks of time and take breaks between blocks. This one mindful approach to work dramatically increases both productivity and satisfaction.

One-mindful walking means bringing full attention to the experience of moving through space. Feel your feet making contact with the ground. Notice the shifting of your weight. Feel your legs moving, your arms swinging. Notice what you see, hear, and smell as you walk. When your mind starts planning or worrying, return to the physical sensations of walking. This practice can be done on any walk, transforming routine journeys into opportunities for presence and awareness.

One mindful household task transforms chores into a mindfulness practice. Washing dishes becomes an experience of warm water, slippery soap, and smooth plates. Folding laundry becomes noticing textures, colours, and the movement of your hands. Sweeping becomes an awareness of repetitive motion, the sound of bristles on the floor, and the gathering of dust.

These mundane activities, done one-mindfully, become rich sensory experiences rather than tedious obligations to rush through.

Common Challenges with One-Mindfully

Challenge 1: The Habit of Multitasking

The most substantial obstacle to one-mindfulness is our deeply ingrained habit of divided attention. We have trained ourselves to multitask constantly. Our attention has become habituated to jumping rapidly between things. Breaking this habit requires intentional practice.

Start small. Choose one activity each day to do completely one-mindfully. Perhaps breakfast, or your morning shower, or your commute. Protect this time from distractions. Turn off devices, close doors, and create an environment that supports focused attention. Gradually extend this practice to more activities. Each one mindful moment strengthens your capacity for sustained attention and weakens the multitasking habit.

Challenge 2: Discomfort with Slowing Down

Many people find one-mindfulness uncomfortable because it requires slowing down and being present in the moment. We are accustomed to rushing, to accomplishing multiple things simultaneously, to constant stimulation. Doing one thing at a time can feel painfully slow or tedious.

This discomfort is actually important information. It reveals how disconnected we have become from direct experience, how dependent we are on constant stimulation, and how uncomfortable we are with simplicity. The practice is to stay with the discomfort. Notice the urge to speed up or add another activity. Acknowledge the discomfort without giving in to it. Gradually, as you build capacity for sustained attention, the richness of fully experienced moments replaces the need for constant stimulation.

Challenge 3: Believing Multitasking Is Necessary

Some people believe they must multitask to accomplish all the tasks they need to do. They worry that one-mindfulness would make them less productive, that they would fall behind, and that they could not manage their responsibilities.

The reality is opposite. One-mindful attention actually increases productivity. You accomplish tasks more quickly and accurately when you give them full attention. You waste less time correcting errors or redoing poorly done work. You experience less stress and exhaustion. You make better decisions. The initial feeling that one-mindfulness slows you down is misleading. In reality, divided attention slows you down because you must constantly reorient, you make more mistakes, and you expend enormous mental energy switching between tasks.

Experiment with this for yourself. Time how long it takes to complete a task with divided attention, then time the same type of task done one-mindedly. Most people find that one-mindful work is actually faster, certainly more accurate, and notably less exhausting.

Challenge 4: Mind Wandering

Perhaps the most common challenge is simply that the mind wanders. You intend to focus one-mindfully, but within moments, you are thinking about something completely different. This can feel frustrating, like you are failing at the practice.

Mind wandering is not failure. It is normal. The wandering mind is what you work with in one-mindful practice. The practice is not achieving perfect focus that never wavers. The practice is noticing when attention has wandered and gently bringing it back. Every instance of catching and returning strengthens your attention capacity. Think of it like lifting weights at the gym; each repetition builds strength. Each noticing and returning is a repetition that builds your attention muscles.

Be patient with yourself. Attention capacity develops gradually. If you can maintain one-minded focus for even thirty seconds at first, that is success. With practice, you will sustain focus for more extended periods, but the wandering mind will never disappear entirely. Working skilfully with the wandering mind is the practice.

Case Studies: One-Mindfully in Practice

Case Study 1: Tom's Work Transformation

Tom, a software developer, constantly felt overwhelmed at work. He would have multiple projects open simultaneously, check email every few minutes, respond to instant messages whilst coding, and attend meetings whilst trying to finish other tasks. He worked long hours but felt he accomplished little. His stress levels were severe, and his work quality was suffering.

His therapist introduced one-mindfulness. Tom was sceptical, believing his workload required constant multitasking, but agreed to experiment. He chose to write code one-mindfully for one hour each morning. He closed email, silenced notifications, told colleagues he was unavailable, and focused entirely on coding.

The first morning felt strange. Tom's hand repeatedly reached for his mouse to check his email. His mind constantly generated thoughts about other tasks. However, he persisted, noticing these urges and refocusing his attention on his code. After the hour, he was surprised to discover he had accomplished more than he typically did in three hours of distracted work. The code was cleaner, with fewer bugs. He felt energised rather than exhausted.

Encouraged, Tom extended the practice. He scheduled focused blocks for different tasks, working on each one mindfully before moving to the next. He checked his email at designated times rather than constantly checking it. He attended meetings fully present rather than multitasking. Within weeks, his productivity dramatically increased whilst his working hours decreased. His stress levels dropped significantly. His sleep improved. Paradoxically, by doing less simultaneously, he accomplished more overall.

Case Study 2: Maria's Relationship Renewal

Maria felt increasingly disconnected from her husband and children. Conversations felt superficial. Family time felt chaotic. Maria was physically present but mentally absent, always thinking about work, checking her phone, or worrying about her endless to-do list. She loved her family, but she couldn't remember the last time she had felt truly connected to them.

Her therapist suggested practising one-mindful attention with her family. Maria decided to implement phone-free family dinners where everyone practised being fully present. The first few dinners felt awkward. No one knew what to do without devices. But gradually, conversations deepened. Maria listened one-mindfully to her children's stories, actually hearing what they were saying rather than formulating responses or thinking about other things. She made eye contact. She noticed details she had been missing—how excited her son became talking about science, how her daughter used humour to deflect when hurt.

Maria extended one-mindfulness to bedtime routines, giving her full attention to reading stories and tucking in her children. She practised one-mindful conversation with her husband, putting away her phone and actually listening. These practices transformed her relationships. Her children sought her out more, sensing that she was truly available. Her marriage regained intimacy and connection. Maria had not gained more time, but the quality of the time she spent with her family had completely changed.

Case Study 3: David's Anxiety Reduction

David experienced chronic anxiety characterised by constant worrying. His mind jumped constantly between concerns: past conversations he regretted, future scenarios he feared, current situations he judged inadequate. He could not remember the last time his mind felt calm. The constant mental chatter was exhausting.

His therapist explained that anxiety thrives on divided attention. When the mind jumps between past and future, between one worry and another, anxiety intensifies. One-mindfulness interrupts this pattern by anchoring attention in present experience.

David began practising one-mindful attention to simple activities. When washing his hands, he focused entirely on sensations of water and soap. When walking, he focused on physical sensations of movement. When talking with someone, he focused entirely on listening. When his mind began its familiar anxious wandering, he noticed this and gently returned attention to his present activity.

The effect was remarkable. David discovered he could not simultaneously worry and focus one-mindfully on present experience. When his attention was fully gathered, anxiety temporarily stopped. At first, he could only maintain this focus for moments before worries returned. But those moments taught him something crucial: anxiety was not constant or uncontrollable. It arose when his attention was scattered and diminished when his attention was focused.

With practice, David learned to interrupt anxious spirals by deliberately shifting to one-mindful attention. When he noticed anxiety building, he would choose something in his immediate environment to focus on completely. This became an effective anxiety management tool. Over months, as one-mindfulness became more habitual, his baseline anxiety decreased significantly. His mind still generated worried thoughts, but they no longer dominated his experience.

Practice Exercises for One-Mindfully

Exercise 1: One-Mindful Eating - Choose one meal or snack this week to eat with complete one-minded attention. Sit down. Put away all distractions. Look at your food. Eat slowly, noticing every aspect of the experience. When your mind wanders, gently bring it back to eating.

Exercise 2: One-Mindful Household Task - Choose a routine household task (washing dishes, folding laundry, vacuuming). Do this task with complete attention. Notice every physical sensation, every movement. When your mind wanders to other concerns, return it gently to the task.

Exercise 3: One-Mindful Conversation - During one conversation this week, practice listening completely one-mindfully. Put down what you are holding. Give the speaker your full attention. When your mind starts formulating responses or wandering, return to listening.

Exercise 4: Technology-Free Period - Designate one hour each day as a technology-free period. Turn off your phone, computer, and television. During this hour, do whatever you do one-mindfully. Notice the difference in your experience.

Exercise 5: One-Task Work Period - Schedule one period of focused work where you do only one task with full attention. Eliminate all distractions. When urges to multitask arise, acknowledge them and return to your single task. Notice the quality and quantity of your work compared to your usual multitasking approach.

Effectively

to practise effectively means to focus on what works rather than what is right, fair, or justified. It means doing what the situation requires to achieve your goals, even when this means letting go of being right, proving a point, or expressing righteous indignation. Effectively is about outcomes, not about being correct.

Many of us sacrifice effectiveness for the satisfaction of being right. We engage in arguments we cannot win because we cannot bear to let someone else have the last word. We refuse to compromise because we insist on fairness. We act in ways that feel justified but create negative consequences because we prioritise expressing our feelings overachieving our goals.

Practising effectively does not mean becoming passive, giving up your values, or never standing up for yourself. It means choosing your battles wisely. It means distinguishing between situations were insisting on being right serves your long-term goals and situations were insisting on being right creates problems. It means being willing to play the long game rather than demanding immediate satisfaction.

Understanding Effectiveness

Effectiveness in DBT is defined by outcomes. An effective behaviour is one that moves you towards your goals whilst maintaining your self-respect and your relationships with others. An ineffective behaviour may feel satisfying in the moment but creates obstacles to your goals or damages things you value.

Consider these examples:

Your colleague takes credit for your work in a meeting. You are angry and want to challenge them publicly. This would feel righteous and justified. However, it might damage your professional reputation, create lasting conflict, and make your workplace uncomfortable. A more effective response might be speaking privately to your colleague or your manager, documenting your contributions, and finding ways to make your work more visible going forward. This is less immediately satisfying but more likely to achieve your actual goals: being recognised for your work and maintaining a functional workplace.

Your partner forgets an important anniversary. You are hurt and want them to understand how thoughtless they have been. You could spend the evening listing their failures and expressing your disappointment. This might feel justified. However, it would create distance, defensiveness, and hurt feelings. A more effective response might be expressing your disappointment briefly and clearly, then suggesting specific ways to remember important dates in future. This is more likely to achieve your actual goals: feeling cared for and improving the relationship.

You are trying to establish a meditation practice. One morning, you sleep through your planned meditation time. You could spend the day berating yourself for failing. This might feel deserved. However, self-criticism would make meditation feel aversive and reduce the likelihood of practising tomorrow. A more effective response would be simply noting that you missed today, problem-solving to prevent it from happening again (setting a louder alarm), and practising tomorrow without self-punishment. This is more likely to achieve your goal of establishing a regular practice.

In each example, the effective choice requires letting go of what feels immediately right or satisfying. Effectiveness often means swallowing your pride, biting your tongue, letting others be wrong, or forgiving yourself and moving on. These choices serve your long-term well-being even when they feel uncomfortable in the moment.

Obstacles to Effectiveness

Several common patterns interfere with acting effectively. Recognising these patterns helps us choose effectiveness more consistently.

The first obstacle is attachment to being right. We often care more about being right than about achieving our goals. We would rather win an argument than preserve a relationship. We would rather prove our point than solve a problem. This attachment to rightness sacrifices effectiveness.

The second obstacle is emotional action. When emotions are strong, we act to express or relieve the emotion rather than to achieve our goals. Anger urges us to attack, even when attacking creates more problems. Hurt urges us to withdraw or retaliate, even when this damages relationships we value. Fear urges us to avoid, even when avoidance prevents us from achieving important goals. Following these emotional urges feels necessary in the moment but often proves ineffective.

The third obstacle is attachment to fairness. Life is not fair. Others will sometimes treat us unjustly. We will face undeserved difficulties. Situations will not work out as they should. We can insist on fairness, but reality does not care about our insistence. Effective action means accepting unfairness when fighting against it would be futile, whilst working to change unfairness when such work might succeed.

The fourth obstacle is short-term thinking. Effective action serves long-term goals, but humans are biased towards immediate gratification. We choose what feels good now over what would serve us better later. We say things that relieve momentary anger but create lasting relationship damage. We avoid temporary discomfort even when facing that discomfort would lead to long-term benefit. Effectiveness requires expanding our time horizon and choosing based on ultimate goals rather than immediate feelings.

The fifth obstacle is pride. Pride makes us unable to back down, apologise, admit mistakes, or compromise. We dig into positions because changing our minds would feel weak. We refuse help because accepting help would acknowledge we need it. We hold grudges because forgiving would feel like condoning wrong behaviour. Pride often sacrifices effectiveness on the altar of ego.

Practising Effectively

Learning to act effectively is a skill that develops through deliberate practice. Several strategies support this practice.

The first strategy is clarifying your goals. You cannot act effectively if you do not know what you are trying to achieve. When facing a decision, ask yourself: What do I actually want to accomplish here? What are my long-term goals? Does this action move me towards those goals, or does it merely satisfy an immediate emotional urge?

Sometimes we think our goal is to make someone understand they have wronged us, when our actual goal is to improve the relationship. We think our goal is to prove we are right, when our actual goal is to solve a problem. Getting clear on what we genuinely want helps us choose actions that serve those wants.

The second strategy is considering consequences. Before acting, play out the likely consequences of your action. If I say this, what will happen? If I do this, what will the other person do? What will this cost me? What will it gain me? Not only immediate consequences, but also those hours, days, or months later. This consequential thinking helps identify ineffective actions that feel satisfying in the moment but create problems later.

The third strategy is being willing to let go. Effectiveness often requires letting go of being right, having the last word, or winning the argument, and embracing immediate satisfaction. Practise the phrase: I can let this go. When you feel the pull to insist, to prove, to fight, pause and ask whether insisting serves your goals. If not, practice letting go.

This does not mean letting go of everything or never standing up for yourself. It means choosing wisely when to stand firm and when to let go. Some battles matter deeply and serve essential values. Others are pointless struggles that create suffering without serving any meaningful goal. Wisdom lies in knowing the difference.

The fourth strategy is separating facts from judgements about fairness or rightness. Often, we resist effective action because the situation feels unfair. But whether something is fair does not determine whether responding to it effectively serves our goals. Acknowledge that life is unjust, then ask: Given that this unfair thing has happened, what action would most effectively serve my goals now? This shifts from fighting against unfair reality to responding effectively to reality as it is.

The fifth strategy is practising humility. Humility means recognising that being right is less important than achieving your goals, that your pride is less important than your wellbeing, that winning arguments is less important than maintaining relationships you value. It means being willing to apologise even when only partly at fault, to compromise even when you believe you are entirely right, to accept help even when you wish you did not need it. This humility paradoxically leads to greater long-term success and satisfaction than rigid insistence on rightness.

Effectiveness in Different Contexts

Effectiveness looks different in different contexts. Understanding how to apply this skill across situations helps integrate it into daily life.

Effectiveness in Relationships

In relationships, effectiveness means prioritising the relationship alongside your individual desires. It means asking: Will this action bring us closer or create distance? Will it solve the problem or escalate the conflict? Will it serve our relationship in the long run, even if it requires me to compromise in this moment?

Effective relationship behaviour often means choosing kindness over rightness. It means apologising even when you were only partly wrong, or when you were technically right but your delivery was harsh. It means letting your partner make mistakes without pointing them out if doing so serves no purpose except to prove you were right. It means picking your battles carefully, addressing issues that genuinely matter, whilst letting go of minor irritations.

Effectiveness in relationships also means communicating clearly about your actual needs rather than expecting others to read your mind or attempting to punish them into behaviour change. Indirect communication may feel less vulnerable than direct requests, but it is usually less effective. State what you want clearly, whilst remaining open to negotiation and compromise.

Effectiveness at Work

In professional contexts, effectiveness means focusing on your actual professional goals: doing good work, advancing your career, maintaining functional relationships with colleagues, earning income. It does not mean being right in every meeting, winning every argument, or expressing every opinion. It means choosing when to speak up and when to let things go based on what serves your professional goals.

Effective professional behaviour often means playing politics wisely rather than pretending politics does not exist. It means building alliances, giving credit generously, handling conflicts privately rather than publicly, and understanding that how you do things often matters as much as what you do. It means being diplomatic even when you would prefer to be blunt and being patient with processes even when you think they are inefficient.

Effectiveness at work also means managing your reputation strategically. This does not mean being fake or manipulative. It means recognising that others' perceptions of you affect your opportunities and taking reasonable steps to ensure those perceptions are accurate and positive. It means owning your mistakes quickly, highlighting your successes appropriately, and understanding the difference between necessary self-promotion and off-putting arrogance.

Effectiveness with Yourself

Acting effectively towards yourself means treating yourself in ways that serve your long-term wellbeing rather than in ways that feel deserved or justified in the moment. When you make mistakes, effectiveness means forgiving yourself and learning, not punishing yourself with harsh self-criticism. When you face difficult tasks, effectiveness means doing them even when you do not feel motivated, because completing them serves your goals.

Self-effectiveness requires distinguishing between what feels good immediately and what serves your actual values and goals. Staying up late watching television feels good in the moment but leaves you exhausted and unable to function well the next day. Effectiveness means going to bed even though you want to keep watching. Avoiding a difficult conversation feels comfortable but allows problems to fester. Effectiveness means having the conversation even though it feels uncomfortable.

Self-effectiveness also means being willing to do things imperfectly rather than waiting until you feel capable of perfection. If your goal is to exercise regularly, going for a ten-minute walk is effective even when you wanted to do an hour at the gym. If your goal is to write, writing badly is more effective than not writing whilst waiting for inspiration. Effective action towards your goals, however imperfect, is perfectly justified inaction.

Common Challenges with Effectively

Challenge 1: Feeling Like Effectiveness Means Being a Doormat

Many people resist practising effectively because they fear it means never standing up for themselves, always letting others win, or accepting unacceptable treatment. They worry that effectiveness requires sacrificing self-respect.

This misunderstanding confuses effectiveness with passivity. Effectiveness actually requires strong self-respect and clear values. You can act effectively only when you know what matters to you and what goals you are working towards. Sometimes effectiveness means firmly setting boundaries, saying no, or ending relationships that are harmful. These actions serve your goals and maintain your self-respect.

The distinction is this: ineffectiveness means acting out of immediate emotional reaction without considering consequences or goals. Effectiveness means choosing your actions deliberately based on your values and goals. This might mean standing firm, or it might mean letting something go. The key is conscious choice based on what serves you, not automatic reaction based on what feels immediately satisfying.

Challenge 2: Difficulty Identifying Goals

Some people struggle to act effectively because they have not clarified their goals. They do not know what they are working towards, so they cannot evaluate whether actions serve those goals. They react to situations without a clear sense of what they want to achieve.

The solution is spending time clarifying your values and goals. What kind of person do you want to be? What kind of relationships do you want? What do you want to achieve professionally? What kind of life would feel meaningful and satisfying? These questions help identify the goals that should guide your choices. Once you are clear on your goals, effectiveness becomes clearer: Does this action move me towards my goals or away from them?

Challenge 3: Emotional Override

Strong emotions can override our commitment to effectiveness. In the grip of intense anger, hurt, or fear, what feels necessary in the moment seems more important than long-term consequences. We know the effective action, but cannot bring ourselves to do it because the emotional pull is too strong.

When emotions are very intense, it may be necessary to use crisis survival skills first to reduce emotional intensity enough that Wise Mind can guide behaviour. Trying to act effectively whilst emotionally flooded is like trying to have a reasoned conversation whilst drowning - the immediate crisis must be addressed first. Once emotions are manageable, return to the question of what action would be most effective.

It also helps to remind yourself in calm moments of your commitment to effectiveness. Write down your goals and effective strategies for common challenging situations. When emotions arise and pull you towards ineffective action, you can refer to what you decided in your Wise Mind. Your emotional mind may resist, but your commitment to your goals can guide your choice.

Challenge 4: Impatience with Long-Term Thinking

Effectiveness requires patience and long-term thinking, but humans tend to be biased towards immediate gratification. We want results now. We want to feel better immediately. Waiting for long-term benefits whilst tolerating short-term discomfort feels intolerable.

The solution is repeatedly connecting current actions to future outcomes. When tempted to act ineffectively for immediate satisfaction, vividly imagine the likely consequences. Picture yourself in a few hours, tomorrow, next week, dealing with the fallout of this impulsive action. Then imagine yourself having acted effectively and picture the better outcomes that result. This mental time travel helps override the bias towards immediate gratification.

It also helps to celebrate small victories in effectiveness. Each time you choose effective action over immediately satisfying action, acknowledge this. You are building the habit of effectiveness and moving towards your goals. These small choices compound over time into significant life changes.

Case Studies: Effectively in Practice

Case Study 1: Sarah's Workplace Conflict

Sarah's colleague, David, repeatedly interrupted her in meetings and dismissed her ideas. Sarah felt angry and disrespected. She wanted to confront him publicly, to make him understand how rude he was being, to put him in his place so he would stop. These urges felt entirely justified.

Her therapist asked Sarah about her goals. Sarah wanted to be respected at work, to have her ideas heard, and to maintain professional relationships. She wanted to advance in her career. Publicly confronting David might feel satisfying, but it risked making her appear unprofessional, creating ongoing tension, and potentially damaging her reputation.

Sarah considered more effective options. She could speak privately to David about the pattern she had noticed. She could speak to their manager if the behaviour continued. She could strategically choose when and how to present her ideas, so they had more impact. She could build alliances with colleagues who respected her work. These approaches were less immediately satisfying than public confrontation but more likely to achieve her actual goals.

Sarah chose to speak privately with David. She described the specific behaviours (interrupting, dismissing ideas) without attacking his character. She explained the impact on their professional relationship and her work. David, when not publicly confronted, was receptive. He had not realised his behaviour was problematic and committed to changing it. When he occasionally slipped back into old patterns, Sarah gently reminded him privately.

Over time, their working relationship improved significantly. Sarah's ideas received more consideration, and her professional reputation strengthened. Acting effectively, not righteously, served her goals.

Case Study 2: Michael's Relationship Repair

Michael's wife, Emma, had an affair. When Michael discovered it, he felt devastated, betrayed, and ragingly angry. He wanted Emma to understand the depth of pain she had caused. He wanted her to suffer as he was suffering. He considered leaving immediately, telling their friends and family what she had done, making her life as difficult as possible. These actions felt justified and deserved.

Michael's therapist did not judge these feelings but asked about Michael's goals. Despite everything, Michael loved Emma and wanted to save their marriage if possible. He wanted to understand why the affair happened and whether the underlying problems could be addressed. Leaving immediately or seeking revenge might feel satisfying but would destroy any possibility of reconciliation. These actions would serve his anger but not his actual goals.

Effective action required Michael to do the hardest thing imaginable: set aside his righteous anger long enough to have honest conversations. This did not mean pretending he was not hurt or immediately forgiving. It meant creating space for Emma to explain, for them to understand what had broken down in their relationship, and for them to decide whether repair was possible.

Michael practised effectiveness by choosing his responses deliberately. He expressed his hurt and anger clearly but without attacking. He listened to Emma's explanations even when they were painful to hear. He sought couple's therapy. He set clear boundaries about what he needed going forward. He gave the process time before making permanent decisions.

This approach was agonisingly difficult. Michael's emotional mind screamed that he should punish Emma, that she deserved his rage, that he was being weak by not leaving immediately. But Michael's Wise Mind recognised that his actual goal was understanding whether the marriage could be saved, not the immediate satisfaction of expressing his anger. Acting effectively meant tolerating extreme discomfort in the service of his long-term goals.

After a year of difficult work, Michael and Emma rebuilt their relationship on more honest foundations. The affair had resulted from problems neither had acknowledged. Addressing these problems transformed their marriage into something stronger than before. Michael's choice of effectiveness over righteousness saved his marriage. Had he followed his initial angry impulses, he would have destroyed what he most wanted to preserve.

Case Study 3: Li's Career Decision

Li worked for a company whose practices increasingly conflicted with his values. Management made decisions Li considered unethical. He felt angry and wanted to speak out publicly about these practices. He wanted his colleagues and the industry to know what was happening. He wanted to hold the company accountable. These urges felt morally right.

Li's therapist explored his goals. Li wanted to work in alignment with his values. He wanted to support his family financially. He wanted to maintain his professional reputation. He wanted to create positive change where possible. Public whistleblowing might feel morally correct, but Li needed to consider the consequences. Would it actually change company practices? Would it damage his career prospects? Would it affect his ability to support his family?

Li researched his options carefully. He could speak to management directly about his concerns. He could document problems and report them to regulatory bodies. He could seek employment elsewhere whilst maintaining professional relationships at his current company. He could stay and work to influence change from within. He could leave and speak publicly after securing other employment. Each option had different consequences.

Li chose to raise concerns internally whilst simultaneously seeking other employment. He presented his concerns to management professionally, documented the responses, and when the concerns were dismissed, began his job search. He left the company on good terms, without public drama. In his new role, he found an organisation whose values aligned with his own. Several months later, with his career secure, he spoke carefully and factually about his concerns regarding his previous employer's practices.

This approach was less immediately satisfying than dramatic public whistleblowing whilst still employed. But it effectively served all of Li's goals: he left a situation that violated his values, he maintained his ability to support his family, he preserved his professional reputation, and he ultimately did speak truth about unethical practices, but in a way that minimised personal cost. Effectiveness meant playing the long game rather than seeking immediate moral satisfaction.

Practice Exercises for Effectively

Exercise 1: Goals Clarification - Write down your major life goals in several domains: relationships, career, health, personal growth. Be specific. Keep this list accessible. When facing decisions, refer to these goals and ask whether your potential action serves them.

Exercise 2: Consequence Prediction - This week, when facing a decision where you feel strong emotions pulling you towards a particular action, pause. Write down the potential consequences of that action at one hour, one day, one week, one month, and one year. Then write down potential consequences of alternative effective actions. Choose based on which consequences best serve your goals.

Exercise 3: Letting Go Practice - Identify three situations this week where you are tempted to insist on being right, to argue your point, or to prove something. Practise deliberately letting go. Choose not to argue, not to defend yourself, not to prove your point. Notice how this feels and what happens as a result.

Exercise 4: Effectiveness Review - At the end of each day this week, review your actions. Identify one moment where you acted effectively, choosing what worked over what felt justified. Acknowledge this success. Also identify one moment where you acted ineffectively and consider what effective action would have looked like. Do this without self-judgement, simply as learning.

Exercise 5: Values Alignment - Choose one area of your life where your actions do not align with your values or goals. Identify specifically what effective action would look like in this area. This week, take one step towards acting effectively in this area, even if it feels uncomfortable or requires letting go of being right.

Mindfulness Practice Programmes

Understanding mindfulness skills conceptually is one thing; integrating them into daily life is another. This chapter provides structured practice programmes that help you develop mindfulness as a lived reality rather than an abstract concept. These programmes offer specific, practical approaches to building a sustainable mindfulness practice.

Mindfulness is a skill that develops through repeated practice. Just as you cannot learn to play piano by reading about it, you cannot learn mindfulness purely through intellectual understanding. You must practise. These programmes provide structure and guidance for that practice.

The programmes range from simple practices suitable for beginners to more intensive practices for those ready to deepen their practice. Choose a programme that matches your current capacity and circumstances. It is better to practise a simple programme consistently than to attempt an ambitious programme sporadically.

Principles of Effective Mindfulness Practice

Before exploring specific programmes, understanding some key principles helps ensure your practice is effective and sustainable.

Consistency matters more than duration. Five minutes of daily practice develops your mindfulness capacity more effectively than an hour of practice once weekly. Your brain learns through repetition. Regular practice creates neural pathways that make mindfulness increasingly accessible. Commit to practising at the same time each day if possible, making it a non-negotiable part of your routine like brushing your teeth.

Start where you are, not where you think you should be. If you can practise mindfully for only thirty seconds before your mind wanders completely, start with thirty-second practices. If sitting still feels intolerable, start with movement practices. Meeting yourself where you are, rather than where you imagine you should be, creates sustainable practice.

Perfection is not the goal. You will not maintain perfect focus. Your mind will wander. You will forget to practise some days. You will fall asleep during meditation. You will become irritated and resistant. All of this is normal and is part of the practice. The practice is not achieving a perfect state; instead, it involves showing up, noticing what happens, and gently persisting.

Gentle persistence beats harsh discipline. Forcing yourself to practise through harsh self-criticism can create an aversion to practise. Instead, cultivate kind persistence. When you miss a practice, notice it without judgement and practice tomorrow. When practice feels difficult, acknowledge the difficulty with compassion and continue gently. This kind of approach creates a sustainable, long-term practice rather than the boom-and-bust cycles of strict discipline followed by complete abandonment.

Formal and informal practice support each other. Formal practice means dedicated time for mindfulness, such as sitting meditation. Informal practice means bringing mindfulness to daily activities. Both are valuable. Formal practice develops concentration and awareness in controlled conditions. Informal practice extends that understanding into the complexity of daily life. Ideally, your practice includes both.

Adapt practices to serve you. The programmes provided here offer structure, but you know yourself and your life. Adapt the practices to fit your circumstances, values, and needs. If a suggested practice does not work for you, modify it or choose an alternative. The goal is to develop mindfulness, not rigidly follow prescribed instructions.

Beginner Programme: Building the Foundation

This programme is designed for people new to mindfulness or returning to practise after a break. It gradually builds basic mindfulness skills, creating a sustainable foundation for long-term practice.

Week 1: Mindful Breathing

Begin with the most fundamental mindfulness practice: attending to breath. This week, practice mindful breathing for five minutes each morning.

Find a comfortable position. You may sit on a chair with feet flat on the floor, or on a cushion on the floor, or even lie down if sitting is uncomfortable. Close your eyes or lower your gaze. Bring your attention to the physical sensation of breathing. Notice where you feel your breath most clearly—perhaps the coolness of air entering your nostrils, the rise and fall of your chest, the expansion and contraction of your belly.

You are not trying to change your breath, only to observe it. Your breath may be shallow or deep, fast or slow. Whatever it is, simply notice it. When your mind wanders—and it will wander, probably within seconds—gently bring your attention back to the sensation of breathing. Do not judge yourself for the wandering. The practice is the returning, not the perfect focus.

Practise this for five minutes each morning this week. Set a timer so you do not need to watch the clock. If five minutes feels too long, start with three minutes. If it feels comfortable, extend to seven or ten minutes. The duration matters less than the daily consistency.

Additionally, throughout this week, pause three times daily to take three mindful breaths. Simply stop whatever you are doing, notice three full breaths with complete attention, then continue. This informal practice helps integrate mindfulness into your day.

Week 2: Body Scan

This week, continue your five-minute morning breathing practice, and add a body scan practice before sleep.

Lie in bed before sleeping. Bring your attention to your feet. Notice any sensations—warmth, coolness, tingling, pressure, or perhaps no particular sensation. You are simply observing, not judging or trying to change anything. After a few breaths attending to your feet, move your attention to your lower legs. Notice whatever is there. Continue moving your attention slowly up through your body: thighs, hips, belly, chest, back, hands, arms, shoulders, neck, face, head.

If you fall asleep during the practice, that is perfectly fine. If you notice tension anywhere, simply observe it without trying to force relaxation. If you notice your mind wandering to thoughts, gently return attention to the body. The entire scan might take five to ten minutes, or you might fall asleep before completing it. Either outcome is acceptable.

Continue your daily three-breath pauses as well. You are building the habit of returning to present-moment awareness multiple times throughout your day.

Week 3: Mindful Movement

This week, maintain your morning breathing practice and evening body scan. Add a ten-minute mindful walk three times this week.

Choose a route where you can walk uninterrupted. This might be around your neighbourhood, in a park, or even back and forth in your home if necessary. Walk at a natural pace. Bring your attention to the physical sensations of walking: your feet making contact with the ground, the shifting of your weight, the movement of your legs, the swing of your arms, the air moving past your body.

You do not need to walk slowly or ceremoniously unless you wish to. Walk at whatever pace feels natural, simply bringing mindful attention to the experience. When your mind wanders to planning or worrying, notice this and return attention to the physical sensations of walking.

If you prefer another movement to walking, substitute any form of exercise or movement. You might run, swim, cycle, do yoga, or dance mindfully. The key is bringing full attention to the physical experience of movement.

Week 4: Mindful Daily Activities

This week, continue your formal practices (morning breathing, evening body scan, three weekly mindful walks). Focus particularly on bringing mindfulness to one routine daily activity.

Choose an activity you do every day: perhaps showering, eating breakfast, washing dishes, brushing your teeth, or commuting to work. This week, commit to doing this activity with complete mindful attention each day. If you choose showering, attend fully to the sensation of water on your skin, the smell of soap, and the sound of water. If you choose to eat, attend to the appearance, smell, taste, and texture of your food. Whatever activity you choose, bring your full attention to it, as if experiencing it for the first time.

By the end of this month, you will have established a basic mindfulness practice foundation: formal morning practice, evening relaxation practice, regular movement practice, and integration into daily life. This foundation supports all further development of mindfulness skills.

Intermediate Programme: Deepening the Practice

This programme is for those who have established basic mindfulness skills and wish to deepen their practice. It assumes you can maintain attention for several minutes and are ready to work with more challenging aspects of experience.

Week 1: Working with Thoughts

This week, extend your morning practice to fifteen minutes. Continue focusing primarily on breath, but when thoughts arise, practice observing them as mental events rather than getting absorbed in their content.

When a thought appears during practice, you might label it simply: thinking. Then gently return attention to breath. Do not try to suppress thoughts or prevent them from arising. Thoughts arising is not a problem or a failure. The practice is noticing thoughts as thoughts, seeing them as mental events that come and go, rather than absolute truths that demand your complete attention.

You might imagine thoughts as clouds passing through the sky of your awareness, or as items floating by on a conveyor belt. You are the observer, watching thoughts pass without needing to grab onto them. Some thoughts will be mundane (need to buy milk), some will be planning (must remember to email), some will be judging (I am terrible at this). Whatever their content, practice the same response: notice, label if helpful, return to breath.

Additionally, this week, in daily life, practice catching yourself getting lost in thought. Several times daily, pause and ask: Where is my mind right now? If you discover you have been lost in thought for the past ten minutes, simply notice this without judgement.

Becoming aware of habitual mind-wandering is the first step in developing more control over attention.

Week 2: Working with Emotions

This week, when emotions arise during your fifteen-minute morning practice or throughout your day, practice observing them mindfully rather than getting swept away or pushing them away.

When you notice an emotion, you might name it: feeling sad, feeling anxious, feeling irritated. Then bring curiosity to the emotion. Where do you feel it in your body? What are the physical sensations? What thoughts accompany it? What urges arise with it? You are investigating the emotion with interested observation rather than immediately acting on it or trying to make it disappear.

If the emotion is mild, you might stay with this observation for several minutes, learning about how this emotion manifests for you. If the emotion is intense and overwhelming, you might observe it briefly, acknowledge it, then return attention to breath or another neutral anchor. The goal is not to force yourself to stay with unbearable distress, but to build capacity to observe emotions without immediately reacting to them.

This practice is particularly valuable with difficult emotions that typically trigger avoidance or impulsive action. Learning to observe anxiety without fleeing, anger without attacking, or sadness without numbing builds emotional resilience and reduces impulsive behaviour.

Week 3: Non-Judgemental Awareness

This week, bring particular attention to practising non-judgementally. During your fifteen-minute morning practice and throughout your day, notice judgemental thoughts as they arise.

You will likely discover you judge almost constantly: This practice is going well, or This practice is going badly. My posture is wrong. That person is irritating. This traffic is terrible. I should be better at this. These judgements arise automatically. The practice is not suppressing them but recognising them as judgements rather than facts.

When you notice a judgement, you might label it: judging. Then return to non-judgemental observation. What are the facts? What sensations, thoughts, or events are occurring without the evaluative overlay? Practise describing your experience factually rather than judgementally.

Be especially vigilant for self-judgements during meditation practice. The mind often judges the quality of meditation: I am doing this wrong; I am terrible at meditating; my mind should not wander this much. Each of these is a judgement. Practise noticing these self-judgements with compassion and returning to non-judgemental observation.

Week 4: Integration

This week, work with all three 'how' skills deliberately. During your morning practice, focus on practising non-judgementally, one-mindfully, and effectively simultaneously.

Non-judgementally: observe without evaluating. One-mindfully: give your complete attention. Effectively: do what works—which means when your mind wanders, simply return attention without self-criticism or elaborate commentary.

Notice how these three skills support each other. Non-judgemental observation is easier when you attend one-mindfully. One-mindful attention is easier when you observe non-judgementally. Both are easier when you focus effectively on what works rather than getting caught in struggles about how things should be.

Throughout daily life this week, practice applying these three skills to challenging situations. When stress arises, pause. Observe non-judgementally: what is actually happening? Attend one-mindfully: be fully present with this moment rather than catastrophising about the future. Act effectively: what response serves your goals rather than just expressing your feelings?

Advanced Programme: Sustaining Deep Practice

This programme is for those committed to making mindfulness a central part of their lives. It requires significant daily time investment and readiness to work with difficult aspects of experience.

Daily Formal Practice

Establish a daily formal sitting practice of thirty to forty-five minutes. This might seem like a large time commitment, but it represents a serious commitment to developing deep mindfulness capacity.

Structure your practice with a timer. You might begin with ten minutes of breath focus to settle attention. Then expand your awareness to include all arising experience: sensations, sounds, thoughts, emotions. Practise observing whatever arises without preference, allowing experience to come and go naturally. When you find yourself caught up in thinking or reacting, return to breath as an anchor, then widen awareness again.

This extended practice time allows you to work through initial restlessness and distraction into deeper states of concentration and awareness. You may experience periods of profound calm, painful boredom, physical discomfort, strong emotions, or strange perceptual shifts. Whatever arises is part of the practice. The instruction remains: observe with non-judgemental awareness.

Weekly Body Scan

Once weekly, practice an extended body scan of forty-five to sixty minutes. This develops detailed awareness of physical sensations and helps identify patterns of tension, numbness, or disconnection from the body.

Move through your body slowly, attending to each region for several minutes. Notice subtle sensations you might typically miss: the feeling of clothes against skin, subtle temperature variations, internal sensations of organs, the pulsing of blood, the movement of breath in different parts of the body. Where you typically feel nothing, bring patient curiosity—what happens when you attend here for three full minutes?

This practice can bring up strong emotions, as body sensations are closely tied to emotional experience. Trauma may be held in the body, and attending to certain areas might trigger difficult feelings or memories. If this happens, you might gently move your attention elsewhere, return to breath, or end the practice if necessary. Consider working with a trauma-informed therapist if you are dealing with significant trauma.

Mindful Walking Meditation

Three times weekly, practice formal walking meditation for twenty to thirty minutes. Unlike mindful walking at a natural pace, formal walking meditation is deliberately slow, almost ceremonial.

Find a path where you can walk back and forth for ten to fifteen metres without interruption. Stand still initially, gathering your attention. Then walk very slowly, breaking down the movement of walking into its component parts: lifting the foot, moving it forward, placing it down, shifting weight, lifting the other foot. Your attention is on the detailed physical experience of each micro-movement.

This practice develops concentration through movement and reveals how much detail exists in simple actions we normally perform automatically. It can feel tedious or awkward at first. Persevere. As attention deepens, the practice becomes absorbing and reveals the richness present in every moment.

All, Day Mindfulness

Once monthly, dedicate an entire day to mindfulness practice. This might be a Saturday or Sunday, or a day taken off work specifically for practice. This extended period of mindfulness offers insights difficult to access in short practices.

Structure the day with alternating periods of sitting meditation, walking meditation, and mindful daily activities. You might sit for forty-five minutes, walk for thirty minutes, eat breakfast mindfully, sit again, walk again, do mindful household tasks, sit again, and so forth throughout the day. Maintain silence if possible, reducing external stimulation to support inward attention.

These intensive practice days reveal patterns in your mind difficult to see in short practices: how quickly restlessness arises, how your energy fluctuates, what thoughts dominate when your mind is not occupied, what emotions sit beneath the surface of busy-ness. This self-knowledge is valuable for understanding your inner landscape and working with it skilfully.

Troubleshooting Common Practice Difficulties

Even with commitment and good structure, mindfulness practice presents challenges.

Understanding how to work with common difficulties helps sustain practice through inevitable rough patches.

Difficulty: Restlessness and Agitation

Problem: You sit to practise but feel intensely restless. Your body wants to move, your mind races, and sitting still feels intolerable.

Solution: Restlessness has physical and mental components. For physical restlessness, try movement practices first—walking meditation or gentle yoga—then sit after releasing physical energy. Ensure you are not consuming excessive caffeine. Check that your posture is not creating discomfort that manifests as restlessness.

For mental restlessness, try breaking practice into shorter periods with brief movement between. Practise for ten minutes, walk for two minutes, practice for ten minutes. Gradually extend the sitting periods as your capacity for stillness increases. You might also try focusing on body sensations or sounds rather than breath, as breath focus sometimes intensifies mental restlessness.

Difficulty: Drowsiness and Sleepiness

Problem: You begin practising but quickly become drowsy or fall asleep.

Solution: First, ensure you are getting adequate sleep. If you are chronically sleep-deprived, meditation time becomes sleep time, and you genuinely need the rest. If you are sleeping adequately but still drowsy during practice, try practising at a different time of day when your energy is higher. Early morning often works better than evening. Practise with eyes open rather than closed. Stand or walk rather than sit. Splash cold water on your face before practising. Ensure the room is not too warm.

Sometimes, drowsiness is avoidance. If difficult emotions or thoughts arise during practice, the mind escapes into sleep. If you suspect this, gently investigate: what was I experiencing just before drowsiness arose? You might need to work with underlying emotions before deep practice becomes accessible.

Difficulty: Physical Pain

Problem: Physical discomfort or pain arises during practice, making concentration impossible.

Solution: Distinguish between harmful pain and discomfort. Sharp, shooting, or intensifying pain suggests you are harming yourself and should adjust your position immediately. Dull, achy discomfort from holding a position is different—this can often be worked with as part of practice.

For harmful pain, modify your position. Use a chair instead of the floor. Add cushions. Lie down. Your practice should not cause injury. For discomfort, practice observing it with curiosity rather than reacting immediately. What exactly is the sensation? Where precisely is it located? How does it change moment to moment? Can you soften around it? This investigative approach sometimes reveals that what seemed intolerable is actually bearable when observed mindfully. If discomfort becomes too intense, move, but be aware of the distinction between genuine necessity and habitual avoidance.

Difficulty: Lack of Time

Problem: You intend to practise but cannot find time in your busy schedule.

Solution: Examine honestly whether this is genuinely a time problem or a prioritisation problem. Most people can find five minutes daily if they truly prioritise it. You might need to wake up earlier, practice during your lunch break, or practice before bed. You might need to reduce the time on other activities.

If time is genuinely scarce, focus on micro-practices: three mindful breaths whenever you remember, one-minute body scans before meetings, mindful tooth brushing, and mindful walking between locations. These brief practices maintain mindfulness in your life even when extended formal practice is not possible. As circumstances change and more time becomes available, return to longer formal practices.

Difficulty: Loss of Motivation

Problem: Your practice has become routine and meaningless. You do not feel motivated to practise and question whether it is worth continuing.

Solution: Motivation naturally fluctuates. Sometimes practice feels valuable and rewarding; sometimes it feels pointless. Neither feeling is the ultimate truth about practice. This is where commitment becomes important. You committed to practise not only when you feel motivated but as an ongoing discipline.

That said, if practice consistently feels deadening, examine what has changed. Are you practising mechanically without genuine attention? Are you practising the same thing repeatedly and need variation? Have life circumstances changed such that you need to adapt your practice? Discuss your practice with a teacher or experienced practitioner who can offer a perspective. Consider reading inspiring texts about mindfulness or attending a group practice to renew motivation.

Sometimes, loss of motivation indicates you are approaching a deeper level of practice. The initial excitement has worn off, but the real work has not yet become apparent. This is the crucial moment to persist through the seeming plateau. Often, just beyond this point of doubt and boredom, practice deepens significantly.

Creating Your Own Practice Programme

The programmes provided here offer structure, but ultimately you must design a practice that fits your life, needs, and values. Use these guidelines to create your own sustainable programme.

Assess your current capacity honestly. How much time can you realistically dedicate to formal practice daily? What time of day works best for you? What type of practice appeals to you most? Start from where you actually are, not where you imagine you should be.

Choose practices that address your specific challenges. If you struggle with anxiety, practices that anchor attention in the present might be most valuable. If you struggle with emotional avoidance, practices that cultivate observation of emotions might be key. If you struggle with chronic rushing and busy-ness, practices that emphasise slowing down might be transformative. Let your practice serve your actual needs.

Build in both formal and informal practice. Formal practice develops your capacity in controlled conditions. Informal practice extends that capacity into real life. A good programme includes both: perhaps fifteen minutes of formal practice daily plus multiple moments of mindfulness throughout your day.

Create accountability structures. You might practise with a friend, join a meditation group, use a meditation app that tracks practice, or keep a practice journal. External structure helps maintain practice through periods of low motivation.

Review and adjust your programme regularly. Every few months, reflect: Is this practice serving me? Am I growing? Do I need to modify, intensify, or simplify my practice? A practice programme is not fixed for life; it evolves as you evolve.

Most importantly, remember that the goal is not perfect practice. The goal is showing up again and again, learning to observe your experience with kindness, and gradually becoming more aware and more responsive to life as it unfolds. This happens through consistent, compassionate practice over time.

Module 2: Distress Tolerance Skills

Life inevitably brings pain, crisis, and distress. Whilst mindfulness helps us observe and accept the present moment, distress tolerance skills provide us with practical strategies to survive crises without making them worse, and to accept reality when we cannot immediately change it.

Many individuals who struggle with emotional regulation have difficulty tolerating distress. When overwhelmed by painful emotions, they may engage in impulsive, destructive behaviours such as substance misuse, self-harm, binge eating, or lashing out at others. These behaviours often provide temporary relief but create additional problems and suffering in the long term.

Distress tolerance skills are not about removing pain or making difficult situations disappear. Rather, they teach us how to bear pain skilfully, to survive crises without making matters worse, and to accept reality as it is in the moment. These skills help us navigate through difficult times whilst maintaining our values and moving towards our goals.

This module is divided into two main categories. Crisis survival skills help us get through intense, short-term crises without engaging in behaviours that will make the situation worse. These are emergency strategies for moments when emotions threaten to overwhelm us and when the risk of impulsive, destructive action is high. Reality acceptance skills help us accept situations we cannot change or cannot change immediately. These skills reduce suffering by helping us stop fighting against reality and find peace with what is, even when it is painful.

Both sets of skills are essential for building a life worth living. Crisis survival skills keep us safe in the moment, whilst reality acceptance skills help us move forward when we face unchangeable circumstances. Together, they form a comprehensive approach to managing life's inevitable difficulties without creating additional suffering.

The Purpose of Distress Tolerance

Distress tolerance serves several crucial functions in emotional regulation and psychological wellbeing. Firstly, these skills help us survive crises without making them worse. When we are in intense emotional pain, our impulse may be to do anything to make the pain stop immediately. However, many of the actions we might take in these moments create new problems or intensify existing difficulties. Distress tolerance skills provide alternative actions that help us tolerate the moment without creating additional suffering.

Secondly, distress tolerance skills help us accept reality. Much of our suffering comes not from painful events themselves, but from our refusal to accept that these events have occurred or are occurring. When we fight against reality, insisting that things should be different than they are, we add mental suffering to our pain. Acceptance does not mean approval or resignation but rather acknowledging what is true in the present moment.

Thirdly, these skills help us make space for wise decision making. In crisis, our emotional mind dominates, and we are likely to make choices we will later regret. Distress tolerance skills help us pause, survive the intensity of the moment, and create space for Wise Mind to emerge. Once we have moved through the crisis, we can make thoughtful decisions about how to address our situation.

Finally, distress tolerance skills help us build resilience. Each time we successfully tolerate distress without making it worse, we learn that we can survive painful moments. We build confidence in our ability to handle difficult situations. This confidence itself reduces anxiety about future challenges and increases our overall capacity to cope with life's difficulties.

When to Use Distress Tolerance Skills

Distress tolerance skills are particularly useful in specific situations. Use these skills when you are in crisis and at risk of acting impulsively in ways you will later regret. A crisis is a situation where your emotions are so intense that you feel you cannot think clearly or make wise decisions. You may feel overwhelmed, desperate, or at the end of your ability to cope. In these moments, crisis survival skills can help you get through without making matters worse.

Use these skills when you are facing a situation you cannot change or cannot change immediately. Perhaps you are waiting for important news, dealing with a loss, facing a difficult but necessary medical procedure, or experiencing unavoidable pain. Reality acceptance skills help you reduce the suffering that comes from fighting against what is.

Use these skills when problem solving is not currently possible or would make the situation worse. Sometimes we face problems that have no immediate solution, or attempting to solve a problem in an emotional state would lead to poor decisions. Distress tolerance helps us pause, survive the moment, and wait until we can address the situation from Wise Mind.

Use these skills when you notice yourself engaging in avoidance that is creating additional problems. If you find yourself turning to substances, excessive sleep, compulsive behaviours, or other avoidance strategies that are interfering with your life, distress tolerance skills provide healthier alternatives for managing difficult emotions.

It is important to note that distress tolerance skills are not a substitute for problem solving or emotion regulation. When problems can be solved, we should work towards solutions.

When emotions can be regulated, we should use emotion regulation skills. Distress tolerance is for those moments when we must simply endure, accept, or survive without making matters worse.

Crisis Survival Skills

Crisis survival skills are your emergency toolkit for moments of intense distress. These are strategies to use when emotions threaten to overwhelm you, when you feel you cannot cope, when urges to engage in destructive behaviours are strong, or when you need to get through an immediate crisis without making your situation worse.

These skills are not designed to solve problems or fix situations. They are designed to help you survive the moment, to keep yourself safe, to prevent impulsive actions that would create new problems. Think of them as emotional first aid. Just as you would apply a bandage to stop bleeding whilst you make your way to hospital for proper treatment, crisis survival skills help you manage intense distress whilst you make your way to more lasting solutions.

Crisis survival skills include several specific techniques, each effective in different situations and for different people. You may find some techniques more helpful than others. The key is building your personal crisis survival toolkit with multiple strategies so that you always have options available when distress strikes.

Recognising When You Need Crisis Survival Skills

Learning to recognise when you are entering crisis territory helps you deploy these skills before you become completely overwhelmed. Several signs indicate you may need crisis survival skills right now.

Your emotional intensity has reached a level where you cannot think clearly. When emotions are extremely intense, they flood your system and make it difficult to access Wise Mind or problem-solving abilities. You feel swept away by your emotions rather than experiencing them as passing states. This emotional flooding is a key indicator that crisis survival skills are needed.

You are experiencing strong urges to engage in impulsive or destructive behaviours. Perhaps you want to harm yourself, use substances, binge eat, lash out at someone, or quit your job. These action urges feel overwhelming and necessary in the moment. When you recognise these urges as symptoms of crisis rather than appropriate responses to the situation, you can intervene with crisis survival skills.

Your usual coping strategies are not working. Perhaps you tried going for a walk, calling a friend, or using mindfulness, but your distress remains overwhelming. When your standard toolkit is not sufficient for the intensity of what you are experiencing, it is time for crisis survival skills.

You cannot effectively problem-solve because emotions are too intense. If someone asked you what would help in this situation, you genuinely could not think clearly enough to answer. This cognitive impairment from emotional overwhelm indicates crisis-level distress requiring survival skills rather than problem solving.

You are thinking in catastrophic, all-or-nothing terms. Thoughts like I cannot bear this, this will never end, everything is ruined, or I cannot survive this moment indicate crisis level thinking. These thoughts suggest emotional overwhelm that requires crisis survival intervention.

The STOP Skill

The STOP skill is the most fundamental crisis survival skill. It is a simple but powerful technique for creating a pause between the crisis moment and your response, allowing you to interrupt an impulsive action before it occurs. STOP stands for: Stop, take a step back, Observe, and Proceed mindfully.

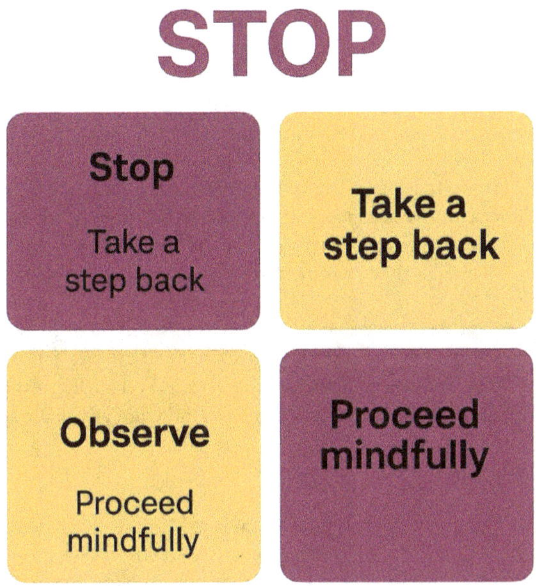

Figure 3: The STOP Skill

This skill can be used in any crisis, particularly when you feel the urge to act impulsively. It takes only seconds to implement but can prevent actions that might take months or years to repair. Learning to STOP has helped countless individuals avoid destructive behaviour during moments of intense distress.

S , Stop

The first step is simply to stop. Freeze. Do not move, do not speak, do not act. When you feel the urge to do something impulsive, the very first intervention is to stop yourself from doing it immediately. This sounds simple, but it requires recognising that a pause is possible even when emotions scream that you must act right now.

In moments of crisis, our body prepares for action. Adrenaline flows, muscles tense, and action urges feel irresistible. The Stop step interrupts this automatic progression from feeling to action. You are inserting a pause, a gap, a moment of non-action between your emotional experience and your behavioural response.

This pause does not need to be long. Even one second of stopping creates space for the next steps. If you can freeze for five seconds, even better. The key is resisting the pull to act immediately on emotional impulse. You are demonstrating to yourself that you have agency, that emotions are strong, but they do not control your actions unless you allow them to.

Some people find physical strategies helpful for the Stop step. You might literally stand still or sit down. You might put your hands in your pockets or sit on your hands if the urge is to hit or throw something. You might close your eyes briefly. You might press your feet firmly into the floor to ground yourself. Whatever helps you interrupt automatic action works.

T , Take a Step Back

The second step is to take a step back, both literally and figuratively. Physically stepping back creates psychological distance from the situation. Metaphorically, you are stepping back from your emotional experience to gain perspective. You are moving from being inside the emotion to observing it.

Physical stepping back can be powerful. If you are in an argument, literally take a step backwards or turn and walk a few steps away. If you are alone and overwhelmed, physically move to a different location—a different room, outside, anywhere that represents a shift. This physical movement disrupts the crisis momentum and creates a felt sense of distance.

Psychological stepping back means cultivating an observer stance towards your experience. Instead of being your emotions, you observe your emotions. You might say to yourself: I am having a thought that I cannot cope, rather than I cannot cope. I am experiencing intense anger, rather than This situation is intolerable. This subtle linguistic shift creates observer distance, reminding you that emotions are experiences you are having, not absolute truths about reality.

Some people find breathing helpful for creating psychological distance. Taking several slow, deep breaths whilst deliberately relaxing your shoulders creates a sense of spaciousness.

You are quite literally making room between the stimulus and your response. You are choosing not to be controlled by the immediate crisis pull.

Taking a step back also means detaching from outcome urgency. Often in crisis, we feel we must resolve everything immediately. We must know now, decide now, act now. Taking a step back means recognising that waiting is possible. The decision can wait one hour, or until tomorrow, or until you are in Wise Mind. Very few situations actually require immediate action, despite what emotional mind insists.

O , Observe

The third step is to observe what is happening. This is where mindfulness becomes your ally. You deliberately notice your internal experience and your external situation without immediately judging or reacting. You are gathering information, seeing clearly, understanding what is actually occurring.

Observe your thoughts. What thoughts are present right now? Notice them without necessarily believing them or acting on them. You might notice I am thinking that this is unbearable. I am thinking that I want to harm myself. I am thinking that everyone hates me. These thoughts arise in crisis but observing them as thoughts rather than facts gives you choice in how to respond.

Observe your emotions. What emotions are you feeling? Try to name them specifically. Is it anger, sadness, fear, shame, disappointment, grief? Often, what feels like overwhelming emotion is actually several emotions layered together. Naming them begins to reduce their overwhelming quality. You are no longer drowning in undifferentiated distress but experiencing named emotional states that you know eventually pass.

Observe your body. What physical sensations are present? Tension, heat, trembling, pain, numbness? Where in your body are you feeling the emotion? Bringing attention to body sensations grounds you in present moment experience and helps discharge some emotional intensity. Body sensations, unlike thoughts, cannot lie or catastrophise. They are what they are.

Observe the situation. What actually happened? Strip away interpretations and judgements for a moment and identify the facts. Your partner said X. You received Y news. Z person did not respond to your message. These are facts. They may be painful facts but seeing them clearly without the overlay of catastrophic interpretation helps you respond more effectively.

Observe your action urges. What do you want to do right now? Yell, leave, hurt yourself, use substances, send an angry message? Observing the urge is not the same as acting on it. You can notice I have a strong urge to send an angry text, without sending the text. Observing urges without automatically following them is a crucial life skill.

P , Proceed Mindfully

The final step is to proceed mindfully. This means choosing your next action deliberately, based on Wise Mind rather than emotional impulse. You ask yourself: What action would be effective here? What response serves my long-term goals and values rather than just relieving immediate distress?

Proceeding mindfully requires checking in with your values and goals. Will this action move me towards the life I want to build, or will it create new problems? Will this action make tomorrow easier or harder? Will this action maintain my self-respect and my relationships, or will I regret it when the emotion passes? These questions help you evaluate potential responses.

Sometimes proceeding mindfully means doing nothing. Not all situations require action. Sometimes the wise response is to wait, to see what develops, to allow emotions to settle before making decisions. Doing nothing mindfully is very different from doing nothing because you are frozen or avoidant. It is an active choice based on wisdom rather than fear.

Sometimes proceeding mindfully means using other DBT skills. You might use TIP skills to reduce physiological arousal, distraction techniques to get through the next hour, or self-soothing to provide comfort. You might recognise that problem solving is not possible right now and consciously choose to wait until tomorrow when you are calmer.

Sometimes proceeding mindfully means taking action, but measured, considered action rather than impulsive reaction. You might decide to have a difficult conversation, but you do it calmly and clearly rather than in angry attack mode. You might decide to leave a situation, but you leave thoughtfully rather than storming out dramatically.

The key to proceeding mindfully is the deliberate choice. You are acting from Wise Mind rather than emotional mind. You have inserted pause, observation, and wisdom between stimulus and response. This is the opposite of impulsivity. This is agency.

STOP in Practice: Case Studies

Case Study 1: Jasmine's Text Message Crisis

Jasmine was waiting for an important text from her boyfriend, Tom. They had argued the previous evening, and Tom had left angry. Jasmine sent several apologetic messages overnight but received no response. By late morning, her anxiety had transformed into rage. How dare he ignore her. This was emotional abuse. She would show him he could not treat her this way. She typed out a long, angry message detailing everything wrong with their relationship and his character, her finger hovering over sends.

In that moment, a small part of her remembered STOP. She literally stopped; finger frozen above the screen. She took a physical step back from her phone, placing it faces down on the table. She walked to the other side of the room. She observed: I am feeling extremely anxious, which has turned into anger. I am having the thought that he is ignoring me to hurt me. I am having the urge to hurt him back. I want to send this message to make him feel the pain I am feeling.

Jasmine recognised these observations. She had been here before. Every time she sent messages like this, the relationship deteriorated further. Every time she acted from rage to relieve anxiety; she regretted it hours later when she saw Tom's perspective more clearly. She asked herself: What do I actually want here? She wanted connection with Tom, reassurance that they were alright, resolution of the conflict. Sending an attacking message would not achieve any of these goals.

Proceeding mindfully, Jasmine deleted the angry message. She decided to wait four hours before sending anything. She used distraction techniques to manage her anxiety in the meantime. Four hours later, Tom texted explaining that his phone had died overnight, and he had been in meetings all morning. He asked if they could talk that evening. Jasmine felt flooded with relief and gratitude that she had not sent the message. Her STOP practice had prevented significant relationship damage.

Case Study 2: Marcus's Workplace Impulse

Marcus's manager criticised his work in a team meeting. The criticism felt unfair and humiliating. Marcus felt his face flush, his hands tremble. He wanted to stand up, tell his manager exactly what he thought of his management style, and walk out. He had been treated poorly for months, and this was the final straw. His body was already tensing to stand when he remembered: STOP.

Marcus stopped. He remained seated, even though his body screamed to move. He deliberately relaxed his muscles and took a deep breath. He took a mental step back: This is happening in a meeting with ten colleagues present. My career matters to me. This feeling will pass. He observed his experience: I am feeling shame and anger. I am having thoughts that this is intolerable, and I must defend myself immediately. I have an urge to storm out dramatically.

Marcus asked himself: What do I value here? He valued his career, his reputation among colleagues, his financial stability. Walking out would serve his immediate need to express anger but would damage everything he valued. Proceeding mindfully, Marcus chose to stay seated. He said calmly: I hear your feedback. I would like to discuss this privately to understand your concerns fully. Can we meet this afternoon?

His manager agreed. In the afternoon meeting, away from colleagues, Marcus was able to respond to the criticism thoughtfully. He acknowledged valid points whilst respectfully disagreeing with others. He maintained his professional relationship and his self-respect. Later, he recognised that STOP had prevented a catastrophic career decision made in emotional mind.

Case Study 3: Claire's Self-harm Urge

Claire had been self-harm free for six months. She felt proud of this achievement and hopeful that her self-destructive patterns were behind her. Then she received devastating news: she had not been accepted to the graduate programme she had applied for. All her hopes for the future collapsed. She felt like a failure, worthless, stupid. The urge to cut arose with such force that she found herself in the bathroom, holding a razor blade, before she fully registered what was happening.

In that moment, she thought: STOP. She literally stopped moving, arms at her sides. She took several steps backward until she was sitting on the edge of the bathtub, as far from the razor as possible. She observed: I am in crisis. I am feeling overwhelming disappointment and shame. I am thinking that I am a failure. I have an extremely strong urge to cut. I want relief from this pain.

Claire had learned that self-harm urges, however strong, pass if she does not act on them. She knew that cutting would bring temporary relief but lasting regret. She would have to tell her therapist, her support group, her family. She would have to restart her self-harm free counter. She would feel additional shame on top of her current pain. She asked herself: What do I need right now? She needed support, comfort, and to get through the next hour without harming herself.

Proceeding mindfully, Claire left the bathroom immediately, leaving the razor blade behind. She called her therapist's crisis line and left a message. She texted two friends from her DBT group. She used TIP skills to reduce her physiological arousal. She wrapped herself in a blanket and watched television to distract herself. The urge to cut remained for about ninety minutes, rising and falling in waves, but she did not act on it. By evening, the crisis intensity had passed. Claire remained self-harm free. STOP had helped her interrupt an automatic pattern and choose a different path.

Practice Exercises for STOP

Exercise 1: STOP Rehearsal - Identify three situations where you typically act impulsively. For each situation, write out exactly how you would use STOP. What would stopping look like? How would you take a step back physically and mentally? What would you observe? What mindful action would you take? Rehearsing STOP in advance makes it more accessible during actual crisis.

Exercise 2: Daily STOP Practice - Each day this week, use STOP in a non-crisis situation. When you feel any impulse—to check your phone, to eat something, to respond to a message—practice STOP first. This builds the habit of pausing before acting, making it more likely you will remember STOP during an actual crisis.

Exercise 3: STOP Response Card - Create a card to carry with you or save on your phone that lists the STOP steps with brief reminders of how to implement each step. In crisis, our memory fails. Having a tangible reminder helps us remember to use the skill when we need it most.

Pros and Cons: Weighing Decisions in Crisis

Pros and Cons is a structured decision-making skill for crisis moments when you are experiencing strong urges to engage in impulsive or destructive behaviours. When emotions are intense, it can feel as though acting on impulse is the only option, that you must do something right now to relieve your distress. The Pros and Cons skill helps you pause and systematically evaluate the consequences of acting on crisis urges versus resisting them, making it more likely you will choose the response that serves your long-term wellbeing.

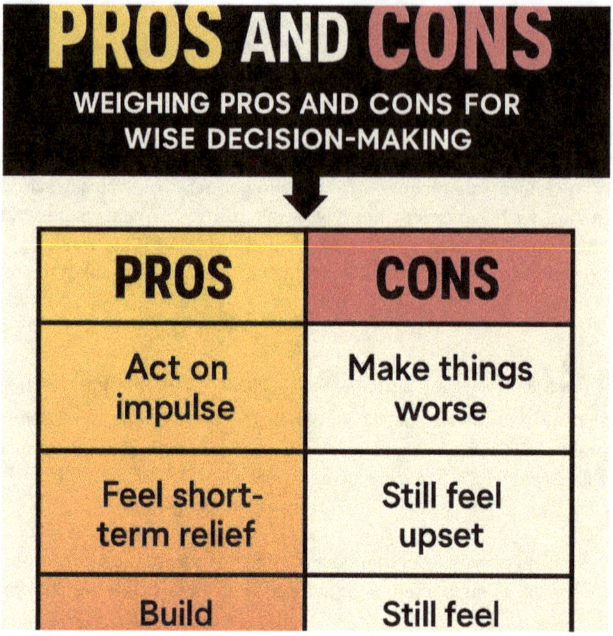

Figure 5: Weighing Pros and Cons

This skill recognises that in a crisis, our thinking narrows dramatically. We can see only the immediate relief that a destructive behaviour might provide, whilst the negative consequences seem distant or irrelevant. Emotions hijack our decision-making capacity, and we lose access to Wise Mind. Pros and Cons is a tool for broadening your perspective when emotions have narrowed it, for bringing Wise Mind back online when emotional mind dominates.

The technique is straightforward: you list the advantages and disadvantages of two options. The first option is acting on the crisis urge—doing the impulsive, destructive behaviour that the emotional mind wants you to do. The second option is resisting the crisis urge—tolerating distress and not engaging in the behaviour. By systematically listing the pros and cons of each option, you create mental space between urge and action, allowing Wise Mind to participate in the decision.

How to Use Pros and Cons. Using Pros and Cons effectively requires a structured approach. Ideally, you should complete this exercise in writing, as writing engages rational thought processes more effectively than simply thinking through options. If writing is not possible in the crisis moment, you can do this mentally, but writing is strongly preferred when feasible.

First, identify the crisis urge clearly. What specific behaviour are you tempted to engage in? Be precise. Rather than "I want to hurt myself", specify "I want to cut my arm". Rather than "I want to escape", specify "I want to leave work without telling anyone and drive somewhere far away". Precision helps you evaluate consequences accurately.

Second, create a four-quadrant grid, either on paper or in your mind. The quadrants are Pros of acting on the urge, Cons of acting on the urge, Pros of resisting the urge, and Cons of resisting the urge. Having all four quadrants is crucial. Many people naturally think only about the pros of acting on an urge (immediate relief) and the cons of resisting it (continued distress), which makes destructive behaviour seem like the obvious choice. Completing all four quadrants provides a balanced picture.

Third, fill in each quadrant honestly and thoroughly. Start with whichever quadrant feels easiest. Do not censor yourself or judge your responses. If a pro of acting on the urge is "I will feel relief", write that down even though it might seem like a poor reason. The goal is honesty, not presenting yourself as already wise and rational. The emotional mind's perspective deserves to be acknowledged, not suppressed.

When listing consequences, include short-term and long-term effects. Include emotional, physical, relationship, practical, and value-based consequences. Consider how this choice affects not just this moment but tomorrow, next week, and next month. Consider the effects on yourself and the effects on others you care about. A comprehensive list is more persuasive to the emotional mind than a brief one.

Fourth, review what you have written. Read through all four quadrants. Notice the patterns. Often, you will discover that the pros of acting on the urge are almost entirely short-term, whilst the cons are long-term and substantial. The pros of resisting may include maintaining your values, protecting relationships, avoiding new problems, and feeling proud of yourself tomorrow. The cons of resisting are usually temporary distress that will pass.

Finally, make a choice. Pros and Cons is not a substitute for decision-making; it is a tool to support wise decision-making. After completing the exercise, you must still choose. Sometimes the choice will feel clear, with resisting the urge obviously serving your wellbeing better than acting on it. Sometimes the choice will feel difficult, with genuine advantages on both sides. In those moments, recommit to your values and long-term goals. Choose the action that tomorrow you will be grateful for, not the action that right now you desperately wants.

Common Crisis Urges and Their Pros and Cons

Understanding typical patterns in crisis urges can help you apply Pros and Cons more effectively. Whilst every situation is unique, certain urges arise commonly, and recognising these patterns helps you think through consequences more completely.

Urge to Self-Harm

Pros of acting: Immediate emotional relief, expression of internal pain, sense of control, distraction from overwhelming emotions, and physical sensation that feels more manageable than emotional pain.

Cons of acting: Physical injury and potential scarring, shame and disappointment in yourself, having to restart self-harm free count, needing to explain injuries to others, reinforcement of maladaptive coping patterns, potential medical complications, disappointing your therapist and loved ones, and moving further from recovery goals.

Pros of resisting: Maintaining your self-harm-free streak, proving to yourself you can tolerate distress without harming yourself, pride and self-respect tomorrow, avoiding shame and regret, moving towards recovery, demonstrating to yourself that emotions pass without self-harm, and strengthening healthier coping patterns.

Cons of resisting: Continued intense emotional distress, feeling as though you cannot cope, needing to use other distress tolerance skills that feel less effective, and experiencing discomfort without immediate relief.

Urge to Use Substances

Pros of acting: Immediate escape from distress, temporary numbness or euphoria, social connection if using with others, relief from cravings, feeling "normal" if substance use has been habitual.

Cons of acting: Potential health consequences, financial cost, shame and disappointment, breaking sobriety, possible legal consequences, disappointing people who support your recovery, worsening of underlying problems that led to the urge, difficulty at work or in relationships the next day, reinforcement of addictive patterns, and potential danger if judgement is impaired.

Pros of resisting: Maintaining sobriety, pride in your strength, avoiding shame and regret, proving you can cope without substances, financial savings, maintaining health, keeping commitments to yourself and others, moving towards recovery goals, waking up tomorrow without a hangover or guilt.

Cons of resisting: Continued experience of distress without immediate escape, strong cravings that feel difficult to tolerate, missing the familiar ritual of substance use, and needing to face problems without a chemical buffer.

Urge to Lash Out at Someone

Pros of acting: Expression of anger, feeling powerful rather than vulnerable, temporary relief from feeling hurt or powerless, communicating that you are upset, possibility that the person will understand how much they hurt you.

Cons of acting: Damage to relationship, possible end of relationship, person becoming defensive rather than understanding, escalation of conflict, saying things you cannot take back, reputation damage if others witness it, shame and regret later, reinforcement of aggressive communication patterns, potential consequences at work or in family.

Pros of resisting: Preserving important relationships, maintaining self-respect, opportunity to communicate effectively later when calm, avoiding escalation, modelling healthy conflict management, ability to see situation more clearly once emotions settle, pride in self-control.

Cons of resisting: Continued feeling of anger or hurt, the person not immediately knowing how upset you are, feeling as though you are suppressing legitimate feelings, and energy required to regulate emotion rather than expressing it.

Making Pros and Cons More Effective

Several strategies can increase the effectiveness of Pros and Cons as a crisis survival skill.

First, prepare Pros and Cons in advance for the urges you experience frequently. If you regularly struggle with self-harm urges, substance use urges, or anger-driven behaviour, create a comprehensive Pros and Cons analysis when you are in Wise Mind, then keep it accessible for crisis moments. Reading through pre-written analysis during a crisis is often more effective than creating one from scratch whilst emotionally flooded.

Second, make consequences vivid and personal. Rather than writing "relationship damage" as a con, write "Sarah will be hurt and may stop trusting me, and I will feel terrible about that for weeks". Rather than "pride" as a pro of resisting, write "I will wake up tomorrow feeling strong and capable, and I will text my sponsor to share my success". Specific, vivid consequences engage the emotional mind more effectively than abstract ones.

Third, include consequences that matter to you personally, not consequences you think should matter. If maintaining your sobriety streak matters enormously to you, that belongs in the pros of resisting, even if it seems superficial. If disappointing your therapist feels devastating, include that even if you wish you cared less about others' opinions, it still feels devastating. The goal is effectiveness, not appearing rational or independent.

Fourth, consider asking someone you trust to help you generate a Pros and Cons list when you are in crisis. Sometimes others can see consequences more clearly than we can when emotions overwhelm us. A supportive person can remind you of your values, goals, and consequences you may be overlooking in the heat of the moment. This is not about them deciding for you, but about them helping you access Wise Mind.

Fifth, review previous Pros and Cons analyses to learn from your patterns. After acting on an urge or successfully resisting one, return to your Pros and Cons list and evaluate its accuracy. Did the pros you anticipated actually occur? Were the cons as bad as predicted, or worse? This review helps you create more accurate analyses in future crises.

Case Study: Emma's Crisis Decision

Emma received feedback at work that her project was not meeting expectations and would need significant revision. She felt humiliated and furious. Her immediate impulse was to send a scathing email to her manager listing everything wrong with the management of this project, then call in sick for the rest of the week to avoid facing anyone. These urges felt overwhelming and necessary.

Instead of immediately acting, Emma remembered Pros and Cons. She found a private space and wrote out the analysis. For the pros of sending the email and avoiding work, she listed: "I would express my anger and feel less powerless. My manager would know how I really feel. I would not have to face colleagues. I could have several days to calm down."

For the cons, she wrote: "I would damage or end my professional relationship with my manager. The email might be forwarded to HR or senior management. I would feel ashamed tomorrow when I re-read it. Taking sick leave when not actually ill is dishonest and could create suspicion. I would still need to face everyone eventually, and avoidance would make that harder. My reputation at work would suffer. I would miss the opportunity to actually address the project issues. I would regret this for months."

For the pros of resisting these urges, Emma listed: "I would maintain my professional reputation. Tomorrow I will feel proud of my self-control. I could address the feedback constructively once I calm down. I would keep my manager's respect. I would model emotional regulation I am trying to learn. I could finish the week with dignity. I would not create a crisis I would have to spend weeks repairing."

For the cons of resisting, she wrote: "I would still feel angry and humiliated right now. My manager would not immediately know how upset I am. I would have to face people at work whilst feeling terrible. I would need to use other skills to get through the day rather than escaping."

Reviewing her analysis, Emma could see that whilst acting on her urges offered immediate emotional relief, resisting them served her long-term wellbeing and values much more effectively. The cons of acting were substantial and long-lasting, whilst the cons of resisting were temporary discomfort that would pass. She decided to resist the urges. She deleted the draft email she had begun writing. She stayed at work through the day, using distraction and self-soothing skills to manage her distress. That evening, she felt proud of her choice. The next day, she was able to meet with her manager calmly to discuss the project feedback. The situation was resolved constructively because she had not damaged the relationship with impulsive communication.

Practice Exercises for Pros and Cons

Exercise 1: Pre-Crisis Planning - Identify the three crisis urges you experience most frequently. For each one, create a comprehensive Pros and Cons analysis whilst you are in Wise Mind. Be thorough and honest. Save these analyses where you can access them during a crisis, perhaps on your phone or in a crisis survival kit. When the urge arises, read through your pre-prepared analysis before making any decision.

Exercise 2: Post-Crisis Review - After experiencing a crisis urge, whether you acted on it or resisted it, complete a Pros and Cons analysis retrospectively. Then evaluate: were the pros and cons you anticipated accurate? What did you overlook? What consequences were more or less significant than predicted? This review improves your future analyses.

Exercise 3: Values Connection - For a recurring crisis urge, create a Pros and Cons list that explicitly connects consequences to your values. For instance, if you value honesty, note how acting on an urge might violate that value. If you value close relationships, note how a behaviour might damage relationships. Connecting pros and cons to your deepest values makes them more emotionally compelling.

TIP Skills: Changing Your Body Chemistry

TIP skills are powerful techniques for rapidly reducing intense emotional arousal by changing your body's physiological state. When emotions are extremely intense, sometimes talking or thinking does not help because you are too flooded to access reasoning. TIP skills work by directly affecting your nervous system, interrupting the physiological crisis state and bringing you back to a level where other coping skills become accessible.

TIP stands for: Temperature, Intense exercise, Paced breathing, and Paired muscle relaxation. Each technique affects your nervous system in specific ways to reduce emotional intensity quickly. These skills are particularly useful when you are emotionally flooded and cannot think clearly, when the urge to act destructively is overwhelming, or when you need rapid relief to prevent impulsive action.

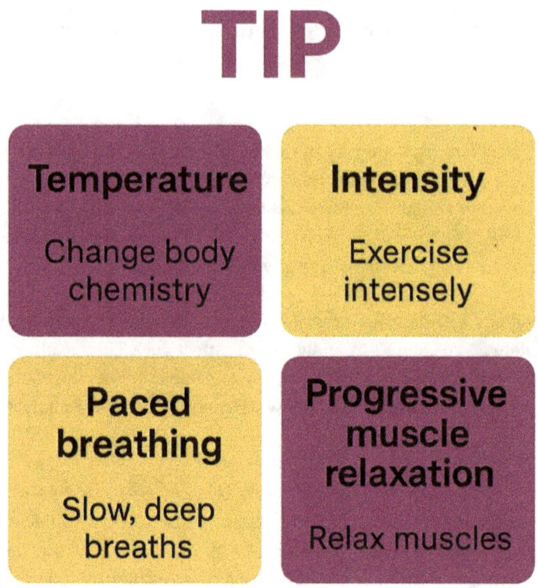

Figure 4: TIPP Skills for Changing Body Chemistry

T , Temperature: Using Cold to Reset Your System

The temperature technique uses cold to activate your body's dive reflex, which automatically slows your heart rate and reduces emotional intensity. This is not about merely feeling cold; it is about triggering a specific physiological response that calms your nervous system rapidly.

The most effective implementation is holding your breath and submerging your face in very cold water (ideally with ice) for thirty seconds. This combination of breath-holding and facial cold exposure most reliably triggers the dive reflex. Your heart rate slows, blood flow redirects to core organs, and emotional arousal decreases. The effect is not psychological; it is biological.

If submerging your face is not practical, alternatives include holding a cold pack or bag of frozen vegetables against your face, particularly covering your forehead, cheeks, and the area under your eyes. Hold the cold against your face for at least thirty seconds whilst breathing slowly. Alternatively, splash very cold water on your face repeatedly, or hold your wrists under very cold running water for several minutes.

Some people resist using cold because it is uncomfortable. This is understandable, but the discomfort is brief and worthwhile. Thirty seconds of physical cold can interrupt emotional crisis that might otherwise last hours or lead to destructive behaviour. The temporary physical discomfort is far less than the lasting emotional pain of impulsive action.

The temperature technique is particularly effective for panic attacks, intense anger, overwhelming urges to self-harm, and emotional flooding where you cannot think clearly. It works quickly, usually within a minute, making it ideal for emergency situations. Keep cold packs in your freezer specifically for crisis use or know where you can access cold water quickly when needed.

Important Safety Note

Do not use the temperature technique if you have certain medical conditions including heart problems or eating disorders. The dive reflex slows heart rate significantly, which can be dangerous for people with cardiac conditions. If you have any health concerns, consult your doctor before using this technique. For most people, it is safe and remarkably effective.

I, Intense Exercise: Burning Off Crisis Energy

Intense exercise changes your body chemistry by metabolising stress hormones and releasing endorphins. When you are in emotional crisis, your body is flooded with adrenaline and cortisol preparing you for fight or flight. If you actually engage in intense physical activity, you complete the stress cycle your body has initiated. The hormones get used for their intended purpose, and your body can return to baseline.

For this technique to work for crisis management, the exercise must be genuinely intense—enough to elevate your heart rate significantly and make you breathe hard. A gentle walk, whilst helpful for general wellbeing, will not provide the crisis relief that intense exercise offers. You need to actually exert yourself: running, fast cycling, jumping jacks, burpees, dancing vigorously, hitting a punching bag, or any activity that makes your muscles burn and your breath come fast.

The exercise does not need to last long. Even five to ten minutes of intense activity can shift your physiological state significantly. Twenty minutes is better if you can manage it, but short bursts are effective. The key is intensity, not duration. Push yourself to the point where you are genuinely working hard, where continuing requires effort.

Intense exercise is particularly effective for anger, as it channels aggressive energy constructively. It also works well for anxiety, as it provides the physical release your body has been preparing for. After intense exercise, people often report feeling physically tired but mentally clearer, emotionally calmer, and more able to think rationally about their situation.

Build an intense exercise crisis plan before you need it. Identify what intense exercise you can access quickly when in crisis. Perhaps you keep running shoes by the door and have a route planned. Perhaps you have a skipping rope or can-do bodyweight exercises at home. Perhaps you have access to a gym or a punching bag. Knowing your plan in advance makes it more likely you will use this skill when you need it.

Safety Considerations

Intense exercise should be used cautiously if you have physical health problems or injuries. Do not exercise to the point of harming yourself. If you have heart problems, respiratory conditions, or physical limitations, consult your doctor about what level of exercise is safe for you. The goal is to help yourself, not create new problems.

P, Paced Breathing: Regulating Your Nervous System

Paced breathing involves deliberately slowing and deepening your breath to activate your parasympathetic nervous system, which calms your body's arousal response. When you are in emotional crisis, you're breathing typically becomes rapid and shallow, which maintains and even intensifies your distress. Deliberately changing your breathing pattern interrupts this cycle.

The most effective paced breathing for crisis involves breathing in through your nose for a count of four or five and breathing out through your mouth for a longer count of six to eight. The longer exhale is crucial—this is what triggers your relaxation response. Continue this pattern for several minutes, ideally for at least five minutes and preferably ten or more, if possible.

Some people find it helpful to breathe into their belly rather than their chest. Place one hand on your chest and one on your belly. As you breathe in, try to make the belly hand rise whilst the chest hand stays relatively still. This diaphragmatic breathing is more efficient and promotes deeper relaxation than shallow chest breathing.

Paced breathing can be combined with counting or focusing on the sensation of breath to keep your mind occupied. If you simply count your breaths (in two three four, out two three four five six), your mind has something to do rather than spinning in crisis thoughts. This dual benefit—physiological calming plus mental focusing—makes paced breathing particularly valuable.

Paced breathing works well for anxiety, panic, and situations where you need to calm down enough to think clearly. It is less effective when you are extremely angry and need to discharge aggressive energy—in those cases, intense exercise works better. But for many crisis situations, paced breathing provides accessible, immediate relief that you can use anywhere without any equipment.

Common Problems with Paced Breathing

Some people find that focusing on breath increases their anxiety rather than decreasing it. If this happens to you, try focusing on other physical sensations instead—the feeling of your feet on the floor, the sensation of your hands resting in your lap—whilst still breathing slowly. The paced breathing works on your nervous system even if you do not focus directly on it.

If you feel lightheaded whilst practising paced breathing, you are likely breathing too deeply or too rapidly. Slow down. Your breaths should be slow and gentle, not forced or gasping.

You are looking for calm, deep breathing, not hyperventilation disguised as relaxation practice.

P , Paired Muscle Relaxation: Releasing Physical Tension

Paired muscle relaxation involves deliberately tensing and then releasing muscle groups whilst breathing in a paced manner. This technique addresses the physical tension that accompanies and maintains emotional distress. When you are anxious, angry, or overwhelmed, your muscles tighten. This physical tension sends signals back to your brain that danger is present, maintaining your distressed state. By releasing physical tension, you interrupt this feedback loop.

to practise paired muscle relaxation, combine paced breathing with progressive muscle tensing and releasing. As you breathe in, tense a muscle group. As you breathe out (the longer exhale), release the tension completely. Move systematically through your body: hands, arms, shoulders, face, jaw, neck, chest, back, stomach, legs, feet.

The tensing should be noticeable but not painful. You are creating contrast so that when you release, you really feel the sensation of letting go. For example, make tight fists as you breathe in, then completely relax your hands as you breathe out. Scrunch your facial muscles as you breathe in, then let your face go soft as you breathe out. The release should feel like melting, like letting go of something you were gripping.

This technique takes longer than the others—perhaps ten to fifteen minutes for a full body progression. It is best used when you have time and space to focus on it, perhaps before bed or when you are alone and can take time for self-care. It is particularly effective for anxiety that manifests as physical tension and for calming yourself before sleep.

Some people prefer recorded guidance for paired muscle relaxation. Many free recordings are available online that talk you through the process. Having external guidance can help you stay focused and not forget any muscle groups. Once you have practised with guidance several times, you can often do it independently.

ACCEPTS: Distraction Techniques

ACCEPTS is an acronym representing seven distraction techniques that help you get through crisis moments by shifting your attention away from overwhelming distress. Distraction is not avoidance when used appropriately. It is a conscious choice to redirect attention temporarily whilst you wait for emotional intensity to decrease to a manageable level.

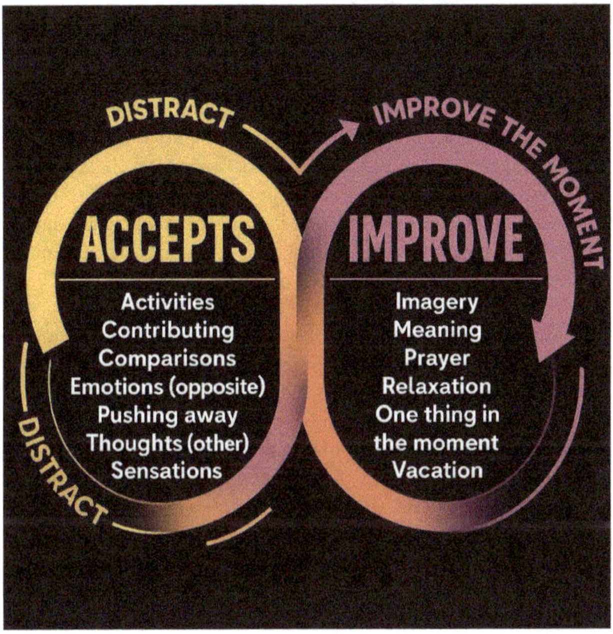

Figure 6: ACCEPTS and IMPROVE the Moment

These techniques work because intense emotions, whilst powerful, are time limited. Emotional peaks typically last between twenty and ninety minutes if we do not continue to fuel them with rumination or impulsive action. Distraction helps you navigate this peak period without exacerbating your situation. Once emotional intensity has decreased, you can then address your problem from the Wise Mind rather than the emotional mind.

ACCEPTS stands for: Activities, Contributing, Comparisons, Emotions, Pushing away, Thoughts, and Sensations. Each technique offers a different way to shift attention during a crisis. Some will work better for you than others, and various techniques work better in different situations. Building familiarity with all seven gives you maximum flexibility in managing crises.

A, Activities: Engaging Your Mind

Distraction activities mean deliberately engaging in an activity that occupies your attention sufficiently so that you cannot simultaneously ruminate on your distress. The activity must capture your mind, not just fill time. Passive activities like watching television often do not work because your mind can still wander whilst your body remains still. You need activities that demand active engagement.

Practical distraction activities vary from person to person but share certain commonalities. They require concentration, involve multiple senses or cognitive processes, and are engaging enough that your mind must focus on them. Examples include puzzles (jigsaw puzzles, crosswords, Sudoku), complex crafts (knitting, drawing, model building), video games that require concentration, reading absorbing fiction, cooking a complex recipe, organising and decluttering, learning something new (a language, an instrument, a skill), or physical activities that require attention (yoga, dance, rock climbing).

The key is matching the activity to your current state. If you are highly agitated, you may need to engage in physical activity that burns energy before you can settle into a quieter distraction. If you are moderately distressed, an engaging cognitive activity may help immediately. If you are in public, you may need a discreet activity, such as a puzzle app on your phone. Planning your distraction activities means you have options ready when a crisis strikes.

Create a distraction menu: a written list of activities that work for you, organised by intensity level and accessibility. Include activities you can do at home, at work, alone, with others, with money, without money. When you are in crisis and cannot think clearly, this menu provides ready options rather than forcing you to brainstorm whilst overwhelmed.

C, contributing: Helping Others

Contributing means deliberately doing something helpful for someone else or for the wider community. This technique shifts focus from your own distress to another person's well-being or to a cause you value. It provides distraction whilst simultaneously building meaning and connection, which are protective factors against emotional suffering.

Contributing can take many forms. You might text or call a friend who is going through a difficult time, offering support. You may consider volunteering for a cause you care about. You might help a neighbour with shopping or gardening. You might donate to a charity. You might spend time on social media offering kind words to people who seem to need support. You might clean up litter in your neighbourhood. You might help a family member with a task. The action can be small or large; what matters is that it genuinely helps someone.

Contributing is particularly powerful because it counteracts feelings of worthlessness or hopelessness that often accompany crisis. When you feel your life has no meaning or that you have nothing to offer, contributing provides immediate evidence that you can make a positive difference. It builds self-worth through action rather than through trying to think your way to feeling valuable.

Some people resist contributing during a crisis, feeling they are in too much pain to help others. This is understandable, but often the best time to contribute is precisely when we are suffering. Contributing does not require feeling good first. In fact, the act of contributing usually improves how we think. It interrupts self-focused rumination and activates our care-giving system, which naturally reduces distress.

Keep a list of quick contributing actions you can take during a crisis: people you can support, causes you can donate to, and helpful actions you can take in your community. Having this list prepared means, you can contribute even when you feel too distressed to think creatively about how to help others.

C, Comparisons: Shifting Perspective

Comparisons as a distraction technique means deliberately comparing your current situation to times when things were worse, or to people who are coping with greater difficulties. This technique must be used carefully, as comparison can become judgemental or dismissive of your own pain. Used skilfully, however, it can provide perspective that reduces the sense that your current situation is unbearable.

Comparing to your own past can be particularly effective. When overwhelmed by current difficulties, you might remind yourself of previous crises you have survived. Perhaps you felt equally hopeless during a past breakup, job loss, or health crisis, yet you managed to survive and eventually find stability again. Remembering that you have coped with difficulty before provides evidence that you can cope with current difficulty. This is not minimising your pain; it is recognising your resilience.

Comparing to others must be done without judgement towards yourself or others. You might think about people managing serious illness, grieving profound losses, living in extreme poverty or danger, or facing challenges far greater than your current ones. This comparison is not about making yourself feel guilty for struggling—your pain is real and valid. Instead, it is about recognising that if others can bear such difficulties, you can bear your current difficulty. If they can find ways to cope, you can find ways to cope.

Some people find it helpful to consider how they would view their current crisis if it were happening to someone they loved. Often, we have more compassion and perspective for others' struggles than we do for our own. If your best friend were in your exact situation, would you tell them that their life was over and that they could not cope? Probably not. You would likely reassure them that they could get through this difficult time. Applying this external perspective to your own situation can reduce catastrophic thinking.

The comparisons technique is less about minimising your experience and more about interrupting thoughts that your situation is uniquely terrible or unbearable. It reminds you that difficulty is an inherent part of the human experience, that others have survived similar or even worse challenges. That survival is possible even when circumstances are painful.

E, Emotions: Creating Opposite Emotions

The emotions technique involves deliberately creating an emotional experience that is different from or opposite to your crisis emotion. You do this by engaging in activities that naturally generate specific emotions. Since it is challenging to feel two strong, incompatible emotions simultaneously, creating a new emotion can temporarily reduce the intensity of your distress.

If you are feeling sad, consider watching a comedy that generates laughter or amusement. If you are feeling anxious, consider listening to calming music that promotes peace. If you are feeling angry, consider watching something tender or heartwarming that evokes feelings of love or compassion. If you are feeling lonely, consider watching uplifting content that evokes feelings of connection or inspiration.

This technique requires knowing what activities reliably generate specific emotions for you. Comedy works for many people, but not everyone finds the same things funny. Some people are moved to tears by classical music, whilst others find it boring. You need to identify your own emotional triggers—the films, music, books, videos, activities, or memories that shift your emotional state.

Create emotion-specific playlists or collections. You might have a playlist of songs that make you feel hopeful, a folder of comedy clips that make you laugh, a collection of photos that make you feel loved, or a list of films that inspire you. Having these collections prepared means you can access them quickly during a crisis rather than searching whilst distressed.

The emotions technique is not about suppressing or denying your original emotion. That emotion is valid and may need to be addressed later. This technique involves creating temporary relief during a crisis, allowing you to survive the moment without resorting to destructive actions. Once the crisis intensity has passed, you can then address the underlying issues that triggered your distress.

P, Pushing Away: Mentally Distancing

Pushing away means mentally creating distance from your distressing situation or thoughts. You consciously decide not to think about your problem right now, postponing its resolution until you are calmer and more capable of addressing it effectively. This is not avoidance if done consciously and temporarily. It is a strategic delay.

One pushing-away technique is imagining placing your problem in a box, closing the lid, and putting it on a shelf. You tell yourself, 'I will deal with this tomorrow at three o'clock.' Right now, I am putting it aside. This visualisation creates psychological distance and permits you to stop ruminating temporarily.

Another technique is the worry time approach. You designate a specific time each day (perhaps thirty minutes in the evening) as your worry time. When distressing thoughts arise outside of this time, acknowledge them and say, 'I will think about this during worry time.' For now, I am setting it aside. During your designated worry time, you can address your concerns thoroughly and effectively. Outside that time, you practise pushing them away.

Some people use physical gestures to reinforce the act of pushing away. When a distressing thought arises, they might make a pushing gesture with their hands whilst thinking, 'Not now.' Later. This physical component can make the mental action feel more concrete and practical.

Pushing away is particularly useful for rumination—repetitive thoughts about problems that have no immediate solution. Suppose you find yourself thinking the same distressing thoughts repeatedly; pushing away interruptions can help break this unproductive cycle. You are not ignoring your problems; you are choosing a better time to address them when you are in a clear, rational mind rather than an emotional one.

This technique requires trust that you will actually return to the problem later. Some people fear that pushing away means avoiding forever. To counter this, actually schedule time to address your concern. Please put it in your calendar. This scheduled attention reassures you that you are not abandoning the issue; you are merely postponing it to a better time.

T, Thoughts: Replacing Unhelpful Thinking

The thought technique involves deliberately filling your mind with various thoughts to replace distressing ruminations. When your mind is occupied with neutral or positive thoughts, it cannot simultaneously spiral into crisis thinking. This technique recognises that we can influence what we think about, even if we cannot always control what thoughts arise initially.

Counting is perhaps the most straightforward thought replacement technique. Count backwards from one hundred by sevens (one hundred, ninety-three, eighty-six, seventy-nine). Count by threes. Count backwards by thirteens. The mathematical challenge occupies your mind sufficiently that distressing thoughts cannot dominate. If you lose track, start over. The point is not completing the task but occupying your mind.

Reciting something from memory works similarly. You might recite song lyrics, poems, prayers, quotations you have memorised, or passages from books you know well. The act of retrieval and recitation fills your mind and crowds out crisis thoughts. Some people memorise specific texts precisely for this purpose—knowing they have mental material they can access during distress.

Mental games also provide thought distraction. You might list all the cities you can think of beginning with B, all the films you have seen in the past year, all the foods you can name in alphabetical order, or all the animals you can think of that live in the ocean. These games engage your mind actively and break the cycle of distressing rumination.

Planning or designing something occupies thoughts constructively. You might mentally design your dream home, plan a fantasy holiday, organise how you would redecorate your bedroom, or imagine what you would do if you won the lottery. This type of pleasant planning gives your mind a place to go that is not crisis focused.

The thought technique is not about positive thinking or trying to convince yourself that everything is fine when it is not. It is simply about giving your mind a temporary alternative focus so that you can get through the crisis peak without adding fuel through rumination. Once you are calmer, you can think about your situation productively rather than destructively.

S, Sensations: Overwhelming Physical Sensations

The sensations technique uses intense physical sensations to interrupt emotional distress. Strong physical sensations can temporarily override emotional sensations because your nervous system has a limited capacity—intense physical input demands attention, leaving less room for emotional experiences. This technique is beneficial when emotions are so intense that they feel physically unbearable.

Cold sensations are highly effective. Holding ice cubes in your hands until they melt, taking a cold shower, biting into something icy, or placing ice on your neck or face creates an intense sensation that captures attention. The cold is uncomfortable, which is precisely why it works—it gives your nervous system something else to process besides emotional distress.

Strong tastes also work well. Biting into a lemon, eating something very spicy, or putting a strong mint or sour-sweet in your mouth creates an intense sensory experience. The robust taste demands attention and temporarily eclipses emotional experience. Some people keep very sour or spicy foods specifically for use in a crisis.

Physical exertion creates an overwhelming sensation. Holding a challenging yoga pose until your muscles burn, squeezing a stress ball as hard as you can for as long as you can, or doing exercises to the point of exhaustion generates physical sensations intense enough to interrupt emotional flooding. This overlaps with intense exercise from TIP skills but focuses specifically on the intense sensation created.

Some people use loud music or sounds, allowing the volume to be almost uncomfortably loud so that the auditory input overwhelms other sensations. Others use strong scents, such as peppermint oil, eucalyptus, or ammonia capsules. The key is intensity—the sensation must be powerful enough to capture your complete attention.

A crucial note: this technique should not involve self-harm. Intense sensation is not the same as hurting yourself. The goal is temporary distraction through intense but safe sensation, not pain that damages your body. If you feel tempted to use harmful sensations, that is a sign you need additional support and should contact your therapist or crisis services.

Using ACCEPTS Effectively

ACCEPTS works best when you use techniques in combination and when you have prepared your distraction toolkit in advance. During a crisis, your ability to think clearly is impaired. Having concrete plans and materials ready makes it far more likely you will actually use these skills.

Create a physical crisis survival kit containing items for ACCEPTS techniques, such as puzzles, craft materials, ice packs, sour sweets or spicy snacks, lists of comedy videos or films, phone numbers for contributing opportunities, and objects with strong scents. Keep this kit accessible so you can reach for it during a crisis.

Write a detailed ACCEPTS plan listing specific activities you will use for each technique. Be concrete: not just watch something funny but watch these three specific comedy clips saved on my phone. Not only do you solve a puzzle, but also complete the jigsaw puzzle in the hall cupboard. Particular plans are more likely to be followed than vague intentions.

Remember that ACCEPTS provides temporary relief, not a permanent solution. After using these techniques to get through the crisis peak, you still need to address underlying issues. ACCEPTS buys you time—time for emotions to decrease enough that you can think clearly, time for the situation to develop or change, time for help to arrive, or simply time for the neurochemical storm to pass so that Wise Mind can re-emerge.

IMPROVE the Moment

IMPROVE the moment is a set of techniques for making an unbearable moment slightly more bearable. Whilst ACCEPTS helps you distract from distress, IMPROVE enables you to change your internal experience of the difficult moment. These skills acknowledge that you cannot always change external circumstances, but you can sometimes shift your internal relationship to those circumstances in ways that reduce suffering.

IMPROVE stands for: Imagery, Meaning, Prayer, Relaxation, One thing in the moment, Vacation, and Encouragement. Each technique offers a different way to make a crisis moment more tolerable. These skills do not eliminate pain, but they can alleviate unbearable distress, making it just bearable enough to survive without resorting to destructive action.

I, Imagery: Creating Mental Refuge

Imagery means using your imagination to create a mental experience that provides relief from current distress. You visualise a place, scene, or scenario that evokes feelings of safety, peace, comfort, or joy. Whilst your body remains in the crisis, your mind temporarily inhabits a different reality, providing respite from emotional overwhelm.

Compelling imagery engages multiple senses. You don't just picture a peaceful beach; you imagine the sound of waves, the warmth of the sun on your skin, the smell of salt air, the feeling of sand between your toes, and the taste of coconut from the drink in your hand. The more sensory detail you include, the more absorbing the imagery becomes and the more effectively it provides relief.

Your safe place imagery might be real or imaginary. Some people visualise actual locations where they have felt peaceful—a grandmother's garden, a childhood bedroom, a favourite holiday destination. Others create entirely imaginary sanctuaries—a castle in the clouds, an underwater palace, a forest grove that does not exist in reality. What matters is that the place evokes feelings of safety and calm for you.

Some people find guided imagery recordings helpful. Many free resources are available online that talk you through visualising peaceful scenarios. Having external guidance can help you stay focused when your mind tends to wander back to distressing thoughts. Once you have practised with recordings several times, you can often create your own imagery without guidance.

Imagery can also involve visualising coping effectively with your situation. If you are dreading a difficult conversation, you might imagine yourself handling it calmly and skilfully. If you are overwhelmed by a task, you might imagine completing it successfully. This type of imagery rehearses competence and can reduce anxiety whilst building confidence.

Develop your safe place imagery through repeated practice when you are not in crisis. The more familiar your safe place becomes, the more quickly and easily you can access it during actual distress. Some people draw or write detailed descriptions of their safe place to strengthen the imagery. This preparation means your mental refuge is readily available when you need it most.

M, meaning: Finding Purpose in Pain

Finding meaning involves seeking purpose, value, or learning from your painful experiences. This does not mean that suffering is good or that pain serves a purpose. Instead, it means that even in unavoidable suffering, we can sometimes find or create meaning that makes the pain more bearable and transforms our relationship to it.

Viktor Frankl, a psychiatrist who survived Nazi concentration camps, wrote extensively about meaning in suffering. He observed that those who found meaning in their experience—whether through maintaining hope, serving others, or committing to future goals—coped better than those who saw their suffering as purely meaningless. Whilst you cannot choose whether you suffer, you can sometimes choose what your suffering means to you.

You might find meaning by recognising growth that results from difficulty. Perhaps this crisis is teaching you resilience, compassion, or strength you did not know you possessed. Perhaps it is showing you who your true friends are. Perhaps it is clarifying your values or priorities. These realisations do not make the pain good, but they create meaning alongside the pain.

You might find meaning by deciding that your struggle will help you understand and support others facing similar challenges. Many therapists, counsellors, and support group leaders were motivated by their own suffering to help others. Many activists working for change experienced the injustice they now fight against. Your pain might become the foundation for meaningful contribution.

You might find meaning through spiritual or religious frameworks. Many faith traditions offer narratives that give suffering meaning—whether through concepts of spiritual growth, divine testing, karma, or afterlife reward. If you hold religious or spiritual beliefs, drawing on those frameworks during crisis can provide comfort and purpose. Even if you are not religious, broader philosophical frameworks about the nature of human existence can offer meaning.

Some people resist finding meaning, feeling it excuses or minimises their pain. This is understandable. Finding meaning should never involve blaming yourself for your suffering or accepting mistreatment as deserved. It is about finding a way to carry pain that makes it slightly lighter, not about convincing yourself that pain is actually good. You can acknowledge that your suffering is real and unjust whilst also recognising that you can create meaning from how you respond to it.

P , Prayer: Connecting to Something Greater

Prayer, broadly defined, means connecting to something greater than yourself. For religious individuals, this might mean traditional prayer to God or a higher power. For non-religious individuals, it might mean connecting to nature, humanity, the universe, or values and principles they hold sacred. The key is stepping outside your individual suffering to connect with a larger context that provides comfort or perspective.

Traditional prayer can be profoundly comforting during crisis. It provides a sense of being held by something larger than yourself, of not being alone in your pain. It offers a way to express suffering, ask for help, and surrender control of what you cannot change. If prayer is part of your religious or spiritual practice, deliberately turning to it during crisis can provide significant relief.

For those without traditional religious belief, the practice might look different but serve similar functions. You might sit quietly and feel your connection to all humans who have suffered and survived. You might go into nature and feel part of something vast and enduring. You might reflect on your values and feel connected to a larger moral framework. You might think about people who have inspired you and draw strength from their example.

Some people find comfort in reading spiritual or philosophical texts during crisis. Whether the Bible, the Bhagavad Gita, Buddhist teachings, Stoic philosophy, or humanist writings, texts that speak to suffering and meaning can provide solace and perspective. Having passages memorised or marked for easy access during crisis provides immediate comfort when you need it.

The prayer practice, in whatever form works for you, helps reduce the isolation of suffering. Pain can feel deeply lonely, as if you are the only person experiencing this particular horror. Connecting to something greater—whether divine, natural, or human—reminds you that you are part of a larger whole, that others have survived similar pain, that you are not utterly alone even in your darkest moment.

R , Relaxation: Releasing Physical Tension

Relaxation involves deliberately releasing physical tension to reduce overall distress. This overlaps with the paired muscle relaxation from TIP skills but focuses more broadly on any technique that promotes physical relaxation. When your body relaxes, signals are sent to your brain that the crisis is diminishing, which can actually reduce emotional intensity. Physical and emotional states influence each other in a bidirectional manner.

Progressive muscle relaxation, as described in TIP skills, is highly effective. Other relaxation techniques include gentle stretching, particularly focusing on areas where you tend to hold tension (neck, shoulders, jaw). Many people unconsciously clench their jaws or tighten their shoulders during periods of stress. Consciously releasing this tension can provide surprising relief.

Breathing practices, when combined with relaxation intention, become more powerful. You might lie down, close your eyes, and breathe whilst deliberately softening your body with each exhale. Imagine tension melting away with each out-breath. Imagine your body becoming heavier, sinking into the floor or bed, releasing all effort to hold tension.

Warm baths or showers can promote physical relaxation, as warmth naturally relaxes muscles. The sensory experience of water combined with warmth creates a conducive environment for releasing tension. Some people add elements like bath salts, dim lights, or calming music to enhance the relaxation effect.

Gentle, mindful movement like slow walking, tai chi, or very gentle yoga can promote relaxation through movement rather than stillness. Some people find static relaxation difficult when anxious, but can relax through gentle, flowing movement. The key is keeping the movement slow and deliberate, focusing on releasing tension rather than achievement or intensity.

Massage, whether self-massage or from another person, can release physical tension effectively. Massaging your own neck and shoulders, hands, or feet whilst breathing slowly promotes relaxation. If you have access to professional massage, this can be a valuable self-care strategy during particularly difficult periods, though it is less accessible during immediate crisis.

O , One Thing in the Moment

This technique means focusing your attention completely on one thing in the present moment. You bring your full awareness to a single object, sensation, or activity, allowing everything else—including your crisis thoughts and emotions—to fade into the background temporarily. This is essentially mindfulness practice applied specifically to crisis survival.

You might focus completely on a single object in your environment. Choose something neutral—a plant, a candle flame, a piece of furniture. Observe it with total attention. Notice every detail: colour variations, texture, shape, shadows, light. Describe it to yourself in minute detail. When your mind wanders to distressing thoughts, gently return attention to the object. This focused observation can interrupt crisis spiralling.

You might focus on a single physical sensation. The feeling of your breath, the sensation of your hands resting in your lap, the contact between your feet and the floor. Attend to this sensation with complete focus. Notice subtle variations and changes. This anchors you in present bodily experience rather than in crisis thoughts about past or future.

You might focus on a single sound. Perhaps rain, music, a fan, traffic noise. Let the sound fill your awareness completely. Notice its qualities—volume, pitch, rhythm, variation. When thoughts intrude, acknowledge them and return to the sound. This auditory focus can be particularly effective because sound naturally captures attention.

You might focus on a single activity, doing it with complete absorption. Washing dishes with full attention to the sensation of water and soap. Walking with complete attention to the physical experience. Drinking tea whilst noticing every aspect of the experience. The activity becomes a meditation, an anchor in the present moment that interrupts crisis consciousness.

This technique requires practice. Our minds naturally wander, and during crisis, they wander specifically to distressing content. Each time you notice your mind has wandered and return attention to your chosen focus; you are strengthening your capacity for present-moment awareness. This is not failure; this is the practice. Over time, your ability to focus one-mindfully during crisis will increase.

V , Vacation: Taking a Mental Break

Taking a vacation does not necessarily mean leaving your physical location. It means giving yourself permission to take a complete mental break from your problems, your responsibilities, and your crisis for a defined period. You consciously decide: For the next hour (or thirty minutes, or three hours), I am on vacation from this crisis. I will not think about it, work on it, or try to solve it. I am taking a break.

This mental vacation might involve doing something purely pleasurable with no productive purpose: watching your favourite show, playing video games, reading escapist fiction, having a long bath, napping, browsing online shops, looking at photos of places you would like to visit, cooking something elaborate just for enjoyment. The activity should be something that gives you genuine pleasure or interest, not something you feel you should do.

The key is giving yourself explicit permission. Many people feel guilty taking breaks during crisis, believing they should be actively solving their problems at every moment. This belief is counterproductive. Your brain needs breaks. Your emotions need breaks. Grinding yourself into exhaustion does not actually help you cope better; it reduces your capacity to cope. Taking defined breaks strengthens rather than weakens your crisis management.

Time-bound your vacation clearly. You are not avoiding your problems forever; you are taking a scheduled break. Perhaps you say: From two until three o'clock, I am on vacation. At three o'clock, I will return to addressing my situation if needed. This boundary makes the break feel safe rather than irresponsible. You know you will return to dealing with reality, so you can fully rest during your vacation period.

Some people find it helpful to physically mark their vacation. They might change location, change clothes, or do something else to create a felt sense of being elsewhere. This physical marking reinforces the psychological permission to take a break and helps you more fully inhabit the vacation mindset.

Mental vacations work best when taken before you are completely exhausted and overwhelmed. If you wait until you absolutely cannot continue, you may be too depleted to rest effectively. Regular mini vacations throughout difficult periods prevent you from reaching total depletion. They are maintenance, not just emergency measures.

E , Encouragement: Supporting Yourself

Encouragement means talking to yourself in the way a wise, compassionate friend would talk to you during difficulty. It means countering the harsh self-criticism that often accompanies a crisis with deliberate self-compassion and realistic encouragement. You become your own supportive coach rather than your harshest critic.

Develop specific encouraging statements that resonate for you. These might include I can get through this. I have survived difficulties before, and I will survive this. This feeling is temporary. I am doing the best I can with what I have right now. I am strong even when I feel weak. I do not have to be perfect; I just have to keep going. This too shall pass. I am worthy of compassion, including my own.

Write these statements down. Keep them in your phone, on a card in your wallet, on sticky notes where you will see them. During a crisis, accessing encouraging thoughts from memory is difficult. Having them written provides concrete reminders when your own mind fails to generate supportive thoughts.

Encouragement is not lying to yourself or forcing positive thinking when your situation is genuinely terrible. It is acknowledging reality whilst also acknowledging your capacity to cope with reality. You can hold both truths simultaneously: This is really hard, AND I can handle hard things. This is painful AND I have survived pain before. I am struggling, AND struggling does not mean failing.

Some people find it helpful to imagine what a loved one would say to them. If your best friend, parent, or partner were watching you go through this crisis, what would they say? Often, we can access compassion for ourselves through imagining others' compassion for us. We can borrow their belief in us when our own belief falters.

Encouragement includes celebrating small victories. If you got through an hour without engaging in destructive behaviour, that is success worth acknowledging. If you used a coping skill, that is success. If you reached out for support, that is success. Crisis management is not about perfect coping; it is about surviving moment by moment without making things worse. Each moment you survive deserves recognition and encouragement.

Combining IMPROVE Techniques

IMPROVE techniques often work best in combination. You might use imagery whilst practising relaxation. You might take a mental vacation, accompanied by encouraging self-talk. You might find meaning whilst praying. Experiment with different combinations to discover what works best for you.

Create an IMPROVE plan for common crisis situations you face. What imagery will you use? What meaning frameworks help you? What encouraging statements resonate? What vacation activities provide genuine relief? Having these prepared means, you can access them quickly when a crisis strikes rather than trying to create them whilst overwhelmed.

Self-Soothing with the Five Senses

Self-soothing means comforting yourself through pleasant sensory experiences. When you are in distress, deliberately engaging your senses in soothing ways can reduce emotional intensity and provide comfort. This technique acknowledges that humans are sensory beings, and our emotional states are significantly influenced by our sensory experiences.

Self-soothing is not indulgence or weakness. It is an essential life skill. Children naturally seek sensory comfort when distressed—a soft blanket, a favourite toy, a parent's hug. As adults, we often lose touch with this natural soothing capacity. Self-soothing skills help us reclaim it. You are learning to provide for yourself the comfort you needed as a child and still need as an adult.

Effective self-soothing engages each of your five senses deliberately. You plan soothing experiences for vision, hearing, smell, taste, and touch. Having a repertoire of soothing options for each sense means you always have tools available, regardless of your situation or location.

Vision: Soothing What You See

Visual soothing involves looking at things that are beautiful, calming, or pleasant. Natural beauty is particularly soothing for most people. You might look at a sunset, watch clouds move across the sky, observe trees swaying in wind, watch birds, look at flowers, or gaze at water. Nature provides endless visual soothing opportunities, and research shows that even brief nature exposure reduces stress.

If you cannot access nature directly, looking at nature images or videos provides benefit. Keep a collection of beautiful nature images on your phone or computer. Watch nature documentaries. Look at photographs of places you find beautiful. The visual cortex does not distinguish sharply between actual experience and vivid imagery, so visual soothing through images can genuinely calm your nervous system.

Art provides visual soothing. Visit galleries, look at art books, or view art online. Different art affects people differently—some find abstract art soothing; others prefer realistic landscapes or portraits. Discover what visual art calms you personally. You might even create your own art as both a soothing activity and a source of pleasant visuals.

Consider your living environment. Can you arrange your space to include visually soothing elements? Perhaps plants, beautiful objects, calming colours, photographs your love, or artwork that brings you peace. Creating a visually soothing environment means you are constantly surrounded by visual comfort rather than needing to seek it out during crisis.

Some people find specific visual stimuli particularly soothing: watching flames in a fireplace or candle, watching fish in an aquarium, looking at the stars, watching rain, observing snow fall. Identify your personal visual soothers and incorporate them regularly into your life, intensifying their use during difficult periods.

Hearing: Soothing What You Listen To

Auditory soothing involves listening to sounds that calm, comfort, or uplift you. Music is perhaps the most obvious and powerful auditory soother. Different music works for different people and different moods. You might find classical music soothing, or ambient electronic music, or gentle folk, or jazz, or specific songs that have particular meaning for you.

Create soothing playlists for different needs. You might have a playlist for sleep, one for anxiety, one for sadness, one for anger. Having these prepared means, you can access appropriate soothing immediately rather than searching whilst distressed. Update your playlists regularly as you discover new music that soothes you.

Natural sounds provide profound auditory soothing: rain, ocean waves, wind in trees, birdsong, flowing water. Many apps and websites provide nature sound recordings. Some people use these sounds for sleep, work focus, or general background soothing throughout the day. If you have access to natural sounds directly—living near water or in a quiet area with birdsong—deliberately taking time to listen provides significant benefit.

Some people find human voices soothing. You might listen to audiobooks, podcasts with calming hosts, guided meditations, or recordings of loved ones. The human voice, when gentle and kind, activates our social bonding system and provides comfort even when we are alone.

Silence itself can be soothing. If you live in a noisy environment, seeking out quiet spaces—a library, a park early in the morning, a quiet room in your home—can provide auditory relief. Some people use noise-cancelling headphones not to play anything, but simply to create silence. In our noisy world, silence has become a luxury worth seeking.

Smell: Soothing Through Scent

Olfactory soothing uses pleasant scents to influence your emotional state. The olfactory system connects directly to the limbic system, the emotional centre of your brain, which means scents can influence emotions rapidly and powerfully. Pleasant scents can quickly shift your state from distressed to calm.

Essential oils provide a concentrated scent for soothing. Lavender is widely known for its calming properties. Other commonly soothing scents include chamomile, bergamot, ylang-ylang, sandalwood, and vanilla. You might use a diffuser, apply diluted oil to your wrists or temples, or simply smell the oil from the bottle. Experiment to discover which scents you find soothing personally.

Natural scents also soothe effectively. The smell of flowers, fresh rain, pine trees, cut grass, ocean air, or fresh bread can evoke feelings of peace and wellbeing. If you have access to these scents naturally, deliberately taking time to notice and appreciate them provides benefit. If not, scented candles, room sprays, or incense can bring nature scents indoors.

Some people find certain scents soothing because of positive associations. Perhaps the perfume your grandmother wore, the smell of your partner's shirt, the scent of a holiday location you loved, or the smell of a favourite childhood food. These personally meaningful scents can be particularly powerful soothers because they connect to positive memories and feelings of safety or love.

Keep soothing scents accessible. You might carry a small bottle of essential oil in your bag, keep a scented candle at home, or use scented hand cream throughout the day. Having a soothing scent readily available means you can access this tool quickly whenever you need comfort.

Taste: Soothing Through Food and Drink

Gustatory soothing utilises pleasant tastes to provide comfort. This must be done mindfully to avoid creating eating problems or using food as your only coping mechanism. Taste soothing is about savouring small amounts of genuinely enjoyable foods, not about mindless eating or bingeing to numb feelings.

Identify foods and drinks you find genuinely soothing. These might include herbal tea, hot chocolate, soup, fruit, chocolate, ice cream, favourite meals, or comfort foods from childhood. The key is foods you truly enjoy and find comforting, not foods you think you should like or foods you eat habitually without real pleasure.

When using taste for soothing, eat slowly and mindfully. Put a small piece of chocolate in your mouth and let it melt slowly, noticing the flavour develop and change. Sip tea slowly, noticing the warmth, the flavour, the aroma. Eat fruit with full attention to its texture and taste. This mindful eating maximizes the soothing effect whilst preventing overconsumption.

Some people find specific tastes soothing beyond the specific food: sweet, sour, spicy, and umami. Experiment with different taste profiles to discover what soothes you. You might find that a sour-sweet calms anxiety, or that spicy food grounds you, or that sweet foods comfort sadness. Understanding your taste-emotion connections helps you use this tool effectively.

Important caveat: if you have a history of eating disorders or struggle with using food to cope with emotions, approach taste soothing carefully. Focus more heavily on other senses, and if you use taste, do so only with support from your treatment team and with clear limits. For some people, taste soothing is not an appropriate tool, and that is perfectly acceptable. The other senses provide sufficient soothing options.

Touch: Soothing Through Physical Sensation

Tactile soothing uses pleasant touch sensations to comfort yourself. Touch is perhaps the most fundamental soothing sense—infants require touch for healthy development, and adults continue to need pleasant tactile experiences for wellbeing. Self-soothing through touch helps you provide for yourself the comforting physical contact you need.

Soft textures provide a reliable touch that soothes. Wrapping yourself in a soft blanket, wearing comfortable clothes, stroking soft fabric, or holding a soft toy can provide comfort. Many people underestimate the power of texture, but our skin is sensitive, and a soft touch activates the calming parasympathetic nervous system.

Temperature provides a soothing touch. A warm bath, a hot water bottle, heated blankets, or sitting in sunshine can soothe through warmth. Conversely, cool air, cold water on your face, or cool cloths can soothe through coolness. Different temperatures work for different emotional states and different people. Experiment to discover what works for you.

Self-massage provides a soothing touch that you can implement immediately. Massage your hands, your neck and shoulders, your scalp, or your feet. The physical touch, combined with the pressure and movement, can release tension and provide comfort. You do not need expertise; a simple, intuitive massage provides benefit.

Physical affection from others—such as hugs, handholding, or a comforting touch—is powerfully soothing, but this requires having someone available and willing. When you do have access to comforting touch from others, accept and appreciate it. When you do not, self-provided touch can still offer significant comfort. Some people find that weighted blankets provide a sense of being held even when alone.

Movement creates touch sensations that can soothe. The feeling of water in a shower, wind on your face whilst walking, the sensation of stretching, or the rhythmic feeling of movement can all provide tactile soothing. Gentle, pleasant movement engages your tactile sense whilst also providing the benefits of activity.

Building Your Self-Soothing Practice

Develop a comprehensive self-soothing plan that incorporates specific soothing strategies tailored to each of the five senses. Write these down in detail. For vision: I will look at the photo album of my holiday, watch nature videos, or go to the park. For hearing: I will listen to my calming playlist, play nature sounds, or listen to a favourite audiobook. And so on for each sense.

Assemble a physical self-soothing kit with items for each of the five senses: beautiful objects or images for vision, calming music for hearing, pleasant scents for smell, your favourite tea or treats for taste, and soft items for touch. Keep this kit readily accessible for use in a crisis. Having these items gathered means you don't need to search for them whilst distressed.

Practice self-soothing regularly, not only during a crisis. Make it a normal part of your daily self-care rather than an emergency measure. Regular practice normalises the techniques, makes them more accessible during an actual crisis, and provides a preventative benefit by reducing your baseline stress level.

Remember that self-soothing is not selfish or indulgent. It is essential for self-care. You deserve comfort. You deserve to feel soothed. Providing this for yourself is not a weakness; it is a strength. It is taking responsibility for your own wellbeing and refusing to make your distress worse through self-neglect or harsh self-treatment.

Reality Acceptance Skills

Crisis survival skills help us get through intense moments without making situations worse. Reality acceptance skills address a different but equally important challenge: accepting situations we cannot change or cannot change immediately. These skills reduce the suffering that comes from fighting against reality, from insisting that things should be different from than they are.

Much of human suffering comes not from painful events themselves, but from our refusal to accept that these events have occurred or are occurring. We waste enormous energy arguing with reality, insisting it should be different, refusing to acknowledge what is true. This refusal to accept reality does not change reality; it simply adds mental anguish to our pain.

Acceptance is perhaps the most misunderstood concept in DBT. Acceptance does not mean approval, resignation, or giving up. It does not mean you like what has happened or that you stop working to change what can be changed. Acceptance means acknowledging what is true in this moment. It means seeing reality clearly rather than through the filter of how you wish things were. It means letting go of the exhausting struggle against facts you cannot change.

This chapter explores four interconnected reality acceptance skills: Radical Acceptance, Turning the Mind, Willingness versus Wilfulness, and Half-Smiling and Willing Hands. Together, these skills provide a comprehensive approach to accepting reality whilst maintaining your dignity, values, and commitment to building the life you want.

Why Reality Acceptance Matters

Understanding why acceptance reduces suffering motivates the difficult practice of accepting painful realities. Acceptance matters for several crucial reasons.

Firstly, fighting reality creates additional suffering. When something painful happens and we refuse to accept it, we experience both the original pain and the additional suffering created by our non-acceptance. We spend energy arguing with what is, wishing it were different, and demanding that it should not be this way. This mental struggle exhausts us and prevents us from moving forward. Acceptance allows us to experience the original pain without adding layers of mental suffering through resistance.

Secondly, acceptance is necessary for effective action. When we refuse to accept reality, we cannot respond to it effectively. If we deny that a relationship has ended, we cannot take steps to care for ourselves and move forward. If we refuse to accept that we have lost a job, we cannot begin the process of seeking new employment. If we cannot accept that we have a health condition, we cannot learn to manage it. Acceptance is the foundation for effective problem-solving and change. You cannot change what you do not first accept exists.

Thirdly, non-acceptance keeps us stuck in the past or in fantasy. When we refuse to accept present reality, we remain caught in how things used to be or how we wish they were. We miss what is actually happening right now. We cannot fully engage with our present life because we are busy fighting against what is true. Acceptance frees us to engage with our actual lives rather than the lives we wish we had.

Fourthly, acceptance reduces bitterness and resentment. When we insist that life should be fair or that others should behave differently, and then life proves unfair or people disappoint us, we become bitter. This bitterness poisons our experience and our relationships. Acceptance of life's fundamental unfairness and human imperfection allows us to respond to disappointments without accumulating toxic resentment.

Finally, acceptance is the only path to peace with unchangeable realities. Some aspects of life simply cannot be changed: our past, other people's choices, ageing, illness, death, the fundamental fact that life includes suffering. We can fight against these realities our entire lives, remaining angry and bitter, or we can accept them and find peace despite them. Acceptance allows us to build meaningful lives even when those lives include unchangeable pain.

Radical Acceptance

Radical Acceptance is the foundational reality acceptance skill. It means completely accepting reality as it is in this moment, without fighting it, without judging it, without demanding it be different. The word radical indicates that this acceptance is total and complete, not partial or grudging. You accept all of reality, not just the parts you like.

Radical Acceptance does not mean you approve of what has happened. It does not mean you think painful events are good or fair or acceptable. It simply means you acknowledge that they have occurred. You stop fighting the fact of what is and instead face reality directly. This facing of reality, paradoxically, is what allows you to move forward and change what can be changed.

Understanding Radical Acceptance

Radical Acceptance is acceptance of facts, not acceptance of unacceptable behaviour or situations that can and should be changed. This distinction is crucial. You can radically accept that someone has treated you badly whilst also setting boundaries and ending the relationship. You can radically accept that you have an addiction whilst also working on recovery. You can radically accept that you are experiencing depression whilst also pursuing treatment.

The acceptance is of what is true right now. This person did treat me badly—that is a fact. I do have an addiction—that is a fact. I am experiencing depression—that is a fact. Accepting these facts does not mean accepting that these situations should remain unchanged. It means seeing clearly what you are working with so that you can respond effectively.

Radical Acceptance is particularly important for aspects of reality that you genuinely cannot change. You cannot change the past. You cannot change other people's thoughts, feelings, or choices. You cannot change many circumstances of your birth and upbringing. You cannot change that you will age and eventually die. You cannot change that life includes pain. Fighting against these unchangeable realities creates only suffering. Accepting them creates possibility for peace and for focusing your energy on what you can influence.

Radical Acceptance is not a one-time event. You do not accept something once and remain perpetually accepting. Acceptance must be practised again and again, sometimes moment by moment. You might accept a difficult reality this morning and find yourself fighting against it this afternoon. When you notice non-acceptance has returned, you choose acceptance again. And again. And again. This repeated choice is the practice of Radical Acceptance.

What to Accept

Radical Acceptance can be applied to a wide range of painful realities. Some common areas where acceptance is necessary include the following.

Accept the past. What has happened has happened and cannot be changed. You can wish your childhood had been different, but it was what it was. You can regret the choices you made, but those choices were made. You can wish traumatic events had not occurred, but they occurred. Fighting against the reality of your past keeps you trapped in it. Accepting your past frees you to focus on creating your future.

Accept other people as they are. You cannot change other people through force of will, through wishing, or through suffering. People change only when they choose to change. Your parents were who they were. Your ex-partner is who they are. Your difficult colleague is who they are. Accepting this does not mean maintaining relationships with people who harm you, but it means stopping the exhausting attempt to mentally remake them into who you wish they were.

Accept your own limitations and humanity. You are not perfect. You have flaws, you make mistakes, you have weaknesses. You have a body that gets tired and ill. You have a mind that sometimes struggles. You cannot be everything to everyone. Accepting your human limitations allows you to work with yourself as you actually are, rather than constantly berating yourself for not being superhuman.

Accept unchangeable losses. Death, ended relationships, lost opportunities, health problems—some losses cannot be undone. Fighting against their reality through denial or bargaining keeps you in perpetual pain. Accepting loss does not mean you are happy about it or that it does not hurt. It means you acknowledge the reality so that you can grieve and eventually move forward.

Accept that life is not always fair. Bad things happen to good people. Effort does not always lead to success. Merit does not always lead to reward. This fundamental unfairness of life is one of the hardest realities to accept, but fighting against it creates lasting bitterness. Accepting that life is not fair allows you to respond to unfair situations pragmatically rather than spending your life in outraged protest.

Accept that pain is part of life. Suffering is not a sign that something has gone wrong with your life or that you have failed. Pain is an intrinsic part of human existence. Everyone experiences loss, disappointment, difficulty, and physical and emotional pain. Accepting this reality allows you to face your pain with less resistance and therefore less additional suffering.

How to Practise Radical Acceptance

Radical Acceptance is a practice, a skill that develops through deliberate, repeated effort. The following steps outline the process of practising Radical Acceptance.

Step 1: Observe that you are fighting reality. Notice your thoughts and feelings that indicate non-acceptance. You might think: This should not be happening. This is not fair. I cannot believe this is true. This must be a mistake. Why me? These thoughts signal that you are fighting against what is. Simply noticing this fighting is the first step towards acceptance.

Step 2: Remind yourself that reality is what it is, regardless of your wishes. The facts are the facts whether you accept them or not. Your non-acceptance does not change reality; it only adds to your suffering. This reminder is not about resignation or defeat. It is simply acknowledging truth: What is, is. What has happened, has happened.

Step 3: Consider the causes that led to this reality. Everything that happens has causes—perhaps multiple, complex causes extending back in time. The reality you are facing arose from all these causes. Understanding causation helps reduce the feeling that reality is random or arbitrary. It also reduces the tendency to blame yourself or others inappropriately. This is what it is because everything that led to this is what it was.

Step 4: Practise accepting with your whole self—your mind, your body, and your spirit.

Mental acceptance means acknowledging facts in your thoughts. Body acceptance means allowing your body to relax rather than holding tension against reality. Spiritual acceptance means accepting on the deepest level, perhaps through prayer, meditation, or any other spiritual practice that is meaningful to you. Full acceptance engages all aspects of yourself.

Step 5: Notice any remaining resistance or non-acceptance. Acceptance is not always immediate or complete. You might partially accept, whilst part of you still fights. Notice this resistance without judgement. Each time you notice resistance, gently return to a state of acceptance. This is the practice: notice resistance, choose acceptance, notice resistance returns, choose acceptance again.

Step 6: Allow disappointment, sadness, or grief if they arise. Acceptance often brings grief. When you stop fighting reality and truly accept a loss or painful fact, you may feel the full weight of sadness. This is natural and healthy. Grief is not the same as non-acceptance. You can fully accept a loss whilst also grieving it deeply. In fact, genuine grieving requires acceptance. Allow yourself to feel your grief whilst maintaining acceptance of what is.

Step 7: Acknowledge that accepting reality does not mean approving of it. You can accept that something has happened whilst wishing it had not. You can accept the present reality whilst working to change the future reality. Acceptance and change are not incompatible. Acceptance of what is provides the foundation for effective action towards what can be.

Common Obstacles to Radical Acceptance

Most people encounter specific obstacles when attempting to practise Radical Acceptance. Recognising these obstacles helps you work through them rather than being stopped by them.

Obstacle 1: Confusing Acceptance with Approval

Many people resist acceptance because they believe it means condoning what has happened or giving up on change. This confusion makes acceptance feel morally wrong. If I accept abuse, does that mean I think abuse is acceptable? If I accept injustice, does that mean I do not care about justice?

The answer is no. Acceptance is acknowledgement of facts, not approval of those facts. You can accept that abuse occurred without thinking abuse is acceptable. In fact, you must accept that abuse occurred in order to protect yourself effectively going forward. You can accept that injustice exists whilst working tirelessly for justice. Fighting against the fact of injustice is different from fighting against injustice itself. Acceptance of what is allows more effective action towards what should be.

Obstacle 2: Fear that Acceptance Means Giving Up

Some people fear that if they accept difficult circumstances, they will stop trying to improve their situation. They believe that maintaining anger, disappointment, or refusal to accept is what motivates change. Acceptance feels like resignation.

In reality, the opposite is true. Non-acceptance tends to keep you stuck. When you are busy fighting against what is, you have little energy left for changing what can be changed. Anger and refusal to accept reality are exhausting and often lead to ineffective, reactive behaviour rather than strategic action. Acceptance frees up energy for effective change. When you clearly see what you are working with, you can develop effective strategies for change. Acceptance is the beginning of change, not the end of it.

Obstacle 3: Attachment to Being Right

Sometimes we resist acceptance because we are attached to being right about how things should be. We know that we should not have been treated this way, that life should be fair, that this should not have happened. We are right about these shoulds, and accepting reality feels like admitting we were wrong.

However, being right does not change reality. You can be entirely correct that something should not have happened and simultaneously accept that it did happen. Reality does not conform to correctness. Letting go of the need to be right allows you to face what actually is rather than what should be. You maintain your values and your sense of justice whilst accepting facts.

Obstacle 4: Grief and Pain

When we fully accept painful realities, we often experience intense grief. As long as we fight against reality, we maintain a kind of denial that protects us from the full weight of our loss or pain. Acceptance removes this protection and confronts us with the reality of our suffering. This is uncomfortable and sometimes feels overwhelming.

This grief is necessary and healthy. It is not an obstacle to acceptance but rather a natural consequence of acceptance. The path forward is through the grief, not around it. Allow yourself to grieve what you have lost, what you wish had been different, what is painful to accept. This grieving, whilst difficult, eventually allows healing that fighting against reality prevents. Trust that you can survive your grief, and that grieving is part of accepting.

Obstacle 5: Believing You Have Already Accepted

Sometimes people intellectually understand and claim to accept reality, whilst emotionally continuing to fight against it. They say: I know my childhood was difficult, and I have accepted that, but their ongoing bitterness and rumination about their childhood suggest that acceptance is incomplete. Intellectual acknowledgement is not the same as genuine acceptance.

True acceptance is evident in your emotional state and behaviour. If you have genuinely accepted something, you experience some peace around it, even if you still feel sad about it. You no longer spend significant energy ruminating, arguing with reality in your mind, or feeling outraged that reality is what it is. If you notice ongoing emotional struggle and mental fighting, that is information that acceptance is incomplete. This is not failure; it simply means you need to continue practising acceptance.

Radical Acceptance in Practice: Case Studies

Case Study 1: Sophia and Childhood Trauma

Sophia spent years in therapy processing childhood abuse. She understood intellectually that her parents had been troubled people who caused her significant harm. However, she remained consumed with rage and bitterness. She frequently thought: They should not have done that. How could parents treat a child that way? It is not fair that I have to deal with this whilst they live without consequences. This ongoing mental fighting exhausted her and prevented her from moving forward.

Her therapist introduced Radical Acceptance. Initially, Sophia resisted fiercely. Accepting that abuse happened felt like saying it was acceptable. She feared that acceptance would make her weak or mean she was giving her parents permission to have harmed her. Her therapist helped her understand that acceptance was acknowledgement of facts, not approval of those facts.

Sophia began practising acceptance by first acknowledging: The abuse happened. This is a fact. My parents did harm me. This is a fact. She noticed how much energy she spent daily arguing with these facts, insisting they should not be true, demanding that reality be different. She began to see how this argument with reality kept her trapped in her past.

The practice was gradual and difficult. Many times, daily, Sophia noticed herself fighting reality: Why did this happen to me? She would pause and choose acceptance: It happened. It happened because of all the causes that led to it—my parents' own trauma, their mental health problems, societal factors. It happened. I do not like that it happened. I wish it had not happened. But it happened. Fighting against this fact does not change it. Accepting it frees me to focus on my healing now.

As Sophia practised Radical Acceptance, a surprising shift occurred. Her rage, which had felt immovable, began to subside. She still felt sadness about her childhood, but the bitter, consuming anger diminished. She found she could think about her past without being hijacked by hours of furious rumination. She had more energy for creating the life she wanted now because she was spending less energy fighting against the unchangeable past. She remained committed to healing and to breaking the cycle of abuse, but from a place of acceptance rather than ongoing outrage. Acceptance had not weakened her; it had freed her.

Case Study 2: Daniel and Job Loss

Daniel was made redundant from a job he loved. The redundancy was not due to his performance but to company restructuring. Daniel was shocked and outraged. He spent months insisting this should not have happened, that it was unfair, that the company had made a terrible mistake. He obsessed over every detail of why and how the decision had been made. He fantasised about the company realising their error and rehiring him. Meanwhile, he made only token efforts to seek new employment because he could not fully accept that his old job was truly gone.

Six months later, Daniel remained unemployed, financially stressed, and consumed with bitterness. His therapist suggested he was suffering from non-acceptance and introduced Radical Acceptance. Daniel's initial response was defensive: Of course, I accept it. I know I lost my job. But his therapist pointed out that his thoughts, emotions, and behaviour suggested ongoing non-acceptance. If he had truly accepted the job loss, would he spend hours daily ruminating about it? Would he feel such intense ongoing rage? Would he be avoiding job searching?

Daniel began practising Radical Acceptance. He acknowledged the facts: I lost my job. The company made a decision. That decision has consequences for me. I cannot change what happened. These are the facts. When he noticed himself starting to ruminate about why or how, he redirected: It happened. The causes that led to it were what they were. Arguing with what happened does not change it. What I can change is what I do now.

The acceptance process brought grief. As Daniel stopped fighting reality and truly accepted his job loss, he felt deep sadness about what he had lost—not just the job but also his identity as someone who worked there, his daily routines, his colleagues, his sense of security. He allowed himself to grieve this loss whilst maintaining acceptance that it was truly lost.

Within weeks of beginning genuine acceptance practice, Daniel's job search became more active and effective. He updated his CV, networked, and attended interviews with real engagement rather than half-hearted going through the motions. Three months later, he accepted a new position. Whilst it was different from his previous job, he approached it with openness rather than constantly comparing it unfavourably to what he had lost. Radical Acceptance had freed him to move forward.

Case Study 3:

Elena and Her Parents' Terminal Illness

Elena's mother was diagnosed with terminal cancer. The prognosis was six to twelve months. Elena heard the diagnosis but could not accept it. She researched alternative treatments, insisted the doctors were wrong, and believed a miracle would occur. She could not bear the reality that her mother was dying, so she fought against this reality with every ounce of her energy.

The months passed with Elena in a state of frantic denial. She argued with her mother about treatment decisions, pushed for experimental therapies, and became angry when her mother began discussing end-of-life wishes. She was so busy fighting against reality that she missed the opportunity to truly be present with her mother during their remaining time together.

When Elena's mother had only weeks left, and her condition deteriorated rapidly, Elena finally faced the reality she had been fighting. Her mother was dying. This was happening. No amount of research, anger, or desperate hope would change this fact. With her therapist's support, Elena began practising Radical Acceptance.

She accepted: My mother is dying. I do not want this to be true, but it is true. This is happening because of causes beyond anyone's control—the cancer, the limits of medicine, the nature of human mortality. I cannot change this. Fighting against this reality has cost me precious time with my mother. I accept what is so that I can be fully present for what time remains.

The acceptance brought overwhelming grief. Elena cried more in one week than she had in the previous six months of frantic fighting. But alongside the grief came a shift. She stopped arguing with her mother about treatment and instead asked what her mother wanted for her final weeks. She listened to her mother's memories and fears. She held her hand and was simply present. She told her mother she loved her and was grateful for everything she had been given.

When her mother died, Elena grieved deeply. But she did not carry the additional burden of regret for time wasted fighting reality. She had accepted what was and used her final time with her mother well. In the years following, Elena found that whilst she missed her mother intensely, she had peace about how they had said goodbye. Radical Acceptance had allowed her to face her mother's death with presence and love rather than with futile resistance.

Practice Exercises for Radical Acceptance

Exercise 1: Identify What You Are Fighting - Make a list of realities you are currently fighting against or refusing to accept. These might include past events, present circumstances, losses, or unchangeable aspects of yourself or your life. For each item, notice how fighting against this reality affects you emotionally and behaviourally.

Exercise 2: Practice Acceptance Statements - For one reality you have identified, write and repeat acceptance statements. Examples: This happened. This is a fact. I cannot change this. Fighting this does not help me. I accept what is. Repeat these statements multiple times daily, noticing any shifts in your emotional experience.

Exercise 3: Observe Non-Acceptance Thoughts - Throughout one day, notice every time you have a thought indicating non-acceptance (should not, it is not fair, why, I cannot believe). Simply notice these thoughts without judgement. Count how many you have. This builds awareness of how much energy you spend fighting reality.

Exercise 4: Acceptance Meditation - Sit quietly for ten minutes. Bring to mind something difficult you are working to accept. Notice all the feelings and thoughts that arise. Practise allowing them to be present whilst repeatedly returning to the statement: It is what it is. I accept what is. Continue for the full ten minutes, building your acceptance capacity.

Exercise 5: Grief and Acceptance - Choose something you have been fighting against. Practise fully accepting it and allow yourself to grieve. Write about your grief or talk to a trusted person about it. Notice whether allowing grief whilst maintaining acceptance provides any relief or shift in your experience.

Turning the Mind

Turning the Mind is the practice of choosing acceptance repeatedly, each time you notice you have fallen back into non-acceptance. It is the action of redirecting your mind from fighting reality back towards accepting reality. This skill acknowledges that acceptance is not a permanent state you achieve once and maintain forever. Rather, acceptance must be chosen again and again, sometimes moment by moment.

The metaphor is of standing at a crossroads. One path leads towards acceptance; the other path leads towards non-acceptance, bitterness, and suffering. You might take the acceptance path, walk along it for a whilst, and then find yourself back at the crossroads or even walking down the non-acceptance path. Turning the Mind means noticing where you are and actively choosing to turn back towards the acceptance path. You turn your mind towards acceptance, away from fighting reality.

Understanding Turning the Mind

Turning the Mind consists of two key elements. First, you notice that you are not accepting reality. Second, you make an active choice to accept. Both elements are essential. You cannot turn your mind if you do not notice it needs turning, and noticing alone without the subsequent choice accomplishes nothing.

The noticing step requires mindfulness. You observe your thoughts and emotions and recognise signs of non-acceptance: thoughts about how things should be different, feelings of ongoing rage or bitterness, rumination about the unfairness of your situation. When you notice these signs, you recognise I am not accepting right now. I am fighting reality again. This awareness without judgement is the first step.

The choosing step requires deliberate action. You cannot simply wait to feel accepting; you must choose acceptance actively. This might be an internal statement: I choose to accept what is. I turn towards acceptance. I let go of fighting. Or it might be a physical gesture—perhaps nodding your head or turning your body. The form matters less than the deliberate choice. You are taking agency, deciding to move towards acceptance rather than waiting passively for acceptance to arrive.

Turning the Mind is not the same as Radical Acceptance itself. Rather, it is the skill you use to return to Radical Acceptance when you have moved away from it. You use Radical Acceptance to accept reality fully. You use Turning the Mind to redirect yourself back towards Radical Acceptance when you notice you are no longer accepting.

Why We Need to Turn the Mind

Non-acceptance is the default human response to painful reality. Our minds naturally resist pain, insist things should be different, fight against unwanted facts. This resistance is automatic and deeply ingrained. Even after we have accepted something, our minds tend to drift back towards non-acceptance. This is not weakness or failure; it is simply how minds work.

Consider physical habits. If you learn a new way of sitting to improve your posture, you do not sit with good posture once and then maintain it forever. You notice yourself slumping and consciously correct your posture. You do this repeatedly, many times daily, gradually retraining your default position. Turning the Mind works similarly. You notice yourself slipping into non-acceptance and consciously redirect towards acceptance. You do this repeatedly, many times daily, gradually retraining your mental default response.

Turning the Mind matters because without it, Radical Acceptance becomes an abstract concept rather than a lived practice. You might understand acceptance intellectually and even experience moments of genuine acceptance. But if you do not notice when acceptance slips away and actively choose to return to it, those moments remain isolated rather than becoming a sustained practice. Turning the Mind is what transforms acceptance from an occasional state into a way of living.

How to Practise Turning the Mind

Practising Turning the Mind involves developing both the awareness to notice non-acceptance and the habit of choosing acceptance in response. The following steps provide a structure for this practice.

Step 1: Notice signs of non-acceptance. Throughout your day, pay attention to your thoughts and emotions. Notice when thoughts arise like: This should not be happening. Why did this have to happen to me? This is so unfair. I cannot stand this. Notice when you feel ongoing bitterness, rage that does not diminish, or resentment that colours your entire mood. These thoughts and feelings signal that you are not accepting reality in this moment.

Step 2: Acknowledge without judgement that you are not accepting. Simply note I am fighting reality right now. I am not accepting what is. There is no need to judge yourself for this. Non-acceptance is natural. The point is not to never experience non-acceptance but to notice it when it occurs so you can redirect towards acceptance.

Step 3: Make an active choice to accept. This choice must be deliberate. You might say internally: I choose to accept what is. I turn my mind towards acceptance. I let go of fighting this reality. Some people find it helpful to make a physical gesture—turning their head, nodding, or making a turning motion with their hand. The physical action reinforces the mental choice.

Step 4: Engage in Radical Acceptance practices. After turning your mind towards acceptance, actually practice accepting. Remind yourself of the facts you are accepting. Acknowledge that reality is what it is. Consider the causes that led to this reality. Allow any grief that arises. Engage whatever Radical Acceptance practices work for you. Turning the Mind is the choice to accept; Radical Acceptance is the accepting itself.

Step 5: Notice when you slip back into non-acceptance and turn your mind again. This will happen. You might accept something fully, feel genuine peace with it, and then an hour later find yourself furious that it happened. When this occurs, do not judge yourself. Simply notice I am fighting again. Then turn your mind back towards acceptance: I choose to accept what is. The practice is the continuous returning, not the perfect maintenance of acceptance.

Step 6: Persist. In the beginning, you may need to turn your mind dozens or even hundreds of times daily. This can feel exhausting and discouraging. You might think: Why do I keep slipping back into non-acceptance? Am I doing this wrong? No. You are doing it right. The practice is the repeated turning. Each time you turn your mind, you are building new neural pathways, weakening old patterns of non-acceptance, and strengthening your capacity for acceptance. Over time, acceptance will require less conscious effort as it becomes more habitual. But in the beginning and during particularly difficult periods, frequent turning is normal and necessary.

Turning the Mind in Practice: Case Studies

Case Study 1: Priya and Chronic Pain

Priya developed a chronic pain condition in her thirties. The pain was constant, limiting her activities and affecting every aspect of her life. She spent years seeking cures, convinced that if she tried enough treatments, the pain would eventually disappear. When each treatment failed, she felt furious and despairing. She could not accept that her life included this pain.

Her pain psychologist introduced her to Radical Acceptance and Turning the Mind. Priya intellectually understood that acceptance might reduce her suffering, but emotionally, she resisted. Accepting pain felt like giving up on ever feeling better. However, the non-acceptance was making her life unlivable. She decided to try.

Priya began by simply noticing how many times daily she fought against her pain reality. When pain arose, her immediate thoughts were: This should not be happening. Why will no one help me? This is unbearable. I cannot live like this. She counted these non-acceptance thoughts—in a typical day, she had these thoughts hundreds of times. She was spending her entire day, every day, fighting reality. No wonder she felt exhausted.

She began practising Turning the Mind. When she noticed fighting thoughts, she would pause and turn I have pain. This is my reality right now. I accept this reality. This does not mean I like it or stop seeking help. It means I acknowledge what is. She made a physical gesture of nodding her head to reinforce the mental turn. Initially, she had to turn her mind towards acceptance every few minutes. The non-acceptance returned constantly.

Over weeks and months, the practice became easier. Priya noticed that whilst the pain had not changed, her suffering had decreased significantly. She was spending less energy fighting reality and more energy actually living her life within her current limitations. She still pursued pain management strategies, but from a place of acceptance rather than desperate denial. When she noticed herself slipping into non-acceptance—and she still did, especially on high-pain days—she recognised this and turned her mind back towards acceptance. The practice had become a natural part of how she related to her chronic condition.

Case Study 2: Ahmed and Divorce

Ahmed's wife left him after fifteen years of marriage. He was devastated. Whilst he rationally understood the marriage was over, emotionally, he could not accept it. He fantasised about her returning. He replayed conversations searching for what he could have done differently. He felt constant bitter anger about the unfairness of her leaving. His entire life felt consumed by the non-acceptance of his divorce.

In therapy, Ahmed learned about Turning the Mind. His therapist explained that he would need to turn his mind towards acceptance, not once but potentially hundreds of times daily, until acceptance became more stable. Ahmed found this daunting but also strangely relieving. He had thought he should be able to accept once and be done with it. Knowing that repeated choosing was normal helped him feel less defective.

Ahmed began noticing his non-acceptance thoughts. Throughout each day, his mind would drift to thoughts like, 'She should not have left.' If only I had done X differently. Maybe she will realise her mistake. I cannot believe this is my life. Each time he noticed these thoughts, he practised turning them around: 'My marriage ended.' This is what it is. I accept this fact. I choose to turn towards acceptance rather than continuing to fight reality.

The early weeks were difficult. Ahmed sometimes turned his mind towards acceptance fifty times in a single day. Each morning, he would wake up and immediately need to turn his mind from fantasy of reconciliation back towards accepting that his marriage was over. But he persisted. He noticed that each day, the bitter rage diminished slightly. The mental energy freed up by fighting less allowed him to begin building a new life.

A year later, Ahmed still occasionally needed to turn his mind towards acceptance. When he saw his ex-wife at family events or when loneliness struck intensely, his mind would slip back into non-acceptance. But now he recognised this immediately and turned quickly back to acceptance. The practice had become almost automatic. He had built a life he valued as a single person. Turning the Mind repeatedly had not made his divorce painless, but it had made it bearable and had freed him to move forward.

Practice Exercises for Turning the Mind

Exercise 1: Count Your Non-Acceptance - For one day, carry a notecard or use a counter app on your phone. Each time you notice a non-acceptance thought, make a mark. This builds awareness of how frequently non-acceptance arises and motivates the practice of turning.

Exercise 2: Develop a Turning Phrase - Create a specific phrase you will use each time you turn your mind towards acceptance. Examples: I choose acceptance. I turn towards what is. I let go of fighting. Practise this phrase so it becomes automatic, ready to use when you need it.

Exercise 3: Physical Gesture - Develop a physical gesture to accompany turning your mind. Perhaps a nod, a hand motion, or turning your body. Practise this gesture combined with your turning phrase. The physical component makes the mental choice more concrete.

Exercise 4: Morning Acceptance Commitment - Each morning, commit to turning your mind towards acceptance whenever you notice non-acceptance during the day. Visualise yourself noticing non-acceptance and choosing to turn towards acceptance. This mental rehearsal primes you for actual practice.

Exercise 5: Turning Log - Keep a log for one week. Each time you turn your mind towards acceptance, write it down briefly: time, what you were not accepting, that you turned your mind. Review this log at week's end. Notice patterns and celebrate each turn as evidence that you are building this skill.

Willingness versus Wilfulness

Willingness and wilfulness represent two fundamentally different stances towards reality. Willingness is openness to doing what the situation requires, accepting reality and working with it. Wilfulness is imposing your will on reality, insisting that reality conform to your wishes and refusing to accept or work with what is. Understanding and practising willingness whilst recognising and letting go of wilfulness is essential for effective living.

Figure 18: Willingness vs Willfulness

These concepts are particularly important because wilfulness often masquerades as strength. We live in a culture that celebrates willpower, determination, and never giving up. These qualities have value, but when they become rigid refusal to accept reality or to adapt to circumstances, they transform from strengths into obstacles. Willingness requires actually greater strength—the strength to face reality as it is and respond flexibly rather than rigidly demanding that reality change to match your preferences.

Understanding Wilfulness

Wilfulness is attempting to control reality through force of will. It is insisting that things be a certain way and refusing to accept or work with any other possibility. Wilfulness says:

This is how it should be, how it must be, how I demand it to be. Reality must conform to my will.

Wilfulness often arises from fear—fear of loss of control, fear that accepting reality means defeat, fear that flexibility means weakness. When we feel frightened or threatened, we tend to grip tighter, insist more rigidly, and demand more adamantly. This gripping and insisting is wilfulness. It feels like maintaining control, but actually represents resistance to reality that exhausts us and prevents effective action.

Wilfulness has several characteristic features. It is rigid: only one outcome is acceptable, only one path is possible. It fights against what is, refusing to acknowledge or work with present reality. It demands that others change to accommodate your preferences. It involves trying to control what cannot be controlled. It often includes blame of self or others when reality does not conform to your will. It exhausts you and often makes situations worse rather than better.

Examples of wilfulness include refusing to accept that a relationship has ended, insisting it must continue despite the other person's clear choice. Refusing to accept limitations imposed by illness or injury, pushing yourself harmfully because you insist your body should function differently. Refusing to adapt plans when circumstances change, rigidly insisting on your original plan even when it no longer makes sense. Refusing help because you insist you should be able to manage independently. Demanding that others behave according to your expectations rather than accepting them as they are.

Wilfulness is not the same as having goals or working towards change. You can want things to be different, work actively for change, and set boundaries without being wilful. The distinction lies in whether you accept present reality whilst working for change or whether you refuse to acknowledge what is true right now. Wilfulness denies reality; willingness acknowledges reality whilst working with or within it.

Understanding Willingness

Willingness is openness and responsiveness to reality. It is accepting what is and asking: Given this reality, what is needed? What makes sense? What will be effective? Willingness means doing what the situation requires, even when that is not what you wanted or planned. It means being flexible, adapting to circumstances, and accepting that you cannot always control outcomes.

Willingness arises from radical acceptance. Once you accept reality as it is, willingness asks: Now what? How do I respond to this reality effectively? What does Wise Mind suggest? You are not passively resigning yourself to circumstances but rather actively engaging with reality as it is, rather than as you wish it were.

Willingness has several characteristic features. It is flexible: you adapt your approach based on circumstances. It works with what is rather than fighting against reality. It involves accepting that you cannot control everything. It responds to what the situation needs rather than rigidly insisting on your preferences. It often includes both/and thinking rather than either/or thinking. It tends to lead to more effective outcomes and less suffering, even when circumstances are difficult.

Examples of willingness include accepting that a relationship has ended and focusing energy on healing and moving forward rather than trying to force reconciliation. Accepting physical limitations and finding ways to live meaningfully within those limitations rather than constantly injuring yourself through overexertion. Adapting plans when circumstances change rather than rigidly adhering to your original plan regardless of new information.

Accepting help when needed rather than insisting you manage everything independently. Accepting people as they are, whilst setting appropriate boundaries rather than demanding they change to meet your expectations.

Willingness is not passivity or giving up. Willing people can be extremely active, goal-oriented, and change-focused. The difference is that they work with reality rather than against it. They accept what cannot be changed whilst actively changing what can be changed. They are flexible and adaptive rather than rigid. This flexibility and reality-acceptance actually make them more effective at creating change than wilful people who exhaust themselves fighting reality.

Recognising Wilfulness and Choosing Willingness

Learning to recognise your own wilfulness is the first step towards choosing willingness. Wilfulness often feels justified and right, which makes it difficult to see clearly. The following signs suggest wilfulness may be present.

You feel rigid or stuck, unable to see alternatives or consider different approaches. You insist there is only one acceptable outcome. You experience intense anger or frustration that circumstances are not as they should be. You find yourself thinking in terms of should, must, or have too extensively. You blame yourself or others when things do not go as planned. You feel exhausted from the ongoing struggle, but cannot seem to let go. You notice others suggesting flexibility or alternatives, but you cannot or will not consider them. These signs suggest wilfulness.

When you recognise wilfulness, the practice is to pause and ask yourself: What am I refusing to accept? What reality am I fighting against? What am I insisting must be true or must happen? These questions help identify the specific non-acceptance underlying your wilfulness. Once you see what you are refusing to accept, you can work with radical acceptance and turning the mind to move towards accepting that reality.

After identifying what you are refusing to accept, ask: What would willingness look like here? If I accepted reality and responded with willingness, what would I do? This question helps you identify a willing alternative to your wilful stance. You might not feel willing initially—that is normal. But you can act willingly even before you feel willing. You can choose the willing behaviour whilst still working on acceptance internally.

Practising willingness involves several specific actions. Accept what you cannot change in this moment. Ask what the situation requires rather than what you wish it required. Be flexible and adapt to circumstances. Do what works rather than what feels fair or right. Let go of rigid insistence on a single outcome. Consider multiple possibilities rather than fixating on one. Ask for help when needed. Allow others to be who they are rather than who you wish they were. Do all of this whilst maintaining your values and self-respect.

Willingness and Wilfulness in Practice: Case Studies

Case Study 1: Robert's Career Wilfulness

Robert had always planned to be a physician. He completed his undergraduate degree with excellent grades and applied to medical schools. He was rejected from all of them. Rather than accepting this reality and considering alternatives, Robert became consumed with wilfulness. He insisted that he must become a doctor, that there were no other acceptable careers, that the rejections were mistakes that would be corrected. He applied again the following year and was again rejected. He applied for a third year with the same result.

By this point, Robert was bitter, depressed, and stuck. He worked in temporary jobs he considered beneath him, waiting for the day when medical schools would recognise their error. He refused to consider other careers in healthcare or science. His entire identity was wrapped up in becoming a doctor, and he refused to accept any other possibility. His wilfulness was making him miserable, but he could not let go.

In therapy, Robert explored his wilfulness. What was he refusing to accept? That he might not become a physician. That his life might look different from what was planned. That he might need to be flexible and consider alternatives. His rigid insistence that only one path was acceptable had trapped him in suffering and prevented him from building any life at all.

Robert's therapist asked: What would willingness look like? If you accepted that medical schools have consistently rejected you, how might you respond? What other possibilities exist for a meaningful career? Robert initially resisted these questions, feeling that considering alternatives meant giving up. But gradually he recognised that his wilfulness was not working. He was not becoming a doctor through sheer force of will, and meanwhile, years of his life were passing in misery.

Robert began practising willingness. He accepted that medical schools had rejected him three times and that continuing to apply might not succeed. He explored other healthcare careers. He discovered physician assistant programmes. Initially, he felt angry that he was considering what he saw as a lesser alternative. But as he learned more, he became genuinely interested. He applied, was accepted, and discovered he loved the work.

Years later, Robert reflected that willingness had opened possibilities his wilfulness had closed. His rigid insistence on one specific path had trapped him in suffering. Accepting reality and responding with willingness had freed him to find meaningful work he genuinely valued. He still sometimes felt wistful about not becoming a physician, but he had built a good life. Willingness had made that possible.

Case Study 2: Maya's Relationship Willingness

Maya's teenage daughter, Jade, was struggling badly, experimenting with drugs, skipping school, staying out late. Maya responded with wilfulness. She set rigid rules, demanded Jade change immediately, grounded her extensively, and monitored her constantly. This approach was not working. Jade became more rebellious, their relationship deteriorated, and the dangerous behaviours continued.

Maya justified her approach through her fear for Jade's safety. She insisted that Jade must stop these behaviours, must obey her rules, must change immediately. Any flexibility felt dangerous. But her wilful approach was pushing Jade further away and preventing the open communication that might actually help.

Maya's therapist asked her to consider her willingness. What was she refusing to accept? That she could not control Jade through force. That Jade was making her own choices regardless of Maya's wishes. That heavy-handed control might push Jade away rather than keep her safe. These realities terrified Maya, but denying them would not protect Jade.

What would willingness look like? Maya explored this question painfully. Willingness might mean accepting that she could not control Jade but could influence her. It might mean adapting her approach based on what was actually working rather than insisting on her original plan. It might mean letting go of some less important rules to preserve their relationship so Jade might actually talk to her. It might mean accepting help from professionals rather than insisting she should manage this alone.

Maya began practising willingness. She relaxed some less important rules whilst holding firm boundaries on truly dangerous behaviours. She started listening to Jade more and lecturing less. She admitted to Jade that she was terrified and did not know how to help. She sought family therapy. She accepted that Jade was going through a difficult period and that this might not resolve quickly.

The changes were not immediate or dramatic. But over the months, Maya and Jade's relationship improved. Jade began talking to Maya more, asking for help occasionally, accepting some guidance. The dangerous behaviours reduced gradually. Maya's willingness to accept what she could not control and work with reality rather than against it proved more effective than her previous wilfulness. Her flexibility, born from acceptance, created space for Jade to change in ways rigid control had prevented.

Practice Exercises for Willingness versus Wilfulness

Exercise 1: Identify Your Wilfulness - Make a list of areas where you might be practising wilfulness. Where are you insisting that reality must be a certain way? Where are you refusing to accept what is? Where are you rigidly holding to one path or outcome? Be honest but not judgemental as you identify these areas.

Exercise 2: Explore the Fear - For one area of wilfulness, explore: What am I afraid will happen if I let go of wilfulness? What am I trying to control? Often, wilfulness arises from understandable fear. Understanding the fear can help you address it directly rather than through wilful attempts at control.

Exercise 3: Willing Alternative - For one wilful stance you have identified, ask: What would willingness look like in this situation? Write down specifically what you would do, think, or say if you were practising willingness. You do not need to do it yet; simply identify what the willing alternative would be.

Exercise 4: Practice One Willing Act - Choose one small situation this week where you will practise willingness instead of wilfulness. Let go of insisting on your way. Be flexible. Do what the situation requires. Notice how this feels and what happens as a result.

Exercise 5: Willingness Affirmations - Write and repeat willingness affirmations: I can be flexible. I can adapt to circumstances. I can accept what I cannot control whilst changing what I can. I can do what the situation requires, even when it is not what I wanted. Repeat these regularly to strengthen your willing stance.

Half, Smiling and Willing Hands

Half-smiling and Willing Hands are physical practices that support acceptance. These skills use your body to influence your mind and emotions. Research in psychology and neuroscience demonstrates that body posture and facial expressions do not just reflect our emotional states; they can actually influence those states. By deliberately adopting postures and expressions associated with acceptance, we can facilitate genuine acceptance.

These practices may feel artificial or silly initially. You might think: How can a slight smile or a particular hand position possibly help with deep suffering or genuine acceptance? The answer lies in the bidirectional relationship between body and mind. Your thoughts and emotions influence your body, but your body also influences your thoughts and emotions. Deliberate use of body posture to influence emotional state is not pretence; it is skilful use of how your system actually works.

Half, Smiling

Half-Smiling means adopting a slight, gentle upward curve of the lips—not a full smile, not a forced grin, but the subtle expression that occurs naturally when you are experiencing contentment or gentle acceptance. The half-smile is the physical expression of serenity. By adopting this expression, you signal to your nervous system that you are safe and accepting of present reality.

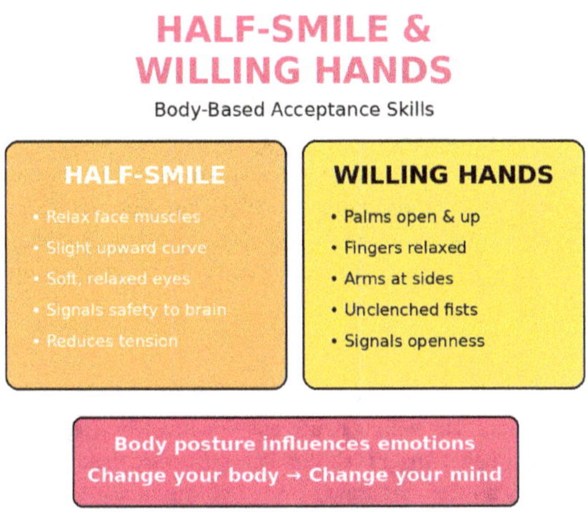

Figure 20: Half-Smile and Willing Hands

to practise half-smiling, relax your face completely. Let tension drain from your jaw, forehead, and around your eyes. Then allow the corners of your mouth to turn upward very slightly, almost imperceptibly. The smile should be so subtle that someone looking at you might not notice it. You are not trying to look happy; you are simply lifting the corners of your mouth a tiny amount. This is the half-smile.

The half-smile works through multiple mechanisms. Physically, it activates facial muscles associated with positive emotion and relaxation. Neurologically, it sends signals to your brain that you are safe and calm. Psychologically, it serves as a reminder to yourself that you are practising acceptance. Socially, if others see your relaxed expression, they may respond more calmly, which can reduce interpersonal stress.

When to use half-smiling: Practise half-smiling when accepting brutal realities. As you work on radically accepting a painful fact, adopt the half-smile. The physical expression supports and reinforces your mental acceptance. Practise half-smiling during meditation or mindfulness practice. The serene expression supports your mindful stance. Practise half-smiling during difficult conversations. The half-smile helps you remain calm and accepting rather than becoming defensive or aggressive. Practise half-smiling when you wake up in the morning. Starting your day with this accepting expression can set a tone of peaceful engagement with whatever the day brings.

Important notes about half-smiling: This practice is for your own benefit, not for others. You are not smiling to convince others you are happy or to hide your genuine feelings. You are adopting this expression to influence your own emotional state towards acceptance. If half-smiling in a particular situation feels invalidating or wrong, refrain from doing it. This skill should support acceptance, not create disconnection from your genuine experience. Some conditions are too acute or painful for half-smiling to be helpful. Use this skill when it genuinely supports acceptance, rather than denying or suppressing genuine pain.

Willing Hands

Willing Hands refers to adopting an open, relaxed hand position that physically conveys willingness and acceptance. The willing hands position involves keeping your hands unclenched, palms up or open, fingers relaxed. This posture is the opposite of clenched fists, which physically convey tension, resistance, and a fighting stance. Willing hands signal openness, receptivity, and acceptance.

to practise willing hands, notice the position of your hands. If they are clenched, gripping, or tense, consciously relax them. Let your fingers unfold naturally. Turn your palms upward or open them towards the front if standing. Allow your hands to rest gently on your lap, palms up or open, if you are sitting. The position should feel relaxed and receptive, not effortful. You are not forcing openness but allowing it.

Willing hands work through several mechanisms. Physically, unclenching your hands releases muscular tension that maintains emotional distress. Symbolically, open hands express receptivity and willingness, whilst clenched fists express fighting and resistance. Your brain reads these physical signals and adjusts your emotional state accordingly. Neurologically, the act of physically releasing your grip can help you mentally release rigid resistance to reality.

When to use willing hands: Practise willing hands when working on acceptance. When you notice yourself mentally gripping and fighting reality, deliberately adopt willing hands. The physical release supports mental release. Practise willing hands during meditation. The receptive hand position supports a receptive mental state. Practise willing hands during difficult conversations, especially when you notice yourself becoming defensive or wanting to argue. The open hand position helps you remain open to others' perspectives. Practise willing hands whenever you notice tension in your hands or body. Physical release often facilitates emotional release.

Important notes about willing hands: Like half-smiling, this practice is primarily for yourself, not for others. You are adopting this position to influence your own state towards willingness and acceptance. If willing hands feels unsafe or inappropriate in a particular situation, do not practice it. Your physical safety takes precedence. Some people find willing hands more powerful than half-smiling, others the reverse. Experiment to discover what works for you. You can practise half-smiling and willing hands simultaneously for combined benefit.

Combining Physical Practices with Acceptance

Half-Smiling and Willing Hands are most powerful when combined with the mental practices of Radical Acceptance and Willingness. The physical practices support and reinforce the mental practices, making acceptance more accessible and sustainable.

A combined practice might look like this: You identify something you are struggling to accept. You sit quietly, adopt willing hands and a half-smile. You breathe slowly and evenly. You state the reality you are accepting: This happened. This is true. I accept what is. You maintain the physical posture whilst repeating the acceptance statements. You notice any resistance and gently return to acceptance and the physical posture. You continue for several minutes, allowing the physical and mental practices to support each other.

This combined practice is particularly valuable during crisis or intense distress. When emotions overwhelm your ability to think clearly, you can return to your body. Adopt willing hands and a half-smile. Focus on the physical sensations. Breathe. These simple physical acts can create a toehold of calm and acceptance even when mental acceptance feels completely inaccessible.

Practice Exercises for Half, Smiling and Willing Hands

Exercise 1: Morning Practice - Each morning this week, upon waking, adopt half-smiling and willing hands for two minutes before getting out of bed. Notice how starting your day with these accepting physical postures affects your mood and your day.

Exercise 2: Acceptance Practice - Choose one difficult reality you are working to accept. Sit for ten minutes in half-smiling and willing hands position. Repeat acceptance statements about this reality. Notice whether the physical posture makes acceptance more accessible.

Exercise 3: Throughout the Day - Set reminders on your phone three times daily. When the reminder goes off, pause and adopt half-smiling and willing hands for one minute wherever you are. Notice your state before and after this brief practice.

Exercise 4: Mindful Activities - Choose one routine daily activity (washing dishes, walking, waiting in a queue). Do this activity whilst maintaining half-smiling and willing hands. Notice whether this changes your experience of the activity.

Exercise 5: Difficult Conversations - Before your next difficult conversation, practice half-smiling and willing hands for several minutes. Maintain this posture during the conversation if possible. Notice whether it helps you remain calm and accepting rather than defensive or aggressive.

Module 3: Interpersonal Effectiveness Skills

Human beings are fundamentally social creatures. Our wellbeing depends significantly on the quality of our relationships with others. Yet for many people, navigating interpersonal situations is fraught with difficulty. We struggle to ask for what we need, to say no when appropriate, to maintain our self-respect whilst also preserving important relationships. We may be too passive, allowing others to take advantage of us, or too aggressive, damaging relationships through hostile communication. We may alternate between these extremes, unsure how to find a balanced, effective middle path.

Interpersonal effectiveness skills provide systematic approaches to navigating relationships and interpersonal situations skilfully. These skills teach you how to ask for what you want effectively, how to say no whilst maintaining relationships, how to resolve conflicts, how to build and maintain healthy relationships, and how to end destructive relationships when necessary. They address the fundamental challenge of balancing multiple goals: getting your objectives met, maintaining positive relationships, and preserving your self-respect.

This module is organised around three core skill sets, each addressing a different aspect of interpersonal effectiveness. DEAR MAN teaches objectives effectiveness—how to ask for what you want or say no to requests in ways that maximise the likelihood of achieving your objectives. GIVE teaches relationship effectiveness—how to act in ways that maintain and strengthen your relationships with others even during disagreements or difficult conversations. FAST teaches self-respect effectiveness—how to maintain your self-respect and integrity whilst interacting with others.

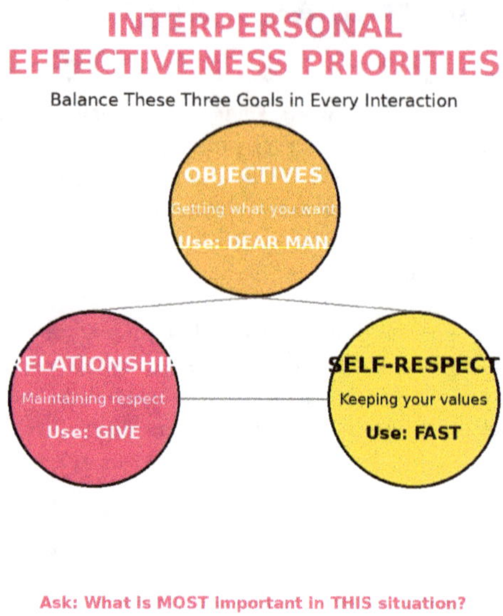

Figure 30: Interpersonal Effectiveness Priorities

Additionally, this module addresses broader interpersonal challenges, including building new relationships, maintaining existing ones, managing conflicts constructively, and ending harmful relationships or no longer serve you. Together, these skills provide a comprehensive approach to creating and maintaining the healthy relationships that are essential for a life worth living.

The Challenge of Interpersonal Effectiveness

Why do so many people struggle with interpersonal effectiveness? Several factors contribute to these difficulties. Many people were never explicitly taught effective interpersonal skills. We may have grown up in families where communication was dysfunctional, where needs were not expressed directly, where conflict was handled poorly or avoided entirely. Without positive models, we never learned what healthy interpersonal interaction looks like or how to implement it ourselves.

Emotional dysregulation significantly interferes with interpersonal effectiveness. When emotions are intense, we often interact in ways we later regret. We may say things we do not mean, react defensively, withdraw completely, or engage in behaviours that damage relationships. Learning to regulate emotions is therefore foundational to interpersonal effectiveness, which is why emotion regulation is another core module in DBT.

Fear often prevents effective interpersonal behaviour. We may fear rejection if we ask for what we want, fear conflict if we say no, fear abandonment if we express our needs, or fear judgement if we show vulnerability. These fears can lead us to avoid necessary conversations, accept unacceptable treatment, or communicate ineffectively in ways that create the very outcomes we feared.

Myths and beliefs about relationships interfere with effectiveness. Some people believe that asking for what you want is selfish, that saying no makes you a bad person, that you should know what others need without being told, or that conflict means the relationship is failing. These beliefs prevent the direct, honest communication necessary for healthy relationships.

Finally, many people struggle with balancing competing priorities. We want to get our needs met, but we also want others to like us. We want to maintain our integrity, but we also do not want to create conflict. We want to say no, but we also fear disappointing others. When we are unclear about how to balance these competing priorities, we often end up sacrificing one entirely—typically our own needs or self-respect—in favour of others' approval.

The Goals of Interpersonal Effectiveness

Interpersonal effectiveness skills aim to help you achieve three primary goals simultaneously. Understanding these goals and learning to balance them is central to effective interpersonal functioning.

Objectives effectiveness means getting your objectives met—getting what you want or need from a situation or successfully refusing an unwanted request. This is about outcome. Did you get the pay rise you requested? Did you successfully decline the invitation you did not want to accept? Did you get your housemate to do their share of cleaning? Objectives effectiveness focuses on the concrete results of interpersonal interactions.

Relationship effectiveness means maintaining or improving the relationship whilst also pursuing your objectives. It is about acting in ways that make the other person feel respected and valued, even when you are saying no to them or asking for something they may not want to give. Relationship effectiveness recognises that in many situations, the ongoing relationship matters as much as or more than the immediate objective. You may win the argument but lose the friendship; interpersonal effectiveness helps you pursue your goals without unnecessary relationship damage.

Self-respect effectiveness means maintaining your own self-respect, integrity, and values whilst interacting with others. It is about not betraying yourself, not compromising your values to please others, and acting in ways you can respect yourself for later. Self-respect effectiveness means you do not leave the interaction feeling you sold yourself out, lied, behaved in ways inconsistent with your values, or allowed yourself to be treated unacceptably.

These three goals sometimes work together easily. You might ask for something politely and clearly (maintaining relationship effectiveness and self-respect effectiveness) and receive a yes (achieving objectives effectiveness). Often, however, these goals create tension. You might need to choose which goal to prioritise in a given situation. Should you push hard for what you want (objectives effectiveness) at the risk of damaging the relationship? Should you prioritise maintaining the relationship even if it means not getting what you need? Should you maintain your values (self-respect) even if it costs you the relationship?

Interpersonal effectiveness skills help you make these decisions wisely. They do not eliminate the reality that sometimes trade-offs are necessary, but they help you consciously choose which goals to prioritise in different situations and provide strategies for maximising all three goals whenever possible.

DEAR MAN—Objectives Effectiveness

DEAR MAN is the skill for objectives effectiveness. It teaches you how to ask for what you want or say no to requests in ways that maximise the likelihood of getting what you want whilst minimising unnecessary conflict or relationship damage. DEAR MAN provides a structure for clear, direct, respectful communication about your needs and boundaries.

The acronym DEAR MAN stands for: Describe, Express, Assert, Reinforce, stay Mindful, Appear confident, and Negotiate. Each element represents a specific component of effective requests or refusals. When combined, these elements create powerful, clear communication that respects both yourself and the other person whilst maximising your chances of achieving your objective.

Before exploring each element in detail, it is important to understand when to use DEAR MAN. Use this skill when you want to ask someone for something, when you want to say no to a request, when you want someone to change their behaviour, or when you want to resolve an interpersonal problem. DEAR MAN is for situations where you have a clear objective you want to achieve through communication with another person.

D , Describe the Situation

Describe means stating the facts of the situation as objectively as possible, without judgement or interpretation. You describe what happened, what is happening, or what the situation is. This factual description provides context for your request or refusal and helps the other person understand what you are responding to.

Effective description is brief, specific, and focused on observable facts rather than assumptions or interpretations. Instead of saying: You are always inconsiderate and never think about anyone but yourself (judgement and interpretation), you might say: You played loud music at midnight last night whilst I was trying to sleep (observable fact). The second statement describes what happened without attacking the person's character.

Avoid long preambles or extensive history. Describe only the facts relevant to your current request. If you are asking your housemate to clean more regularly, you need only describe the current state: The kitchen has unwashed dishes from several days. You do not need to recount every time in the past when cleaning has been an issue. Long descriptions become complaints rather than clear communication.

If the situation is ongoing or has happened repeatedly, you can acknowledge this without making it an accusation: This is the third time this month that I have had to complete your portion of the project. This states the pattern factually without becoming an attack. The tone remains descriptive rather than accusatory.

When describing, stick to what you directly know rather than assumptions about others' intentions or motivations. Instead of: You obviously do not care about my feelings (assumption about intention), say: You left without saying goodbye after we argued (observable fact). You can rarely know with certainty what others think or intend; describing observable behaviour keeps the communication clear and inarguable.

E , Express Your Feelings or Opinions

Express means clearly stating your feelings about the situation or your opinion about it. This step personalises your request and helps the other person understand why this matters to you. People are generally more motivated to respond positively when they understand the emotional context and impact of the situation.

Express your feelings using I statements rather than you statements. I feel frustrated is very different from You are frustrating. The first takes responsibility for your emotional response; the second attacks the other person. I statements reduce defensiveness and keep the focus on your experience rather than on judging the other person.

Be specific about your emotion rather than vague. Instead of I am upset about this, specify I feel disappointed and concerned. Specific emotion words communicate more clearly and help the other person understand the situation's impact more fully. If you struggle to identify specific emotions, refer to an emotion word list to build your emotional vocabulary.

If you are expressing an opinion rather than an emotion, make this clear: I believe that sharing household tasks fairly is important. My opinion is that this deadline is unrealistic. Clearly labelling statements as opinions rather than facts prevents confusion and allows space for the other person to have different opinions.

Keep the expression brief and sincere. You are sharing your internal experience to provide context, not to manipulate through emotional displays. A simple, genuine statement of feeling or opinion is more effective than lengthy emotional explanations or dramatic presentations. The goal is clarity, not performance.

A , Assert Your Needs or Wants

Assert means clearly asking for what you want or clearly saying no to what you do not want. This is the heart of DEAR MAN—the actual request or refusal. Everything else in the skill supports this central assertion, but without a clear assertion, the communication fails.

Make your request or refusal direct and specific. Avoid hints, indirect communication, or expecting the other person to read between the lines. Instead of: It would be nice if the flat were cleaner (hint), say directly: I would like you to wash your dishes each evening. Instead of I am quite busy lately (indirect refusal), say: No, I cannot help you move this weekend.

Use clear, simple language. Do not bury your request in qualifications, apologies, or lengthy explanations. The assertion should be unmistakable. The other person should never leave the conversation wondering what exactly you wanted or whether you really meant no. If you find yourself being indirect, pause and ask yourself: What exactly am I asking for? Then state that directly.

For requests, be specific about what you want, when you want it, and how you want it done if relevant. Instead of: I need you to be more responsible (vague), say: I need you to text me if you will be more than thirty minutes late (specific). Vague requests are difficult to fulfil because the other person is unclear about what success looks like. Specific requests are actionable.

For refusals, a clear no is often sufficient. You do not need lengthy justifications for saying no, though you may choose to offer a brief reason. No, I am not available to work late tonight is complete. If you add a reason, keep it brief: No, I cannot work late tonight because I have a prior commitment. Extensive justifications often signal uncertainty and invite pressure to change your mind.

Avoid undoing your assertion with qualifiers. Do not say: I would really like you to stop interrupting me, but I know you probably do not mean anything by it. The second half undermines the first half. State your assertion clearly and stop. Trust that your request or refusal is legitimate and deserves to stand without apology or qualification.

R , Reinforce the Positive Consequences

Reinforce means explaining the positive consequences of the other person agreeing to your request or accepting your refusal. This step provides motivation for the other person to respond in a positive manner. People are generally more inclined to say yes when they understand what benefit they will gain or what problem they will avoid.

Positive reinforcement might involve explaining the benefit to them: If you complete your portion by Friday, you will have your weekend free. If you wash dishes promptly, you will always have clean dishes available when you need them. People respond to incentives; helping them see the advantage makes cooperation more likely.

Positive reinforcement might involve explaining the benefit to the relationship: If we can resolve this, I think we will both feel more comfortable, and our working relationship will improve. Framing your request as beneficial to the relationship appeals to people who value connection and harmony.

Positive reinforcement might involve positive consequences for you that matter to the other person: If I can get enough sleep, I will be much better company. If you respect my no on this, I will feel more comfortable saying yes to things I genuinely can do. When people care about you, your wellbeing can motivate them to respond positively to your requests or respect your boundaries.

Be genuine with reinforcement. Do not make promises you cannot keep or exaggerate consequences. False promises damage trust and reduce your effectiveness in future interactions. If you tell someone that agreeing to your request will transform your entire relationship and it does not, they will be less responsive to future requests.

It is also possible to mention negative consequences of not agreeing but do this carefully. Negative consequences should be genuine and stated calmly, not as threats. For example: If we cannot resolve this, I will need to speak with our manager might be appropriate workplace communication. However, if you do not do this, you will regret it is a threat that will likely create resistance and damage the relationship. Focus primarily on positive consequences and mention negative ones only when necessary and genuine.

M , Stay Mindful of Your Objective

Stay Mindful means keeping your attention focused on your objective throughout the interaction. Do not be distracted by attacks, attempts to change the subject, or emotional manipulations. Continue returning to your request or refusal calmly and persistently until you achieve your goal or decide to let go of the objective.

The other person may attempt to sidetrack you. They might bring up past grievances, attack your character, or try to make the conversation about something else entirely. Stay Mindful means recognising these distractions and redirecting back to your objective. I understand you are upset about last week, but right now I am asking about cleaning schedules. Can we discuss that?

Use the broken record technique when necessary. This means calmly repeating your request or refusal without getting angry, defensive, or sidetracked. The other person says: But I am so busy. You respond I understand you are busy, and I need you to complete your portion by Friday. They say: You are so demanding. You respond I need you to complete your portion by Friday. You simply keep returning to your objective like a broken record stuck on one phrase.

Staying Mindful also means not being derailed by your own emotions. If you become angry, hurt, or defensive during the interaction, acknowledge the emotion to yourself but keep your focus on your objective. You came into this conversation wanting something specific. Emotions may arise, but do not let them take over the interaction. Pause, breathe, return to your objective.

Know when to stop. Staying Mindful includes recognising when you have achieved your objective or when continuing the conversation is no longer productive. If the person agrees to your request, thank them and end the conversation gracefully. If it is clear they will not agree and further discussion is futile, you may need to accept this reality and consider alternative strategies. Mindfulness includes knowing when to persist and when to let go.

A , Appear Confident

Appear Confident means using body language, tone of voice, and demeanour that convey confidence in your right to make this request or refusal. How you present yourself significantly influences how others respond to you. Confident presentation increases the likelihood that your request will be taken seriously and respected.

Make eye contact. Looking directly at the person whilst you make your request communicates that you believe in what you are saying and deserve their attention. Avoiding eye contact suggests uncertainty or shame about your request. You need not stare intensely, but comfortable, natural eye contact is important.

Use a clear, steady voice. Speak loudly enough to be heard easily, at a normal conversational pace. Mumbling, speaking too quietly, or rushing through your words suggests discomfort with your request. Take your time. You have a right to be heard, so speak clearly.

Maintain good posture. Stand or sit up straight. Do not hunch your shoulders, curl in on yourself, or make yourself small. Physical confidence supports verbal confidence. Your body language should communicate that you have a right to occupy space and make requests.

Avoid unnecessary apologies or qualifiers. Do not begin with I am so sorry to bother you, but... or I know this is probably a terrible idea, but... These phrases undermine your request before you even make it. If you are making a reasonable request, you need not apologise for it. State it confidently.

It is important to note that appearing confident is different from being aggressive or domineering. Confidence is calm and self-assured; aggression is hostile and attacking. You want to convey I have a right to make this request, and I expect you to take it seriously, not I am going to force you to comply. The distinction is crucial.

If you do not feel confident, appearing confident may feel like acting or being false. Remember that you are not lying about your feelings; you are using your body and voice to support your legitimate request. Over time, as you practise appearing confident and experience positive results, your internal confidence will grow to match your external presentation. Act as if you are confident, and confidence will follow.

N , Negotiate

Negotiate means being willing to give to get. It means looking for solutions that work for both parties rather than rigidly insisting on getting everything exactly as you want it. Negotiation demonstrates respect for the other person's needs and increases the likelihood of reaching an agreement that satisfies both of you.

Before the conversation, identify what aspects of your request are negotiable and which are non-negotiable. You might need your housemate to do their share of cleaning (non-negotiable), but be flexible about exactly which tasks they do or when they do them (negotiable). Knowing your bottom line helps you negotiate effectively without compromising on what truly matters.

Ask the other person for their input. What would work for you? Do you have suggestions about how we could make this work? invites collaboration rather than imposing your solution. The other person may see possibilities you have not considered. Their suggestions may be better than your original request, or at a minimum, involving them in problem-solving increases their investment in the solution.

Look for win-win solutions. Can you find a way for both people to get what they need, or at least for neither person to feel they lost entirely? Perhaps you want your colleague to stop interrupting you in meetings, and they want to ensure their ideas are heard. A win-win might be: You wait until I finish speaking, and I commit to asking for your input before moving on. Both needs are addressed.

Be willing to compromise on means whilst holding firm on ends. You want to reach your objective, but there may be multiple paths to that objective. If you need your partner to contribute more to household work, does it matter whether they cook or clean, whether they do it daily or in a weekend batch? Being flexible about implementation whilst clear about the desired outcome often leads to solutions both parties can accept.

However, negotiation does not mean always meeting halfway or accepting unfair solutions. If your bottom line is non-negotiable and the other person is unwilling to respect it, negotiation has limits. You can negotiate how needs are met, but you should not negotiate away your fundamental rights or needs. No is a complete sentence, and some things are not open to negotiation. Knowing the difference between healthy compromise and inappropriate self-sacrifice is essential.

DEAR MAN in Practice: Case Studies

Case Study 1: Natalie's Workplace Request

Natalie had been working unpaid overtime for months. Her manager regularly asked her to stay late or work weekends, and Natalie always agreed despite feeling exhausted and resentful. She finally decided to use DEAR MAN to address this pattern.

Describe: Natalie stated the facts: Over the past three months, I have worked late at least twice weekly and worked two full weekends. This overtime has been unpaid.

Express: She shared her feelings and opinion: I feel exhausted and overwhelmed. I believe this amount of unpaid overtime is unsustainable.

Assert: She made her request clearly: I would like to work only my contracted hours going forward, or if overtime is necessary, I would like to discuss compensation or time off in lieu.

Reinforce: She explained positive consequences: If I work reasonable hours, I will be more productive and focused during my working day. I will also be less likely to burn out and need extended leave.

Stay Mindful: When her manager said: But we really need your dedication right now, Natalie stayed focused on her objective: I understand the team needs support. I am asking about compensation or time off in lieu of overtime work. When the manager mentioned another colleague who always helps out, Natalie used broken record: I would like to discuss compensation or time off in lieu of my overtime.

Appear Confident: Natalie maintained eye contact, spoke clearly and firmly, and did not apologise for her request. She sat up straight and projected confidence in her right to fair working conditions.

Negotiate: When her manager seemed resistant to paying overtime, Natalie suggested: If paying overtime is not possible, I would be happy to take compensatory time off. Perhaps for every four hours of overtime, I could leave four hours early another week? This provided flexibility whilst maintaining her core objective of fair treatment.

The result was that Natalie's manager agreed to the compensatory time arrangement. Natalie had achieved her objective of fair treatment for overtime whilst maintaining her working relationship and her self-respect. Using DEAR MAN had structured her communication effectively.

Case Study 2: James's Refusal

James's brother regularly asked to borrow money. James had lent him money multiple times, and the money was never repaid. When his brother called asking for another loan, James decided to use DEAR MAN to say no.

Describe: James stated the facts: You have asked to borrow £500. Over the past two years, I have lent you approximately £3,000, and none of it has been repaid.

Express: He shared his feelings: I feel uncomfortable continuing to lend money that is not repaid. I believe this pattern is not healthy for either of us.

Assert: He stated his refusal clearly: No, I cannot lend you money.

Reinforce: He explained a positive consequence: If I stop lending money, it removes a source of tension between us, and our relationship can be based on something other than financial transactions.

Stay Mindful: When his brother said: But I am your family, James stayed focused: Yes, you are my family, and I cannot lend you money. When his brother mentioned a crisis that required immediate funds, James remained consistent: I understand you are in a difficult situation. I cannot lend you money. He used a broken record calmly and kindly but firmly.

Appear Confident: Despite feeling guilty and anxious, James maintained a calm, clear tone. He did not apologise excessively or justify at length. He stated his no with confidence, conveying that this was a firm decision.

Negotiate: James offered a non-financial alternative: I cannot give you money, but I am happy to help you make a budget or research other resources that might help with your situation. This showed willingness to support in other ways whilst maintaining his boundary about money.

His brother was initially angry, but James maintained his no. Over time, their relationship improved because the financial strain was removed. James had successfully set a boundary whilst keeping the relationship intact. His use of DEAR MAN had made a difficult conversation manageable.

Case Study 3: Amara's Conflict Resolution. Amara's flatmate, Chen, repeatedly left the common areas messy. Amara had hinted and complained to other friends but had never addressed it directly with Chen. She decided to use DEAR MAN.

Describe: Amara stated observable facts: When you cook, the kitchen is often left with unwashed dishes, food on the counter, and spills not cleaned up. This has happened most evenings this week.

Express: She shared her feelings and opinion: I feel frustrated when I come home to a messy kitchen. I believe keeping shared spaces clean should be a shared responsibility.

Assert: She made a clear request: I would like you to clean up completely after cooking each evening.

Reinforce: She provided positive consequences: If we both keep the kitchen clean, we will both always have a pleasant space to cook in, and we will not have tension about housework. We will probably enjoy living together more.

Stay Mindful: When Chen said: You are so uptight about mess, Amara stayed on topic: I am asking about cleaning up after cooking. Can you commit to doing that? When Chen mentioned times, Amara had been messy. Amara acknowledged this without being derailed: You are right that I sometimes leave things out. Right now, I am asking about cleaning up after cooking. Can we agree on that?

Appear Confident: Amara spoke clearly and maintained eye contact despite feeling nervous about potential conflict. She kept her tone friendly but firm, conveying that this was an important issue worthy of discussion.

Negotiate: When Chen said cleaning up immediately after cooking felt restrictive, Amara suggested: How about cleaning up before you go to bed each night? That way dishes are not left overnight but you have flexibility about timing. Chen agreed to this compromise.

The result was that their kitchen stayed cleaner, and their living situation improved. Amara felt respected, Chen did not feel attacked, and they had worked out a solution together.

DEAR MAN had provided structure for a conversation that could have turned into an unproductive argument.

Common Problems with DEAR MAN

Problem: Being Too Indirect or Too Aggressive

Some people struggle to find the middle ground between passive, indirect communication and aggressive, hostile communication. They either hint at what they want rather than ask directly, or they demand it in ways that feel attacking. DEAR MAN provides the structure for assertive communication that is neither passive nor aggressive.

Solution: Follow the DEAR MAN structure closely, particularly the Describe and Assert steps. Keep your description factual rather than accusatory. Make your assertion clear and direct. If you notice yourself hinting or becoming aggressive, pause and return to the structure. Practise with minor requests before attempting DEAR MAN in high-stakes situations.

Problem: Forgetting Your Objective When Emotions Arise

During interpersonal interactions, emotions can derail you from your objective. You might become angry and shift from requesting behaviour change to attacking the person's character. Or you might become anxious and abandon your request entirely. Emotions interfere with staying mindful of your objective.

Solution: Write out your DEAR MAN script before important conversations. Having your objective written down helps you return to it when emotions threaten to pull you off course.

If you notice yourself becoming emotionally flooded during a conversation, take a brief pause. Use TIP skills if necessary to reduce emotional intensity, then return to your objective. The broken record technique also helps—simply repeat your assertion calmly when you notice yourself being pulled away from it.

Problem: Negotiating Away Your Bottom Line

Some people negotiate so much that they end up agreeing to solutions that do not actually meet their needs. They want to be nice, to avoid conflict, or to be seen as reasonable, so they compromise on things that should be non-negotiable. They leave the interaction having gotten nothing they needed.

Solution: Before using DEAR MAN, clarify your bottom line. What is the minimum acceptable outcome? What needs are non-negotiable? Once you know your bottom line, you can negotiate everything else freely whilst protecting what truly matters. If negotiations approach your bottom line, state firmly: This is really important to me, and I need this aspect to be addressed. Some people find it helpful to practise saying: I am willing to be flexible about X, but Y is non-negotiable for me.

Practice Exercises for DEAR MAN

Exercise 1: Script a Request - Identify something you want to ask for. Write out a complete DEAR MAN script: Describe (facts), Express (feeling/opinion), Assert (clear request), Reinforce (positive consequence), how you will stay Mindful (your objective and broken record phrase), how you will appear Confident (specific behaviours), and what you are willing to Negotiate.

Exercise 2: Script a Refusal - Identify something you want to say no to. Write a DEAR MAN script for your refusal. Pay particular attention to your assertion (clear no) and how you will stay mindful if the person pressures you to change your mind.

Exercise 3: Practise Broken Record - With a friend or in your imagination, practice staying mindful by using a broken record. Have the other person try to distract, guilt, or sidetrack you. Practise calmly returning to your objective repeatedly without becoming angry or giving in.

Exercise 4: Confidence Building - Practise appearing confident even when you do not feel confident. Stand in front of a mirror and request whilst maintaining eye contact with yourself, speaking clearly, and projecting confidence. Notice how confidence in your body affects your sense of entitlement to make the request.

Exercise 5: Real-Life Application - Choose a low-stakes situation to practise DEAR MAN this week. Perhaps asking a shop assistant for help, requesting your housemate not to leave dishes in the sink overnight, or declining an invitation you do not want to accept. Start with easier situations to build skill and confidence before attempting high-stakes DEAR MAN interactions.

GIVE and FAST—Relationship and Self, Respect Effectiveness

Figure 8: GIVE Skills for Relationship Effectiveness

DEAR MAN focuses on getting your objectives met. However, objective effectiveness is only one aspect of interpersonal effectiveness. Two other crucial dimensions are maintaining positive relationships and preserving your self-respect. GIVE skills address relationship effectiveness, whilst FAST skills address self-respect effectiveness. Together with DEAR MAN, they provide a comprehensive approach to interpersonal situations.

In many situations, maintaining the relationship matters as much as or more than getting your immediate objective. You might win the argument but lose the friendship. You might get what you want, but damage the relationship in the process. GIVE skills help you pursue your goals in ways that strengthen rather than weaken your relationships with others.

Similarly, getting what you want or maintaining relationships means little if you betray yourself in the process. If you achieve your objectives through manipulation or lies, if you maintain relationships by completely abandoning your values, you will lose self-respect. FAST skills help you interact with others in ways that allow you to respect yourself afterwards.

GIVE: Relationship Effectiveness

GIVE is the skill for maintaining and strengthening relationships during interpersonal interactions. GIVE stands for: be Gentle, act Interested, Validate, and use an Easy manner. These elements help you interact in ways that make the other person feel respected and valued, even when you are saying no to them, disagreeing with them, or asking for something they may not want to give.

Use GIVE whenever the relationship is important to you. If you need to maintain a working relationship, if you value the friendship, if the person is family you will continue to interact with, or if you simply want to be kind to another human being, GIVE skills help you do this whilst also pursuing your objectives or maintaining your boundaries.

G , Be Gentle

Being gentle means communicating without attacks, judgements, or threats. It means being kind and respectful even when you are frustrated, disappointed, or need to set a firm boundary. Gentleness reduces defensive reactions and keeps the interaction constructive rather than deteriorating into conflict.

Avoid attacking the person's character, intelligence, or worth. Do not call names, make sweeping negative statements about who they are, or attribute malicious motives to their behaviour. Instead of: You are so selfish, and you never think about anyone but yourself, describe the specific behaviour: When you made plans without checking with me first, I felt disappointed. The first attacks the person; the second addresses the action.

Avoid physical threats, verbal threats, or implied threats. Threats create fear and resistance, not cooperation. Do not say: If you do not do this, I will make your life miserable. Instead, you might state a natural consequence calmly: If we cannot resolve this, I will need to speak with our supervisor about how to proceed. The first is a threat designed to intimidate; the second is a statement of necessary next steps.

Express anger or frustration without hostility. You can communicate that you are upset whilst remaining respectful. I feel angry about this situation works very differently from You make me so angry, you are unbearable. The first expresses your emotion; the second blames and attacks the person.

Use appropriate humour if it comes naturally, but never sarcasm or mockery at the other person's expense. Genuine, kind humour can defuse tension. Sarcasm or mockery damages relationships. If you are unsure whether humour will land well, err on the side of straightforward communication.

Being gentle does not mean being weak or passive. You can be simultaneously gentle and firm. You can set clear boundaries, make strong requests, or say firm no's whilst remaining respectful and kind. In fact, gentle firmness is often more effective than aggressive demands because it does not trigger the other person's defensiveness.

I , Act Interested

Act Interested means showing genuine interest in what the other person is saying, thinking, and feeling. It means listening attentively rather than simply waiting for your turn to speak. When people feel heard, they are more likely to hear you in return. Interest creates connection, and connection facilitates cooperation.

Listen actively. Give the person your full attention. Put away your phone. Make eye contact. Nod or make verbal acknowledgements that show you are following what they are saying.

Do not interrupt. Let them complete their thoughts before you respond. This attentive listening communicates respect and value for their perspective.

Ask questions to understand their viewpoint better. What led you to that conclusion? Can you help me understand your perspective on this? How did that affect you? Questions demonstrate genuine interest and often provide information that helps resolve the situation more effectively. They also communicate that you see the other person as someone worth understanding, not merely an obstacle to your objectives.

Acknowledge their feelings and concerns, even if you disagree with their conclusions. I can see this is important to you or I understand you are frustrated can be said truthfully even when you maintain a different opinion. Acknowledging their experience is not the same as agreeing with their position. It simply recognises their humanity.

Avoid checking your phone, looking around the room, or showing other signs of disinterest. These behaviours communicate that the person and their concerns are not important to you. If you cannot give someone your full attention right now, it is better to say: Can we discuss this in an hour when I can give you my full attention? than to have a conversation whilst obviously disengaged.

Acting interested is particularly important when saying no or disagreeing. If you refuse someone's request whilst simultaneously communicating that you do not care about their needs or feelings, you damage the relationship unnecessarily. If you disagree whilst showing no interest in understanding their perspective, you create an adversarial dynamic. Interest maintains a connection even during disagreement or refusal.

V , Validate

Validate means acknowledging and communicating that the other person's feelings, thoughts, or actions make sense in context. It means finding the kernel of truth or an understandable response in what they are expressing, even if you do not agree with everything they are saying. Validation is perhaps the most powerful relationship-building skill because it communicates respect and understanding at a deep level.

Validation does not mean agreement. You can validate someone's feelings without agreeing with their interpretation of events or their proposed solutions. I understand why you feel disappointed is validation. It does not require you to agree that disappointment is the objectively correct response or that the situation truly warrants disappointment. It simply acknowledges that, given this person's perspective and experience, disappointment makes sense.

Look for what is valid in what the person is expressing. Perhaps their facts are wrong, but their feelings about those facts are understandable. Perhaps their conclusion is flawed, but their concern is legitimate. Perhaps their solution is unworkable, but the problem they identified is real. Find the valid element and reflect it back: You are right that this is a significant problem. I can see why you would be worried about this. That does make sense given what you experienced.

Validate based on context. Even if you would not feel or think the way this person does, can you understand why they might, given their history, values, or current circumstances? I can see why that would be particularly difficult for you, given your past experiences validate their response as sensible, given their context, even if it might not be your response in similar circumstances.

Express validation clearly and specifically. I hear you, or I understand, can feel dismissive if said automatically or without specific reference to what you are validating. Instead, I understand why you would feel excluded when plans were made without your input, clearly states what you are validating. The specificity communicates genuine understanding rather than formulaic acknowledgement.

Avoid invalidating language. Do not say: You should not feel that way. Do not be so sensitive. That is not a big deal. You are overreacting. These statements dismiss the person's experience and damage the relationship. Even if you genuinely believe their response is disproportionate, find a way to validate the feeling whilst perhaps offering perspective: Anyone would feel disappointed by that. Let me share how I am seeing the situation, which might offer a different angle.

Validation is powerful because most people do not feel validated in their daily lives. When you offer genuine validation, you often defuse defensiveness, open the person to hearing your perspective, and strengthen the relationship. People are more willing to consider alternative views and compromise solutions when they feel understood and respected. Validation creates the foundation for effective problem solving.

E , Use an Easy Manner

Use an Easy Manner means being pleasant, light-hearted when appropriate, and not overly intense or serious about every interaction. It means smiling, using a warm tone, and approaching interactions with friendliness rather than heaviness. An easy manner makes interactions more pleasant for both parties and facilitates cooperation.

Be pleasant in your tone and demeanour. A warm, friendly approach invites reciprocal warmth. A cold, hostile, or overly serious approach invites defensiveness. You can address serious matters with a fundamentally pleasant demeanour. Pleasant does not mean fake cheerfulness when addressing difficult issues; it means maintaining basic friendliness and respect.

Smile when appropriate. A genuine smile communicates warmth and goodwill. Obviously, you would not smile when delivering terrible news or addressing very serious conflicts, but in many everyday interactions, a smile softens the interaction and builds connection. If you struggle to smile genuinely, think of something that brings you warmth towards the person or simply relax your face into a soft, open expression.

Use appropriate humour. If humour comes naturally to you and fits the situation, it can ease tension and create connection. However, ensure humour is kind and does not minimize serious concerns. Humour should add lightness, not dismiss or avoid important issues.

Avoid being overly intense or taking everything too seriously. Not every disagreement is a crisis. Not every request requires dramatic presentation. An easy manner means maintaining perspective and not escalating situations unnecessarily. If you tend towards intensity, consciously soften your approach. Imagine how you would discuss this issue with a beloved friend and bring that gentler energy to other interactions.

Match your manner to the situation. An easy manner does not mean being inappropriately casual about serious matters. If someone is sharing something deeply painful, an easy manner would be gentle warmth and presence, not joking or lightness. Easy manner is about creating pleasant, comfortable interaction appropriate to the context, not about forcing light-heartedness regardless of circumstances.

Using GIVE with DEAR MAN

GIVE, and DEAR MAN work together. You use DEAR MAN to structure what you say—your request or refusal and the supporting information. You use GIVE to determine how you say it—the tone, manner, and approach you take to maintain the relationship whilst pursuing your objective.

A DEAR MAN request delivered without GIVE might achieve the objective, but damage the relationship. You might get your housemate to clean the kitchen (objective achieved), but create ongoing resentment (relationship damaged). DEAR MAN, with GIVE increases the likelihood of achieving your objective whilst maintaining or even strengthening the relationship.

When preparing to use DEAR MAN, consider: How can I be gentle in my description and assertion? How can I show interest in the other person's perspective? What can I validate about their experience or concerns? How can I use an easy manner to make this conversation more pleasant? Building GIVE into your DEAR MAN practice creates interpersonally effective communication.

FAST: Self, Respect Effectiveness

FAST is the skill for maintaining self-respect during interpersonal interactions. FAST stands for: be Fair to yourself and others, do not apologise excessively, stick to your values, and be Truthful. These elements help you interact with others in ways that allow you to respect yourself afterwards, even when the interaction is difficult or does not go as you hoped.

Use FAST whenever your self-respect is at stake. If you are tempted to betray your values to avoid conflict, if you find yourself apologising for legitimate requests or needs, if you are considering lying to smooth over difficulties, or if you are treating yourself unfairly in order to please others, FAST skills help you maintain your integrity.

F , Be Fair

Be Fair means treating yourself as fairly as you would treat someone you care about. It means not sacrificing your legitimate needs and rights to please others. It means considering your own wellbeing as important as others' wellbeing, not more important but certainly not less important.

Many people are unfair to themselves. They automatically give others the benefit of the doubt whilst harshly judging themselves. They accommodate others' needs whilst ignoring their own. They give others second, third, and fourth chances whilst being unforgiving of their own mistakes. Being fair requires recognising and correcting this self-directed unfairness.

Check your requests and boundaries for fairness. Am I asking for something reasonable? If someone asked this of me, would I think the request was fair? If the answer is yes, you can make your request without guilt. Your request is fair, and you deserve to ask for fair treatment. Do not diminish legitimate needs because you fear being seen as demanding.

Consider what you give versus what you receive in relationships. Relationships need not be exactly equal at all times—sometimes you give more, sometimes the other person does—but over time, healthy relationships involve reciprocity. If you consistently give far more than you receive, you are being unfair to yourself. Fairness requires addressing imbalances, not endlessly accepting them.

Treat your mistakes and shortcomings as fairly as you would treat a friend's mistakes. If a friend made the same error you made, would you condemn them as harshly as you condemn yourself? Probably not. Apply the same compassion and understanding to yourself that you naturally extend to others. Self-respect requires fair self-treatment.

Being fair to yourself does not mean being unfair to others. You are not seeking special treatment or demanding that your needs always take precedence. You are simply ensuring that your needs receive equal consideration to others' needs. Fairness means neither martyring yourself nor exploiting others. It means balanced consideration of all parties' legitimate interests.

A , Do Not Over, Apologise

Do Not Over-Apologise means apologising when you have actually done something wrong, but not apologising for existing, having needs, or making reasonable requests. Excessive apology communicates that your needs, feelings, and requests are inherently burdensome or inappropriate. This undermines your self-respect and often reduces others' respect for you as well.

Notice how often you apologise unnecessarily. I am sorry to bother you, but... I am sorry to ask, but... I am so sorry about this; I know you are busy... These apologetic preambles suggest that making a request is inherently wrong. If your request is reasonable, you need not apologise for making it. Simply make your request directly.

Distinguish between an appropriate and excessive apology. If you genuinely wronged someone, apologise sincerely once: I apologise for forgetting our meeting. That was inconsiderate. But endless, grovelling apology (I am so, so sorry, I am such a terrible person, I cannot believe I did that, I am so sorry...) is excessive and suggests you deserve harsh judgement for a simple mistake. One clear apology is sufficient.

Do not apologise for your feelings. I am sorry I am upset, or I am sorry for crying, or I am sorry I feel this way, all apologise for being human. Emotions arise naturally. You need not apologise for having them. You might need to manage how you express certain emotions, but the emotions themselves require no apology.

Do not apologise for saying no. No, I cannot help you move this weekend; it needs no apology. If you want to soften the refusal, you might express regret: I wish I were available to help, but I cannot. These express regret about circumstances whilst maintaining your boundary. It does not apologise for having boundaries or limitations.

Replace unnecessary apologies with thank you statements when appropriate. Instead of: Sorry, I am late, try: Thank you for waiting. Instead of: Sorry to burden you with this, try: Thank you for listening. This shift acknowledges the other person's kindness without unnecessarily positioning yourself as wrong or burdensome.

S , Stick to Your Values

Stick to Your Values means acting in accordance with your personal values and morals even when doing so is difficult or unpopular. It means not betraying yourself to please others, avoid conflict, or achieve short-term gains. Your values define who you are; abandoning them to smooth over interpersonal difficulties damages your self-respect profoundly.

Clarify your values if you have not already. What principles guide your life? What kind of person do you want to be? Common values include honesty, loyalty, fairness, compassion, integrity, responsibility, and respect. Knowing your values explicitly helps you recognise when situations challenge them and when you need to actively stick to them despite pressure.

When facing interpersonal pressure to act against your values, pause and check in: If I do this, will I respect myself afterwards? If I agree to this, am I betraying something important to me? If the answer is yes to either question, hold firm to your values even if it creates conflict or disappoints others. The temporary discomfort of holding firm is far less painful than the lasting damage of self-betrayal.

Communicate your values when relevant. I am not comfortable with that because honesty is very important to me, or I need to decline because this conflicts with my commitment to fairness helps others understand your decision. You are not lecturing them about values; you are explaining your position. People often respect clear value-based positions even when they disagree with them.

Recognise that sticking to your values sometimes costs you socially or practically. Some people will be frustrated when you do not join in gossip if honesty is your value. Some opportunities may close if you do not compromise your integrity. These losses are real, but the loss of self-respect from betraying your values is ultimately more damaging. You have to live with yourself forever, and maintaining your integrity matters.

Do not use values rigidly to avoid all flexibility or compassion. Sticking to values does not mean being harsh or unforgiving. If kindness is your value, that might mean being flexible with someone who made an honest mistake. If fairness is your value, that includes being fair to yourself and others. Values should guide you towards the best action, not justify rigidity or cruelty.

T , Be Truthful

Be Truthful means not lying, exaggerating, or acting helpless when you are not. It means being honest about your thoughts, feelings, abilities, and limitations. Lies and deception create distance in relationships and damage self-respect. When you lie to manage others' reactions or perceptions, you sacrifice authentic connection and your own integrity.

Tell the truth even when it is uncomfortable. If you made a mistake, admit it rather than making excuses or blaming others. If you do not know something, say: I do not know, rather than pretending knowledge you lack. If you do not want to do something, say so directly rather than inventing excuses. Truthfulness may feel risky in the moment, but it builds trust and respect over time.

Do not exaggerate your distress, helplessness, or inability to cope to manipulate others into helping you or letting you off the hook. If you genuinely need help, ask directly. If you made a mistake, take responsibility. Acting more helpless than you are to avoid responsibility is a form of dishonesty that damages self-respect and relationships.

Be truthful about your feelings. If you are angry, do not pretend you are fine. If you are hurt, do not laugh it off. Authentic expression of your emotions, whilst managing how you express them appropriately, maintains your connection to yourself and allows genuine intimacy with others. Constant false fronts create isolation and internal fragmentation.

Truthfulness includes being honest about your limitations and boundaries. Do not promise what you cannot deliver. Do not agree to things you genuinely cannot or will not do. Do not pretend you are fine with situations you are not fine with. These dishonest agreements create problems down the line and require you to maintain pretences that exhaust you.

Balance truthfulness with kindness. Being truthful does not mean brutally sharing every negative thought. You can be honest whilst also being kind. You might think: This person is boring but saying this would be unnecessarily hurtful. Instead, when declining further socialisation, you might say truthfully: I am not feeling up for company today. Truthfulness means not lying, not sharing every unfiltered thought.

Using FAST with DEAR MAN and GIVE

FAST works alongside DEAR MAN and GIVE to create fully effective interpersonal interactions. DEAR MAN structures your communication for objectives effectiveness. GIVE determines your manner for relationship effectiveness. FAST ensures your actions maintain self-respect effectiveness. Together, they create balanced interpersonal functioning.

When preparing for important interactions, consider all three skill sets. What is my objective and how will I use DEAR MAN to pursue it? How can I use GIVE to maintain this relationship? How can I use FAST to maintain my self-respect? This comprehensive approach helps you balance competing priorities and navigate complex interpersonal situations skilfully.

Sometimes these skill sets create tension. Being gentle (GIVE) whilst being truthful (FAST) about a difficult reality requires finesse. Getting your objective (DEAR MAN) whilst sticking to your values (FAST) may cost you the relationship. These tensions are real. The skills do not eliminate difficult choices; they help you make those choices consciously and navigate them as effectively as possible.

Building and Managing Relationships

DEAR MAN, GIVE, and FAST provide tools for specific interpersonal interactions. However, interpersonal effectiveness encompasses more than managing individual conversations. This chapter addresses broader relationship challenges: how to build new relationships, how to maintain and deepen existing ones, how to navigate common relationship difficulties, and how to recognise and end relationships that have become harmful.

Factors Affecting Interpersonal Effectiveness

Before exploring relationship building and management, understanding factors that affect interpersonal effectiveness helps you make wise decisions about when and how to use your skills. Several factors influence whether particular interpersonal approaches are likely to succeed.

Capability: Can the Other Person Give You What You Want?

Consider whether the other person can meet your request. If you ask someone without financial resources to lend you money, the request will fail regardless of how skilfully you ask. If you ask someone without expertise to teach you a skill, they cannot comply, however much they might want to. If you ask someone with severe depression to be cheerful, you are asking for something beyond their current capacity.

Before making requests, honestly assess capability. Does this person have the resources, skills, time, knowledge, or emotional capacity to give what I am asking? If the answer is no, either adjust your request to something they can provide or direct your request to someone with appropriate capability. Skilful asking cannot overcome genuine inability.

Priorities: Does the Other Person Have Reasons Not to Give What You Want?

Even when someone is capable of meeting your request, they may have competing priorities that make agreeing difficult or impossible. They may have other commitments, limited resources, or conflicting obligations. Understanding their priorities helps you frame requests effectively or recognise when timing is poor.

If you ask your manager for time off during the company's busiest period, their priorities conflict with your request, regardless of your skill in asking. If you ask a friend already stretched thin to take on another commitment, their self-care priorities may prevent them from agreeing. Sometimes the answer is no, not because of how you asked but because of genuine priority conflicts.

When priorities conflict, you might negotiate timing, modify your request to fit their constraints, or accept that this person cannot help with this particular need right now. You might also explore whether you can help address the conflicting priorities, creating space for them to assist you. Flexibility and understanding of their priorities increase effectiveness.

Relationship: How Is the Relationship?

The quality and history of your relationship significantly affect how requests are received. People are generally more willing to help those they feel close to, trust, and have a positive history with. If the relationship is strained, even reasonable requests may meet resistance.

If you have damaged the relationship through past behaviour, address this before making significant requests. Apologise for harm done, demonstrate behaviour change, and rebuild trust. Then your requests are more likely to be received positively. If you have been unreliable, demonstrating reliability before asking for favours increases your effectiveness.

Consider also whether you have been giving as well as taking in the relationship. If every interaction involves you asking for something, the relationship becomes one-sided, and the other person understandably becomes less responsive to requests. Ensure reciprocity—offer help, show interest in their life, provide support—before making additional requests.

Rights: Do You Have the Right to Ask or Refuse?

Consider whether you have the legitimate right to make your request or refusal. If your landlord asks for overdue rent, you have limited grounds for refusal because rent payment is your contractual obligation. If your employer asks you to complete work within your job description, this is their right as your employer. Understanding legitimate authority and obligations helps you recognise when refusal may not be viable.

However, you always have the right to ask for fair treatment, to say no to unreasonable requests, to set boundaries about your person and your time, and to request things you need. Do not automatically assume you lack rights. Many people underestimate their legitimate entitlement to ask for what they need or refuse what they do not want. Check whether your hesitation about rights is accurate or reflects low self-worth.

Authority: What Is Your Relative Power?

Power dynamics affect interpersonal effectiveness. If you are in a position of less power—employee to employer, child to parent, junior colleague to senior—your ability to refuse or make demands is constrained. If you are in a position of more power, you must use that power responsibly rather than coercively.

When you have less power, frame requests carefully, use GIVE skills extensively to maintain the relationship and recognise that some requests may not be viable. Consider carefully which battles are worth fighting and which may create more problems than they solve. This is not about accepting mistreatment, but about a realistic assessment of what you can change in a particular power dynamic.

When you have more power, be aware that your requests may feel like orders even if you intend them as requests. People with less power may feel unable to refuse you freely. Use your power ethically. Make genuine requests that the other person can decline without fear of negative consequences. Do not exploit power imbalances to get what you want.

Building New Relationships

Many people struggle with building new relationships. They may feel shy, anxious about rejection, or uncertain about how to initiate and develop connections. The following guidance provides structure for relationship building.

Finding Potential Relationships

New relationships require proximity and shared interests or experiences. You cannot build relationships with people you never encounter. Actively put yourself in situations where you will meet potential friends or partners: classes, clubs, interest groups, volunteer organisations, community events, social gatherings, online communities focused on your interests.

Choose environments aligned with your interests and values. If you love books, join a book club. If you value service, volunteer. If you enjoy hiking, join a hiking group. Shared interests provide natural conversation topics and activities, making relationship building easier. You also ensure you meet people with at least some compatibility with you.

Show up consistently. Relationships require repeated exposure. Attending one meeting or event is insufficient. Regular attendance over weeks and months allows others to become familiar with you and provides opportunities for relationships to develop naturally. Consistency signals your genuine interest in the community and makes you a recognisable presence.

Initiating Connection

Once you encounter potential friends, initiate conversation. Many people wait passively for others to approach them. Active initiation significantly increases relationship opportunities. Start with small, low-risk interactions: greet people, ask questions, make observations, offer compliments. These brief exchanges build familiarity and can develop into deeper conversations over time.

Show genuine interest in others. Ask questions about their experiences, thoughts, and interests. Listen actively to their responses. People generally appreciate when others show interest in them, and genuine curiosity creates a connection. Remember details they share and ask follow-up questions in future interactions. This demonstrates that you value them.

Share appropriately about yourself. Relationship building involves reciprocal disclosure. If someone shares something personal, sharing something comparable builds intimacy. However, match the depth of disclosure to the stage of the relationship. Oversharing too early can overwhelm people. Under-sharing indefinitely prevents relationships from deepening. Calibrate disclosure to create gradual intimacy.

Suggest shared activities. Once you have had a few positive interactions, suggest doing something together: getting coffee, attending an event, or working on a project. These shared experiences build the relationship beyond brief encounters. Start with time-limited, public activities to feel safe, then expand as comfort and trust develop.

Overcoming Relationship Building Obstacles

Fear of rejection prevents many people from initiating relationships. Remember that most people appreciate friendly overtures. If someone does not respond warmly, this reflects their circumstances or preferences, not your inadequacy. Not every person you approach will become a friend, and this is normal. Friendship requires mutual interest and chemistry. Some incompatibility is inevitable and acceptable.

If you struggle with social anxiety, start small. Set goals like: This week I will say hello to three people, or I will ask one person about their weekend. Small, consistent social actions build confidence gradually. Use TIP skills before social situations if anxiety is high. Consider whether therapy specifically for social anxiety might help.

If you tend to be judgemental of others, practice radical acceptance. People have different interests, styles, and preferences. This diversity is normal, not wrong. Approach potential friends with curiosity rather than judgement. Look for what is interesting or appealing about them rather than immediately dismissing them for not matching your ideal friend template.

Maintaining and Deepening Relationships

Building initial connections is one challenge; maintaining and deepening relationships over time is another. The following strategies help sustain and strengthen relationships.

Regular Contact

Relationships require ongoing contact to be maintained. Reach out regularly, even briefly. Text, call, suggest meetings, and engage on social media. The form matters less than the consistency. Regular contact signals that the person matters to you and keeps the relationship alive through life's inevitable busy periods.

Take initiative rather than waiting for the other person to always reach out first. Balanced relationships involve both parties initiating contact. If you consistently wait for others to contact you, relationships often fade. Active investment in maintaining contact demonstrates that you value the relationship.

Reliability and Consistency

Be someone others can count on. Follow through on commitments. Arrive when you say you will arrive. Do what you say you will do. If something prevents you from keeping a commitment, communicate as soon as possible. Reliability builds trust, and trust deepens relationships. Unreliability erodes connection even in otherwise positive relationships.

Consistency in behaviour helps others feel safe with you. This does not mean being the same at all times, but rather being predictably yourself. If you are warm one day and cold the next without explanation, people feel uncertain around you. Consistent warmth, kindness, and responsiveness help relationships flourish.

Reciprocity

Relationships thrive on reciprocity—giving and receiving, supporting and being supported, sharing and listening. Notice the balance in your relationships. Do you always talk about your problems without asking about theirs? Do you always take help without offering it? Do they always initiate whilst you passively participate? Imbalances create resentment over time.

If you notice you tend to take more than you give, consciously increase your giving. Offer help, ask about their lives, provide support, initiate contact. If you notice you tend to give far more than you receive, this may indicate an unhealthy relationship pattern requiring attention. Healthy relationships involve a relatively balanced exchange over time.

Vulnerability and Depth

Deep relationships require vulnerability—sharing fears, struggles, hopes, and authentic feelings. Surface-level interaction keeps relationships friendly but not intimate. Appropriate vulnerability creates intimacy. This requires emotional risk. The other person might respond poorly or use information against you. However, without vulnerability, relationships cannot reach depth.

Increase vulnerability gradually. Share progressively more personal information as the relationship proves safe. Notice how the other person responds to your vulnerability. Do they reciprocate with their own? Do they maintain confidentiality? Do they respond with empathy? These responses help you assess whether deeper vulnerability is safe in this relationship.

Managing Conflict Constructively

All relationships involve conflict. Healthy relationships are not conflict-free; they are relationships in which conflict is managed constructively. When issues arise, address them rather than avoiding or exploding. Use DEAR MAN to express concerns. Use GIVE to maintain the relationship whilst addressing problems. Use FAST to maintain your self-respect.

Listen genuinely to the other person's perspective during conflict. Conflict often involves two valid but incompatible needs or perspectives. Understanding their position does not require abandoning yours, but it creates the possibility for solutions that work for both parties. Be willing to apologise when you have genuinely wronged the other person. Clean up your mistakes promptly.

Know when to let go of minor irritations. Not every annoyance warrants a conversation. Choose your battles. Address issues that genuinely affect the relationship or your wellbeing. Let go of minor preferences. Constant criticism erodes relationships; selective addressing of important issues maintains them.

Recognising and Ending Destructive Relationships

Not all relationships are healthy or worth maintaining. Some relationships are destructive—they damage your wellbeing, violate your values, or drain you without reciprocity. Learning to recognise destructive relationships and end them when necessary is an essential interpersonal effectiveness skill.

Signs of Destructive Relationships

Destructive relationships have characteristic patterns. Recognising these patterns helps you identify when a relationship may need to end. The relationship is consistently one-sided, with you giving far more than you receive. You feel worse about yourself when you spend time with this person rather than better. The person regularly violates your boundaries despite clear communication. The relationship involves abuse—physical, emotional, sexual, or financial. The person is actively harmful to your recovery or wellbeing.

The relationship requires you to constantly compromise your values or pretend to be someone you are not. You feel exhausted rather than energised by interactions. The person gossips about you, shares your confidences, or undermines you to others. The relationship involves active addiction or behaviours that endanger you. After using your interpersonal effectiveness skills extensively, the relationship shows no improvement.

One or two of these signs does not necessarily indicate a relationship should end. All relationships have difficult periods. However, persistent patterns of these issues, particularly when you have attempted to address them without success, suggest a destructive relationship that may need to end.

Deciding to End a Relationship

Ending relationships is difficult and painful. Many people stay in destructive relationships far longer than they should because ending them feels unbearable. However, maintaining destructive relationships damages your well-being, prevents you from investing in healthy relationships, and keeps you stuck in painful patterns.

Consider these questions when deciding whether to end a relationship: Have I clearly communicated my needs and boundaries to the other person? Have I given the person a genuine opportunity to change? Have things improved or remained the same despite my efforts? Is staying in this relationship preventing me from building the life I want? Is this relationship actively harmful to my well-being or recovery? Would I advise someone I love to stay in this relationship if they described it to me?

If, after honest consideration, you conclude the relationship needs to end, trust this decision.

Ending destructive relationships is an act of self-respect and self-preservation, not selfishness or cruelty. You have the right to protect yourself from relationships that harm you.

How to End Relationships

How you end a relationship depends on the relationship type and circumstances. For casual friendships or acquaintances, gradual distancing is often appropriate. You reduce contact frequency, decline invitations, and allow the relationship to fade naturally. No formal announcement is necessary for relationships that were never very close.

For closer relationships or when gradual distancing is not working, direct communication is more respectful. You might say: I have realised this friendship is not working for me anymore, and I have decided we should not continue spending time together. I wish you well. This is clear and allows both parties to move on without confusion or false hope.

For relationships involving abuse or safety concerns, prioritise your safety over politeness.

You need not have a final conversation if doing so is dangerous. You can end the relationship by ceasing all contact, blocking communication channels, and informing mutual acquaintances if necessary. Safety always takes precedence over relationship norms.

After ending relationships, especially significant ones, allow yourself to grieve. Ending even destructive relationships often involves loss and sadness. These feelings are normal. Use your distress tolerance skills to manage the grief. Seek support from healthy relationships. Remind yourself why you made this decision when you doubt yourself. Over time, the pain diminishes, and you will likely feel relief that the destructive pattern has ended.

Balancing Relationship Effectiveness Goals

Throughout this module, we have explored three relationship effectiveness goals: getting your objectives met, maintaining relationships, and preserving self-respect. These goals sometimes align easily; other times they create tension requiring difficult choices. This final section addresses how to make these choices wisely.

In relationships you value highly, prioritise relationship effectiveness even when it means compromising on objectives. If your objective is less important than the relationship, let go of the objective or moderate your approach significantly. Use GIVE extensively. Be willing to accept less than you hoped for to preserve the relationship. This is not weakness; it is recognising what matters most to you.

When your objective is very important and the relationship is less important, prioritise objectives effectiveness. Use DEAR MAN assertively. Push for what you need. Be willing to damage or lose the relationship if necessary to get your objective met. This makes sense when your need is significant, and the relationship is casual or already problematic.

Always prioritise self-respect effectiveness over pleasing others or achieving objectives. If achieving an objective or maintaining a relationship requires betraying your values, lying, or accepting unacceptable treatment, the cost is too high. FAST skills protect your fundamental integrity and self-worth. Without these, no achievement or relationship is worthwhile.

In many situations, you can achieve reasonable balance among all three goals. You get much of what you want, the relationship remains intact or even strengthens, and you maintain your self-respect. These balanced outcomes are most common when you use all three skill sets together skilfully. However, sometimes trade-offs are inevitable. Making conscious, value-guided choices about these trade-offs is itself an interpersonal effectiveness skill.

Integration and Practice

Interpersonal effectiveness skills require practice to become natural. In the beginning, using these skills feels artificial and effortful. You may need to write out DEAR MAN scripts, consciously remind yourself to use GIVE, and deliberately check your FAST alignment. This conscious effort is normal and necessary. With practice, the skills become increasingly automatic.

Start practising with lower-stakes situations. Use DEAR MAN to make a minor request from a friend or decline a small invitation. Practise GIVE skills in everyday pleasant interactions. Notice when you are being unfair to yourself and practice FAST. These small practices build skill and confidence for more challenging situations.

Reflect after interpersonal interactions. What went well? What could you improve? Did you achieve your objectives? How is the relationship? Do you respect how you handled yourself? This reflection helps you learn from experience and refine your approach over time. Do not judge yourself harshly for imperfect implementation; simply notice and adjust.

Remember that interpersonal effectiveness is about skill, not perfection. You will make mistakes. You will sometimes prioritise the wrong goal, misjudge situations, or execute skills poorly. This is part of learning. What matters is your ongoing commitment to developing these skills and your willingness to keep trying despite setbacks. Over time, your interpersonal effectiveness will grow significantly, and your relationships will reflect this growth.

Module 4: Emotion Regulation Skills

Emotions are central to human experience. They provide information, motivate action, and communicate to others. However, for many people, emotions feel overwhelming, uncontrollable, and destructive. They may experience emotions as too intense, too frequent, or lasting too long. They may feel hijacked by their emotions, engaging in impulsive behaviours they later regret. They may fear their emotions, attempting to suppress or avoid them, which paradoxically intensifies emotional suffering.

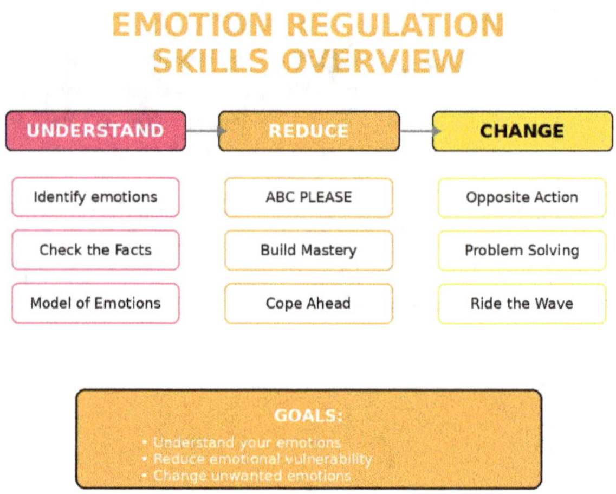

Figure 31: Emotion Regulation Skills Overview

Emotion regulation skills address these difficulties. These skills teach you to understand your emotions, reduce your vulnerability to negative emotions, build positive emotional experiences, and change emotions that are causing problems. Emotion regulation does not mean eliminating emotions or maintaining constant happiness. It means developing a healthier, more flexible relationship with your emotional experience that allows you to experience the full range of human emotions without being controlled or overwhelmed by them.

This module begins by helping you understand emotions—what they are, how they work, and what functions they serve. Understanding emotions is essential for regulating them effectively. The module then provides specific skills for reducing emotional vulnerability, building positive emotions, and changing unwanted emotions. Together, these skills create a comprehensive approach to emotional wellbeing.

Why Emotion Regulation Matters

Difficulties with emotion regulation create significant suffering and life interference. When emotions are dysregulated, they dominate your experience, influence your decisions, and damage your relationships. Understanding why emotion regulation matters motivates the often-challenging work of developing these skills.

Firstly, unregulated emotions lead to impulsive, destructive behaviours. When overwhelmed by emotion, you may engage in actions that provide temporary relief but create lasting problems: substance use, self-harm, aggressive outbursts, reckless spending, binge eating, or impulsive relationship decisions. These behaviours often occur because you lack effective strategies for managing intense emotions. Emotion regulation skills provide those strategies.

Secondly, emotion dysregulation interferes with your ability to pursue goals and build the life you want. When emotional reactions are intense and prolonged, they consume your energy and attention. You may avoid situations that trigger difficult emotions, which limits your opportunities. You may make decisions based purely on temporary emotional states rather than your long-term values and goals. Emotion regulation allows you to experience emotions without being controlled by them, freeing you to pursue what matters to you.

Thirdly, emotional dysregulation damages relationships. Intense, unpredictable emotional reactions can frighten or overwhelm others. Emotional outbursts create conflict. Emotional withdrawal prevents intimacy. People may distance themselves from you or walk on eggshells around you. Emotion regulation skills help you interact with others in emotionally balanced ways that build rather than damage relationships.

Finally, chronic emotion dysregulation is exhausting and demoralising. Living in emotional chaos is draining. You may feel hopeless that things could ever change, believing you are fundamentally broken or defective. Emotion regulation skills demonstrate that emotional difficulties are not fixed character flaws but patterns that can be changed through skill development and practice. As you build these skills, emotional life becomes more manageable and hope for wellbeing becomes realistic.

Understanding Emotions

Before you can effectively regulate emotions, you must understand what emotions are and how they work. Many people have misconceptions about emotions that interfere with regulation. This chapter provides accurate information about emotional experience and functioning that forms the foundation for all other emotion regulation skills.

What Are Emotions?

Emotions are complex responses involving multiple components. When you experience an emotion, several things happen simultaneously. You have physiological changes (your body reacts), cognitive changes (your thinking shifts), action urges (you feel pulled to behave in particular ways), and subjective experience (you feel something). Understanding these components helps you recognise and work with emotions more effectively.

Physiological changes are physical sensations that accompany emotions. When anxious, your heart may race, you may sweat or feel tension in your chest. When angry, you may feel heat, muscle tension, or energy surging. When sad, you may feel heavy, tired, or lump in your throat. These body sensations are real and measurable. They prepare your body for action appropriate to the emotion.

Cognitive changes are shifts in how you think and what you attend to. Fear narrows your attention to threats. Anger focuses you on perceived injustices. Sadness draws your attention to losses. Each emotion changes both what you notice in your environment and how you interpret what you notice. These cognitive shifts can be subtle but significantly influence your experience.

Action urges are inclinations to behave in specific ways. Fear urges you to escape or avoid. Anger urges you to attack or confront. Sadness urges you to withdraw or seek comfort. Shame urges you to hide. These urges are automatic and powerful, but urges are not the same as actions. You can experience an urge without following it. Recognising the difference between urges and actions is crucial for emotion regulation.

Subjective experience is the felt quality of the emotion—what it is like to be anxious, angry, sad, or joyful. This internal experience is difficult to describe fully to others but is immediately recognisable to you. The subjective experience combines all other components into a unified emotional state that you identify with a name: I am anxious, I am angry, I am sad.

The Functions of Emotions

Emotions are not arbitrary or meaningless. They serve important functions. Understanding these functions helps you appreciate emotions rather than viewing them as purely problematic. Even painful emotions have value and purpose.

Emotions provide information about your environment and your needs. Fear tells you that you perceive danger. Anger tells you that a boundary has been violated or an injustice has occurred. Sadness tells you that you have lost something important. Guilt tells you that you have violated your own values. These emotional signals help you understand what is happening and what matters to you.

Emotions motivate action. The action urges that accompany emotions push you to respond to situations. Fear motivates protective action. Anger motivates you to address injustices or protect boundaries. Sadness motivates you to slow down and process loss. Joy motivates you to continue or repeat actions that bring pleasure. Without emotional motivation, you would struggle to prioritise amongst competing demands.

Emotions communicate to others. Your facial expressions, tone of voice, and body language convey your emotional state, often unconsciously. This communication serves important social functions. Your fear may warn others of danger. Your sadness may elicit comfort and support. Your anger may signal to others that they need to adjust their behaviour. Emotional expression facilitates social coordination and relationship maintenance.

Emotions can influence others' behaviour. When you express emotion authentically, others often respond in predictable ways. Your crying may evoke comfort. Your anger may cause others to reconsider their actions. Your enthusiasm may inspire others to join you. This influence can be used consciously or may occur automatically, but it represents a significant function of emotional expression.

Understanding these functions does not mean all emotional experiences are helpful or should be indulged. Sometimes emotional responses are disproportionate to situations, based on inaccurate information, or lead to unhelpful actions. Sometimes emotions served valuable functions in past circumstances, but no longer serve you in present circumstances. Emotion regulation involves recognising when emotions are serving their functions appropriately and when they need to be regulated or changed.

The Emotion Regulation Model

Understanding how emotions arise and persist helps you identify points where you can intervene to regulate them. The emotion regulation model describes the typical sequence of events in emotional episodes and reveals multiple opportunities for regulation.

Emotions typically begin with a prompting event—something that happens in your environment or in your thoughts that triggers an emotional response. This might be an external event (someone criticises you; you receive bad news, you encounter a feared situation) or an internal event (a memory, a physical sensation, a thought). The prompting event starts the emotional sequence.

Your interpretation of the event influences which emotion arises and how intensely. The same event can trigger different emotions depending on interpretation. If someone does not respond to your text message, you might interpret this as rejection (triggering sadness or anxiety), as disrespect (triggering anger), or as simply that they are busy (triggering no particular emotion). Your beliefs, assumptions, and attributions shape your emotional response.

Based on your interpretation, an emotion arises with all its components: body changes, cognitive shifts, action urges, and subjective experience. This emotional response happens quickly, often before conscious awareness. You may notice you are angry before you consciously recognise what you are angry about.

Your response to the emotion—what you think about it and what you do—influences whether the emotion intensifies, diminishes, or maintains. If you act on destructive urges, you may intensify the emotion. If you ruminate on triggering thoughts, you maintain the emotion. If you use emotion regulation skills, you can reduce the emotion's intensity or duration. Your response to your emotion is as important as the emotion itself in determining your overall experience.

This model reveals multiple regulation points. You can modify vulnerability factors that make you more emotionally reactive. You can change the situations you encounter (problem-solving). You can change your interpretation of events (cognitive change). You can change your response to emotions once they arise (opposite action, distraction, self-soothing). Effective emotion regulation involves strategically intervening at the most appropriate point for particular situations.

Figure 2: The DBT Model of Emotions

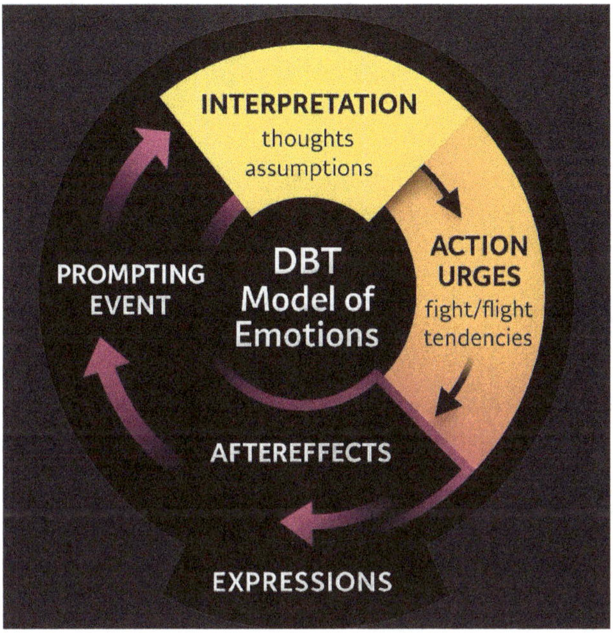

Figure 2: The DBT Model of Emotions

Components of the Model

Prompting Event

The initial trigger for an emotion.

Can be **external** (e.g., someone criticises you) or **internal** (e.g., a painful memory).

Interpretation

How you **perceive and interpret** the prompting event.

Influenced by past experiences, beliefs, and assumptions.

Example: "They ignored me, so they must dislike me."

Biological Changes

Physical reactions in the body.

Includes changes in **heart rate**, **breathing**, **hormones**, and **muscle tension**.

Action Urges

The impulse to act in a certain way based on the emotion.

Example: Anger → urge to shout; Fear → urge to avoid.

Expressions

How the emotion is shown outwardly.

Includes **facial expressions**, **tone of voice**, and **body language**.

Aftereffects

The consequences of the emotional episode.

Can influence future emotions and interpretations, creating a feedback loop.

Why This Matters

By breaking down emotions into these components, DBT teaches skills to:

Identify triggers and interpretations.

Change biological responses through relaxation.

Modify action urges using the opposite action.

Reduce harmful aftereffects by choosing skilful behaviours.

Common Myths About Emotions

Many people hold beliefs about emotions that interfere with effective regulation. Identifying and correcting these myths is essential for emotional wellbeing.

Myth 1: Negative emotions are bad and should be avoided. Reality: All emotions, including painful ones, provide information and serve functions. Attempting to avoid or suppress emotions typically intensifies them and creates additional problems. Acceptance and effective management of all emotions, not avoidance, leads to wellbeing.

Myth 2: Letting others know how I feel is weak. Reality: Emotional expression is a normal human behaviour that facilitates connection and support. Appropriate expression of emotions strengthens relationships. Chronic suppression of emotions damages both your wellbeing and your relationships.

Myth 3: My emotions are who I am. Reality: Emotions are temporary states you experience, not fundamental aspects of your identity. You are not your anger, your sadness, or your fear. You are a person who experiences these emotions. This distinction creates space for change.

Myth 4: Emotions happen for no reason. Reality: Emotions always have causes, even if those causes are not immediately apparent. Prompting events, interpretations, and vulnerability factors all contribute to emotional responses. Understanding causes helps you regulate emotions more effectively.

Myth 5: Painful emotions will last forever. Reality: All emotions are temporary. Even intense emotional states diminish over time if you do not continuously fuel them through rumination or dysfunctional behaviour. Trusting that emotions pass helps you tolerate distress without impulsive action.

Myth 6: If I ignore an emotion, it will go away. Reality: Ignored or suppressed emotions typically do not disappear. They may manifest in physical symptoms, leak out in uncontrolled ways, or intensify over time. Acknowledging and appropriately addressing emotions is more effective than ignoring them.

Myth 7: There is a right way to feel in every situation. Reality: Emotional responses vary based on individual history, biology, current circumstances, and interpretation. Your emotional response is your emotional response. Judging emotions as right or wrong adds suffering without helping you regulate them.

Reducing Emotional Vulnerability—ABC PLEASE

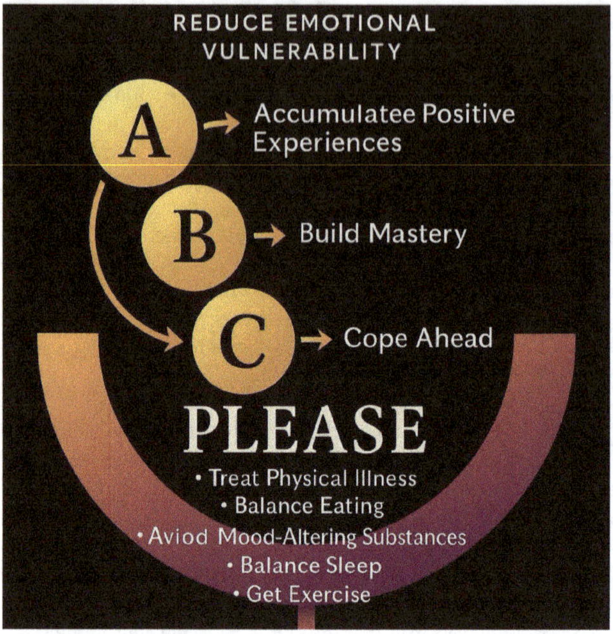

Figure 7: ABC PLEASE Skills

Some approaches to emotion regulation focus on changing emotions once they arise. ABC, PLEASE takes a different approach: reducing your vulnerability to negative emotions in the first place. This skill addresses the physical and lifestyle factors that contribute to increased emotional reactivity. When you prioritise your physical health and maintain a balanced life, you are less susceptible to emotional dysregulation.

ABC, PLEASE stands for: Accumulate positive experiences, build mastery, Cope ahead of time, treat Physical illness, balance Eating, avoid mood-Altering substances, balance Sleep, and get Exercise. These elements work together to reduce emotional vulnerability and build emotional resilience.

Figure 22: Build Mastery

Accumulate Positive Experiences

Accumulate positive experiences means deliberately building pleasant events into your life. Many people struggling with emotional dysregulation has lives dominated by demands, problems, and unpleasant necessities. Without positive experiences to balance the negative, emotional reserves deplete and vulnerability increases. Deliberately accumulating positive experiences builds emotional resilience.

Start by identifying what activities bring you pleasure or satisfaction. Make a list of activities you enjoy, people you like spending time with, places you find pleasant, and experiences that make you feel good. Include both small pleasures (a good cup of tea, sunshine on your face) and larger ones (holidays, concerts, significant achievements). This list is your resource for accumulating positive experiences.

Schedule pleasant activities regularly. Do not wait until you feel like doing them or until you have spare time. Build them into your routine deliberately. Aim for at least one pleasant activity daily, even if brief. These scheduled positive experiences counterbalance life's inevitable difficulties and prevent emotional reserves from complete depletion.

Be mindful during positive experiences. It is not enough to merely participate in pleasant activities; you must actually experience them as pleasant. Avoid multitasking, worrying about the future, or ruminating on problems during pleasant activities. Bring your full attention to the positive experience, noticing pleasant sensations, thoughts, and feelings. This mindfulness amplifies the benefit.

Work towards long-term goals that align with your values. Whilst immediate pleasant activities provide short-term emotional benefit, progress towards valued goals provides lasting satisfaction and meaning. Identify goals in areas like relationships, work, education, health, or personal development. Take concrete steps towards these goals regularly. Progress creates a sense of purpose that reduces emotional vulnerability.

Build Mastery

Build mastery means doing things that make you feel competent, capable, and accomplished. Mastery experiences counteract feelings of helplessness and build self-efficacy. When you regularly engage in activities where you can see your skill developing or where you successfully meet challenges, you feel more confident in your ability to handle whatever life presents.

Choose activities that are challenging but achievable. If too easy, they do not build mastery. If too difficult, they lead to frustration. Find the balance where you must stretch yourself but can succeed with effort. This might be learning a new skill, completing a difficult task, engaging in a hobby that requires practice, or taking on challenges slightly beyond your comfort zone.

Break larger mastery goals into smaller steps. If you want to learn to play guitar, start with learning basic chords rather than attempting complex pieces. If you want to run a marathon, start with running for five minutes. Small, achievable steps allow you to experience frequent success, which builds confidence and motivation for continued progress.

Engage in mastery activities even when you do not feel like it. Motivation often follows action rather than preceding it. You may not feel capable or motivated initially, but starting the activity and experiencing even small success generates motivation and positive feelings. Do not wait to feel confident before building mastery; build mastery to develop confidence.

Acknowledge your accomplishments. Many people dismiss or minimise their achievements. Actively notice and appreciate what you accomplish. Keep a record of mastery activities and review it regularly. Recognising your competence and progress builds the sense of mastery that reduces emotional vulnerability.

Cope Ahead

Cope ahead means rehearsing how you will handle difficult situations before they occur. When you have planned your response to challenging circumstances, you feel more confident and less overwhelmed when they arise. Preparation reduces anxiety and improves actual performance when the situation occurs.

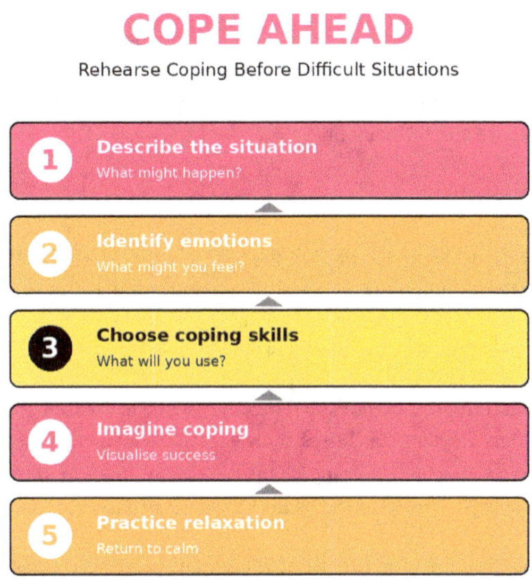

Figure 23: Cope Ahead

Identify situations that typically trigger emotional difficulties for you. These might include specific interactions (family gatherings, performance reviews at work), circumstances (being alone, financial stress), or general challenges (rejection, criticism, conflict). Make a list of predictable difficult situations.

For each identified situation, imagine yourself in it vividly. What will happen? What will you see, hear, and experience? How will you likely feel? What thoughts might arise? What urges might you experience? Creating a detailed mental picture of the situation prepares your mind to handle it effectively.

Decide which skills you will use to cope with the situation. Will you use mindfulness to stay present? TIP skills to manage physiological arousal. DEAR MAN to communicate effectively? Opposite action to counter problematic urges? Choose specific skills appropriate to the particular situation and rehearse using them.

Imagine yourself using the skills successfully. Visualise yourself handling the situation with skill and composure. See yourself noticing difficult emotions arising, implementing your planned skills, and managing the situation effectively. This mental rehearsal builds confidence and makes successful coping more likely when the actual situation occurs.

Revise your plan based on experience. After encountering the situation, reflect on how your coping plan worked. What went well? What could be improved? Adjust your plan accordingly and rehearse the revised approach. Coping ahead is an iterative process that improves with practice and refinement.

Treat Physical Illness

Treat physical illness means attending promptly and appropriately to your physical health. Physical illness increases emotional vulnerability significantly. Pain, fatigue, and physiological stress from illness make emotional regulation more difficult. Taking care of your physical health supports your emotional health.

Attend medical appointments. Do not avoid healthcare due to anxiety, cost concerns, or minimising symptoms. Regular check-ups allow early detection and treatment of problems. When symptoms arise, seek appropriate medical care promptly rather than waiting until problems become severe. Your physical health deserves attention and professional care.

Take prescribed medications consistently. If you have chronic conditions requiring medication, take your medications as prescribed. If you experience problematic side effects, discuss these with your doctor rather than simply stopping medication. Many people's emotional dysregulation worsens significantly when they discontinue necessary medications.

Manage pain effectively. Chronic pain profoundly affects emotional wellbeing. Work with healthcare providers to manage pain as effectively as possible. This might involve medication, physical therapy, mindfulness-based pain management, or other approaches. Do not suffer unnecessarily with untreated pain.

If you are avoiding medical care due to anxiety or past negative experiences, address this directly. Perhaps take someone with you to appointments for support or seek a different healthcare provider if past experiences were poor. Your physical health is too important to neglect due to anxiety or avoidance.

Balance Eating

Balance eating means maintaining regular, adequate, balanced nutrition. Whilst this seems simple, many people struggling with emotional dysregulation has problematic relationships with food. They may restrict, binge, eat chaotically, or use food to manage emotions. Balanced eating supports emotional stability.

Eat regular meals rather than skipping meals or eating chaotically. Aim for three meals daily at relatively consistent times. Regular eating maintains stable blood sugar, which significantly affects mood and emotional regulation. Skipping meals often leads to increased irritability, anxiety, and emotional reactivity.

Eat sufficient quantities. Chronic undereating, whether due to food restriction, poverty, or disordered eating patterns, increases emotional vulnerability. Your brain and body need adequate fuel to function effectively. If you struggle with eating enough, consider working with a dietitian or therapist specialising in eating issues.

Eat a variety of nutritious foods. Whilst perfection is not necessary, generally prioritising whole foods, fruits, vegetables, proteins, and whole grains over highly processed foods supports both physical and emotional health. Adequate nutrition provides the building blocks for neurotransmitters that regulate mood.

Avoid using food as your primary emotion regulation strategy. Many people eat to cope with difficult emotions. Food can provide temporary comfort, but relying on food as your main coping mechanism often creates additional problems. Develop other emotion regulation skills so food is one option amongst many, not your only tool.

If you have an eating disorder or significantly disordered eating patterns, seek specialised treatment. Eating disorders require professional intervention. The suggestions here are for generally balanced eating, not treatment for clinical eating disorders. Do not attempt to treat an eating disorder on your own.

Avoid Mood, Altering Substances

Avoid mood-altering substances means limiting or eliminating use of alcohol, recreational drugs, and misuse of prescription medications. Whilst substances may provide temporary relief from difficult emotions, they significantly increase emotional vulnerability over time and interfere with emotion regulation skill development.

Substance use provides short-term emotional relief but creates long-term emotional instability. Alcohol may temporarily reduce anxiety, but it disrupts sleep, interferes with emotional processing, and often leads to depressed mood. Stimulants may temporarily boost energy or mood, but they increase anxiety and emotional volatility. The temporary benefit is vastly outweighed by the lasting harm.

Substance use interferes with emotion regulation skill learning. When you use substances to manage emotions, you never learn to regulate emotions through skill. You remain dependent on external substances rather than developing internal capacity. Sobriety is often necessary for effective emotion regulation skill development.

If you use substances regularly to cope with emotions, begin reducing use gradually whilst simultaneously building alternative coping skills. Do not simply stop substances without developing replacements, as this often leads to relapse. Build your emotion regulation skill toolkit whilst gradually reducing substance dependence.

If you have a substance use disorder, seek specialised treatment. Substance use disorders require professional intervention, often including medical support for safe withdrawal and ongoing treatment for maintaining sobriety. DBT emotion regulation skills support recovery but do not replace addiction-specific treatment.

Be aware of prescribed medications that can affect mood. Some medications have emotional side effects. If you notice mood changes after starting a medication, discuss this with your prescriber. There may be alternatives that do not affect your emotions as significantly. Never discontinue prescribed medications without medical guidance but do advocate for medications that support rather than undermine your emotional wellbeing.

Balance Sleep

Balanced sleep means getting adequate, regular, good-quality sleep. Sleep deprivation is one of the most potent factors increasing emotional vulnerability. When sleep-deprived, you are more reactive, more irritable, and less able to regulate emotions effectively. Conversely, adequate sleep supports emotional resilience.

Aim for seven to nine hours of sleep nightly. Whilst individual needs vary, most adults function best with sleep in this range. Chronic sleep deprivation of even one or two hours nightly accumulates and significantly affects emotional functioning. Prioritise sleep as essential for wellbeing, not an optional luxury.

Maintain consistent sleep and wake times. Going to bed and waking at similar times daily, even on weekends, regulates your circadian rhythm and improves sleep quality. Erratic sleep schedules disrupt this rhythm and often lead to poor sleep and increased emotional vulnerability.

Create conditions conducive to good sleep. Keep your bedroom dark, quiet, and cool. Avoid screens for at least an hour before bed, as blue light interferes with sleep initiation. Avoid caffeine in the afternoon and evening. Develop a relaxing bedtime routine that signals to your body that sleep is approaching. These sleep hygiene practices significantly improve sleep quality.

If you struggle with insomnia, address this directly. Chronic insomnia profoundly affects emotional wellbeing and should not be ignored. Consider cognitive-behavioural therapy for insomnia, which is highly effective. Avoid long-term reliance on sleep medications, if possible, as they often create dependency without addressing underlying sleep problems. However, short-term medication uses whilst building better sleep habits may be appropriate; discuss options with your healthcare provider.

Recognise that improving sleep often requires difficult changes. You may need to adjust your schedule, limit activities, or change habits. These changes may feel inconvenient or unpleasant initially. However, the emotional benefits of adequate sleep are profound. Prioritising sleep is one of the most effective ways to reduce emotional vulnerability.

Get Exercise

Get exercise means engaging in regular physical activity. Exercise is perhaps the single most effective natural emotion regulation tool. It reduces anxiety and depression, improves mood, enhances sleep, and increases stress resilience. Regular exercise should be a cornerstone of any emotion regulation programme.

Aim for at least thirty minutes of moderate physical activity most days. This might include brisk walking, cycling, swimming, dancing, or any activity that elevates your heart rate. The activity need not be intense to be beneficial. Even gentle movement provides emotional benefit, particularly if you are currently sedentary.

Choose activities you can sustain. The best exercise is the exercise you will actually do consistently. If you hate running, do not force yourself to run. Find movement you enjoy or at least tolerate. This might be walking in nature, dancing, playing sports, gardening, or practising yoga. Variety is also acceptable; you need not do the same activity always.

Start where you are, not where you think you should be. If you are currently inactive, start with five or ten minutes of gentle activity and build gradually. Attempting too much initially often leads to injury, exhaustion, and abandonment of exercise altogether. Small, sustainable increases in activity accumulate into significant change over time.

Exercise even when you do not feel like it, particularly when you do not feel like it. Depression and low mood often sap motivation for movement. However, exercise itself improves mood, so waiting until you feel motivated creates a trap. Commit to exercise as a non-negotiable self-care practice regardless of momentary motivation. The mood improvement that follows exercise will reinforce the behaviour.

If you have physical limitations or health conditions affecting exercise capacity, work within your limitations. Consult healthcare providers about appropriate exercise for your circumstances. Even very limited movement provides benefit. The goal is regular movement at whatever level you can safely manage, not achieving athlete-level fitness.

ABC PLEASE in Practice

ABC, PLEASE works best when all elements are addressed together. They are mutually reinforcing. Regular exercise improves sleep. Adequate sleep supports making healthy eating choices. Balanced eating provides energy for exercise. Pleasant activities and mastery experiences make life feel worth the effort of maintaining physical health. Together, these elements create a foundation of resilience that makes emotional regulation far more achievable.

Start by assessing your current functioning in each area. Rate yourself honestly on each element: accumulating positives, building mastery, coping ahead, treating illness, balanced eating, avoiding substances, balanced sleep, and exercise. Identify your weakest areas—these are your priorities for improvement.

Choose one or two elements to focus on initially. Attempting to overhaul all aspects of your life simultaneously is overwhelming and usually leads to failure. Select one or two areas where improvement would provide maximum benefit, or where change seems most achievable. Once these become more habitual, add another element.

Make specific, concrete plans. Instead of I will sleep better, plan: I will go to bed by 10:30 pm on weeknights. Instead of I should exercise, plan: I will plan to walk for twenty minutes every Monday, Wednesday, and Friday morning. Specific plans are actionable. Vague intentions rarely translate into behaviour change.

Track your progress. Keep a simple record of your ABC PLEASE activities. You might check off each element daily or weekly, rate your overall functioning, or keep notes about what you are noticing. Tracking makes your efforts visible, which motivates continued work and helps you identify what makes a difference for you.

Be patient with yourself. Lifestyle changes take time to implement and even more time to show emotional benefits. You may not notice dramatic mood improvements immediately after starting to exercise regularly or eating better. The benefits accumulate gradually. Trust the process and persist even when immediate results are not apparent. Over weeks and months, the cumulative effect of ABC PLEASE dramatically reduces emotional vulnerability.

Opposite Action

Opposite Action is one of the most powerful emotion regulation skills. It is based on a simple yet profound principle: emotions are accompanied by action urges, and acting on those urges often reinforces or intensifies the feeling. If you act opposite to the emotion's urge, you can change the emotion itself. This is not suppression or denial; it is a strategic use of behaviour to shift emotional states.

Understanding Opposite Action

Emotions and actions influence each other in a bidirectional manner. Not only do emotions drive actions, but actions also influence emotions. If you smile, even if it's artificial, you may start to feel happier. If you stand in a confident posture, you may begin to feel more confident. Opposite Action uses this principle deliberately to change unwanted emotions.

Use Opposite Action when an emotion is not helpful in your current situation, when the emotion does not fit the facts, or when acting on the emotion would make your situation worse. Not all feelings require Opposite Action. Sometimes, emotions align with the facts, and acting on them is appropriate. Opposite Action is for problematic emotions, given your circumstances and goals.

When to Use Opposite Action for Specific Emotions

Fear and Anxiety

Use Opposite Action for fear when the feared situation is not actually dangerous or when avoiding it interferes with your life. The urge when afraid is to avoid or escape. Opposite Action means approaching and staying in the situation rather than avoiding it. Face your fears gradually and repeatedly. Do what you are afraid of, over and over, whilst using coping skills to manage the anxiety. Over time, repeated approaches without harm occurring reduce the fear response.

Engage fully in what you are afraid of, rather than half-heartedly participating whilst planning an escape. If you're afraid of social situations, attend them and engage actively rather than standing in the corner planning when you can leave. If fearful of particular activities, do them thoroughly and mindfully rather than rushing through them to finish quickly. Full engagement maximises the learning that reduces fear.

Sadness and Depression

Use Opposite Action for sadness when a current loss does not cause it or when withdrawing and isolating is making depression worse. The urge when sad is to withdraw, isolate, lie in bed, and become inactive. Opposite Action means taking action, approaching rather than avoiding, and doing things even when you don't feel like doing them.

Engage in activities that are meaningful, pleasant, or build mastery. Force yourself to participate in life even when every fibre of your being wants to withdraw. Call friends even when you want to isolate. Exercise even when you feel you cannot move. Do enjoyable activities even when nothing feels enjoyable. The activity itself, even without immediate pleasure, begins to shift mood over time.

Approach problems rather than avoiding them. When depressed, everything feels overwhelming, and you may avoid dealing with anything. Opposite Action means tackling one issue at a time, even if progress is slow. Taking action, however small, counteracts the helplessness that maintains depression.

Anger

Use Opposite Action for anger when the situation does not warrant anger, when expressing anger would make things worse, or when anger is disproportionate to the problem. The urge when angry is to attack—verbally or physically, overtly or passive-aggressively.

Opposite Action means avoiding the person or situation temporarily if possible, doing something kind or gentle, and adopting a nonjudgemental stance.

If you cannot avoid the person, act with kindness and gentleness rather than hostility. This does not mean pretending you are not angry or accepting unacceptable treatment. It means expressing yourself constructively rather than destructively. Use DEAR MAN with extensive GIVE skills. The gentle approach often resolves situations more effectively than aggression, whilst also reducing your own anger.

Change your body posture from aggressive to relaxed. Unclenching your jaw and fists, relaxing your shoulders, and softening your facial expression can reduce anger physiologically. Try half-smiling whilst internally raging—the smile often shifts the emotion.

Shame and Guilt

Use Opposite Action for shame when you have not actually done anything wrong or when the shame is disproportionate to any wrongdoing. Shame urges you to hide, avoid eye contact, make yourself small, and isolate. Opposite Action means doing the opposite: maintain eye contact, hold your head up, stay in the situation, and interact with others rather than hiding.

For guilt, if you have actually violated your values, the appropriate action is to repair the harm: apologise sincerely, make amends, and commit to different future behaviour. However, for disproportionate guilt about minor mistakes or guilt about things beyond your control, use Opposite Action. Rather than ruminating and punishing yourself, forgive yourself and move forward.

How to Implement Opposite Action

Check whether Opposite Action is appropriate. Not all emotions require opposite action. If your fear is of genuine danger, the proper action is protective behaviour, not approaching danger. If your sadness is appropriate grieving of a real loss, attempting to suppress it through forced activity may interfere with healthy processing. Consider: Does this emotion fit the facts? Is acting on the urge effective? If the emotion aligns with facts and acting on it is effective, consider using other emotion regulation strategies rather than Opposite Action.

Identify the emotion and its urge. Name what you are feeling specifically. Then identify the action urge: What does this emotion pull me to do? This clarity about the urge helps you identify the opposite action.

Do the complete opposite of the urge, all the way. Half-hearted opposite action is less effective. If fear urges you to avoid, approach comprehensively and stay in the situation. If sadness urges you to withdraw, engage actively with others and activities. If anger prompts you to lash out, be kind and gentle. The action must be genuinely opposite to the urge, not a compromise.

Act opposite with your body, face, and posture. Change your body language to match the opposite action. If doing the opposite of fear, hold your body confidently rather than tensely. If you're trying to counteract sadness, hold your head up, make eye contact, and move energetically rather than slumping. Physical expression reinforces the opposite action.

Repeat the opposite action until the emotion changes. Opposite Action is not a one-time intervention. You may need to act opposite repeatedly for hours or days before the emotion shifts substantially. Continue until you notice the emotion has decreased or changed. Trust that repeated opposite action will eventually affect the emotion, even if not immediately.

Building Positive Emotions and Problem Solving

Emotion regulation is not only about reducing negative emotions; it also involves cultivating positive emotions and solving problems that generate negative emotions. This chapter addresses these proactive approaches to emotional well-being.

Building Positive Emotions

Building positive emotions involves deliberately creating experiences that generate pleasant emotional states. Many people assume positive emotions should occur spontaneously, but in reality, positive emotions often require deliberate cultivation, particularly when struggling with emotional dysregulation or depression.

Identify what brings you joy, contentment, interest, love, or other positive emotions. Make an extensive list of activities, people, places, sensory experiences, achievements, or anything else that generates positive feelings for you. Include small pleasures and large ones, immediate pleasures and longer-term satisfactions.

Schedule positive experiences regularly. Do not wait for positive emotions to occur spontaneously. Plan pleasant activities, social connections, sensory pleasures, and meaningful pursuits deliberately. Treat these as necessary appointments that you keep, not optional activities to fit in if convenient. Regular positive experiences create baseline positive emotion that buffers against negative emotions.

Be mindful during positive experiences. Actually, experience them rather than being physically present but mentally elsewhere. When eating something delicious, truly savour the taste. When with people you care about, truly be present with them. When in nature, honestly notice the beauty. Mindfulness amplifies positive experiences.

Build a life worth living by aligning your activities with your values. Beyond immediate pleasant experiences, work towards goals that matter to you. Make progress in relationships, work, health, learning, creativity, or service. This progress generates lasting satisfaction and meaning that sustained positive emotion.

Problem Solving

Many negative emotions arise from actual problems in your life. Whilst emotion regulation skills help you manage emotions, solving the underlying issues is often the most effective long-term approach. Problem-solving is an emotion-regulation skill because it addresses the causes of negative emotions directly.

Use problem-solving when you face a solvable problem that generates negative emotions. Not all situations are solvable—sometimes reality is difficult and requires acceptance rather than problem-solving. However, when genuine issues exist that could be solved or improved, addressing them reduces negative emotions more effectively than merely managing them.

Steps for Effective Problem Solving

Step 1: Define the problem clearly and specifically. Vague problem definitions make it difficult to identify solutions. Be as specific and concrete as possible. Instead of: My life is a mess, I am behind on my bills, my flat is very untidy, and I am not sleeping enough. Specific problems can be addressed; vague distress cannot.

Step 2: Brainstorm possible solutions without judgement. Generate as many potential solutions as possible, including unconventional or seemingly imperfect ones. Do not evaluate solutions during brainstorming; evaluation kills creativity. List every possible approach you can imagine; however impractical some may seem.

Step 3: Evaluate solutions. Consider the likely consequences, feasibility, and alignment with your values of each potential solution. Some solutions may be impractical. Some may solve one problem but create new ones. Some may work in the short term but not the long term. Evaluate thoughtfully.

Step 4: Select the most suitable solution based on your evaluation. Select the solution most likely to address the problem effectively without creating new problems, that you have the resources to implement, and that aligns with your values. If no single solution is perfect, choose the best available option.

Step 5: Implement the solution. Make a specific, concrete plan for implementing your chosen solution. When will you do it? What steps are involved? What resources do you need? Actually, follow through on your plan. Implementation is where problem-solving succeeds or fails.

Step 6: Evaluate the outcome. After implementing your solution, assess whether it solved the problem. If so, celebrate your successful problem-solving. If not, or only partially, return to your list of potential solutions and try a different approach. Problem solving is often iterative—the first solution may not work, but trying multiple approaches usually leads to improvement.

When Problem Solving Is Appropriate

Problem solving works when situations are actually changeable and when you have the capacity to implement solutions. It is less helpful when situations are unchangeable (requiring acceptance instead) or when you are in crisis (where crisis survival skills take priority over problem-solving).

If you are overwhelmed with multiple problems, choose one to solve first rather than attempting to solve everything simultaneously. Success with one problem builds confidence and skills for tackling others. Prioritise problems that are solvable and whose solution would provide maximum benefit.

Combine problem-solving with other emotion-regulation skills. Use mindfulness to see problems clearly. Use ABC PLEASE to ensure you have resources for problem-solving. Use distress tolerance to manage emotions whilst implementing solutions. Problem-solving does not exist in isolation, but instead works in conjunction with other skills.

Managing Difficult Emotions

This final chapter integrates emotion regulation skills and addresses common difficult emotions: anxiety, depression, anger, shame, and grief. Managing these emotions effectively requires understanding their specific characteristics and knowing which skills are most effective for each.

Managing Anxiety

Anxiety is characterised by worry, physical tension, and fear about future threats. It ranges from mild unease to panic. Managing anxiety requires both immediate strategies for high anxiety and long-term approaches for chronic anxiety.

For immediate anxiety relief, use TIP skills, particularly temperature and paced breathing. These rapidly reduce physiological arousal. Use mindfulness to stay present rather than catastrophising about the future. Use self-soothing to comfort yourself. Use distraction to interrupt worry spirals.

For longer-term anxiety management, use Opposite Action consistently. Approach rather than avoid feared situations. Face what makes you anxious repeatedly until it no longer triggers such intense reactions. Use ABC PLEASE to reduce overall vulnerability, particularly by ensuring adequate sleep and regular exercise. Use problem-solving to address actual problems generating anxiety. Use coping ahead to prepare for anxiety-triggering situations.

Managing Depression

Depression involves persistent sadness, loss of pleasure, low energy, hopelessness, and withdrawal. It is one of the most difficult emotional states to manage because depression itself undermines motivation to use skills. Managing depression requires both self-compassion and persistent action.

Use Opposite Action extensively. Get active even when every instinct urge withdrawal. Do pleasant and meaningful activities even when nothing feels enjoyable. Connect with others even when you want to isolate. The activity itself begins to shift depression even before you feel like doing it.

Use ABC PLEASE rigorously. Depression is powerfully affected by sleep, exercise, nutrition, and routine. Maintain these even when—especially when—depression makes it difficult. Use accumulating positive experiences and building mastery consistently, even if immediate pleasure or sense of accomplishment is absent. Over time, these practices shift depression.

Seek professional help if depression is severe or persistent. Depression can be life-threatening and often requires treatment beyond self-help skills. Therapy and medication can be essential components of recovery. Using DBT skills alongside professional treatment is powerful, but skills alone may be insufficient for severe depression.

Managing Anger

Anger arises from perceived injustice, boundary violations, or obstacles to goals. It ranges from irritation to rage. Whilst anger can motivate appropriate action, it often leads to destructive behaviour if unregulated.

Use Opposite Action when anger would make situations worse or is disproportionate. Be gentle and kind rather than aggressive. Temporarily avoid the triggering person or situation if possible, allowing yourself to calm before addressing issues. Use half-smiling and willing hands to shift your physical state.

Use DEAR MAN with extensive GIVE skills to address situations generating anger constructively. Express concerns clearly but respectfully. Focus on solving problems rather than attacking people. Use TIP skills, particularly intense exercise, to discharge angry energy safely. Use mindfulness to observe anger without acting on it impulsively.

Examine whether your anger fits the facts. Sometimes situations truly are unjust, and anger is appropriate. Other times, our interpretations create anger where circumstances do not warrant it. Check your thinking for inaccuracies, mind-reading, or catastrophising. Correcting thinking errors often reduces anger.

Managing Shame and Guilt

Shame is feeling defective, exposed, or worthless. Guilt is feeling you have violated your values. Both are painful self-conscious emotions that can be paralysing if unregulated.

For shame, use Opposite Action. Hold your head up, maintain eye contact, stay in social situations rather than hiding. Challenge shame-based thoughts: I made a mistake does not mean I am defective. Everyone makes mistakes. This does not define my worth. Use self-compassion extensively. Treat yourself with the kindness you would offer a friend.

For guilt, first assess whether you actually violated your values. If yes, repair the harm: apologise sincerely, make amends, and commit to different future behaviour. This is appropriate guilt serving its function. If no actual value violation occurred, use Opposite Action and self-forgiveness. Let go of inappropriate guilt and move forward.

Managing Grief

Grief is the natural response to loss. It involves sadness, yearning, and periods of intense pain. Grief is not an emotion to eliminate but rather to move through skilfully. Managing grief means allowing the process whilst caring for yourself through it.

Accept that grief is necessary and will take time. Do not try to rush through grief or convince yourself you should be over it by some arbitrary timeline. Grief unfolds according to its own schedule. Allow yourself to feel the waves of sadness when they come without judging yourself for grieving.

Use self-soothing and self-compassion extensively. Grief is painful, and you deserve comfort. Provide yourself with the care and kindness you need. Use distress tolerance skills to survive the most intense moments. Use mindfulness to stay present rather than adding suffering through fighting the grief or worrying about whether it will ever end.

Balance allowing grief with engaging in life. Whilst grief requires space and time, withdrawing completely from life prolongs suffering. Continue basic self-care. Maintain some connections. Engage in small, pleasant activities even whilst grieving. This is not avoiding grief but rather ensuring you maintain functioning whilst you grieve.

Seek support. Grief is not meant to be carried alone. Talk to trusted others about your loss. Consider grief counselling or support groups. Connection with others who understand grief can provide comfort and hope that healing is possible.

Integration and Conclusion

Throughout this module, you have learned numerous emotion regulation skills. In real life, you will use different skills for different situations. Sometimes you will reduce vulnerability through ABC PLEASE. Sometimes you will change emotions through Opposite Action.

Sometimes you will solve problems. Sometimes you will simply tolerate emotions using distress tolerance skills. The key is developing skill in recognising which approach fits which situation.

Practice Worksheets

39 Professional Practice Worksheets for DBT Skills Development

Mindfulness • Distress Tolerance • Interpersonal Effectiveness • Emotion Regulation

These worksheets are designed to be used alongside the skills training content in this manual. Each worksheet provides structured exercises to help you practise and integrate DBT skills into your daily life.

MINDFULNESS

WORKSHEETS

Mindfulness Worksheet 1

Three States of Mind Practice

Use this worksheet to develop awareness of Reasonable Mind, Emotion Mind, and Wise Mind. Complete each section as you notice and practise accessing different states throughout the week.

Understanding the Three States of Mind
Reasonable Mind: Logical, rational, fact-focused thinking. Cool, task-oriented. • Emotion Mind: Emotions control thinking and behaviour. Hot, mood-dependent. • Wise Mind: The integration of both - intuitive knowing that honours both logic and emotion.

Part 1: Identifying Reasonable Mind

Prompt	Your Response
Describe a situation where you were in Reasonable Mind (focused on logic, facts, practical thinking):	
What specific logical thoughts did you have?	
What physical sensations did you notice?	
What was helpful about Reasonable Mind here?	
What (if anything) was unhelpful?	

Part 2: Identifying Emotion Mind

Prompt	Your Response
Describe a situation where you were in Emotion Mind (feelings controlled your thinking and behaviour):	
What emotions were you feeling? Rate intensity (0-10):	

What physical sensations accompanied these emotions?	
What urges did you have? What did you want to do?	
What did you actually do (your behaviour)?	
How did Emotion Mind affect your thinking? Were facts distorted?	

Part 3: Accessing Wise Mind

Prompt	Your Response
Situation requiring a decision or response:	
What did Reasonable Mind say? (logical analysis)	
What did Emotion Mind say? (emotional urges)	
How did you access Wise Mind? (breathing, expanding awareness, asking "what feels right?", stepping back)	
What did Wise Mind know to be true?	
What action did you take? How effective was it (0-10)?	

Part 4: Weekly Practice Log

Day	Reasonable Mind Moment	Emotion Mind Moment	Wise Mind Moment
Monday			
Tuesday			

Wednesday

Thursday

Friday

Saturday

Sunday

Part 5: Reflection

What made it challenging to access Wise Mind this week?

What helped you access Wise Mind?

What will you do differently next week to access Wise Mind more readily?

Mindfulness Worksheet 2

Observing Practice

Observing is the act of noticing or attending to something without reacting to it. When you observe, you experience with your senses and with your mind. Practise observing without attaching to what you observe.

Key Principle
The goal of observing is to notice experiences without trying to change them, push them away, or hold onto them. Simply witness what is happening in the present moment.

Part 1: Observing External Environment

Sense	Date/Duration	What Did You Observe?	Ability to Observe Without Judgement (0-10)
SIGHT (3 minutes)			
SOUND (3 minutes)			
SMELL/TASTE/TOUCH (3 minutes)			

Part 2: Observing Internal Experience

Internal Focus	What Did You Notice?	Ease of Letting Go (0-10)
THOUGHTS (5 minutes)		
EMOTIONS (5 minutes)		

BODY SENSATIONS (5 minutes)

Part 3: Reflection on Observing

What was difficult about just observing without reacting or clinging?

When did you notice yourself clinging to or pushing away what you observed?

What helped you return to just observing?

Part 4: Daily Observing Practice Log

Day	What I Practised Observing	Key Observations	Rating (0-10)
Day 1			
Day 2			
Day 3			
Day 4			
Day 5			
Day 6			
Day 7			

Mindfulness Worksheet 3

Describing Practice

Describing means putting words on your experience. When you describe, you label what you observe. Describe just the facts, without adding interpretations or judgements.

Key Principle

Stick to the facts: Describe only what you observe through your senses. Avoid interpretations, assumptions, or judgements. Instead of "She was rude," describe "She did not make eye contact and spoke in short sentences."

Part 1: Describing External Events

Event/Situation	Factual Description (no judgements)
Describe a recent interaction with another person:	
Describe a situation that triggered an emotion:	

Part 2: Distinguishing Facts from Interpretations

Situation	Initial Thought/Interpretation	Just the Facts (What Would a Camera See?)

Part 3: Describing Internal Experience

Emotion Noticed	Body Sensation	Thought Content	Action Urge

Part 4: Practice Converting Judgements to Descriptions

Judgement Statement	Descriptive Statement
Example: "He is so inconsiderate"	*Example: "He did not ask about my day when he came home"*

Part 5: Reflection

What did you learn from describing rather than judging?

How did describing change your emotional response?

Mindfulness Worksheet 4

Participating Practice

Participating means throwing yourself completely into activities. Become one with whatever you are doing. Let go of self-consciousness and fully engage in the present moment.

Key Principle
Participate fully without being self-conscious. Become one with your experience. Act intuitively from Wise Mind. Practice becoming one with whatever you are doing, completely forgetting yourself.

Part 1: Activities for Full Participation

Activity	Level of Participation (0-10)	Self-Consciousness Level (0-10)	What Helped You Fully Engage?

Part 2: Barriers to Full Participation

Barriers I Experienced	Strategies to Overcome
Self-consciousness:	
Worry about doing it right:	
Distraction/mind wandering:	

Part 3: Participating in Everyday Activities

Routine Activity	How I Can Participate More Fully	Result When I Did This
Eating a meal		
Conversation		
Walking/exercise		
Work task		

Part 4: Weekly Practice Log

Day	Activity I Fully Participated In	What I Noticed	Participation Rating (0-10)
Mon			
Tue			
Wed			
Thu			
Fri			
Sat			
Sun			

Mindfulness Worksheet 5

Non-Judgemental Stance Practice

Practise taking a non-judgemental stance. See, but do not evaluate as good or bad. Accept each moment like a blanket spread upon the ground, accepting each leaf that falls upon it.

Key Principle
Focus on the "WHAT" not the "GOOD" or "BAD." Acknowledge the consequences, not judge them. When you find yourself judging, do not judge your judging. Simply notice it and return to describing the facts.

Part 1: Noticing Judgements

Situation	Judgement I Made	Type (self/other/situation)	Effect of the Judgement

Part 2: Replacing Judgements with Descriptions

Judgement	Non-Judgemental Description	Consequences/Preferences
Example: "This is a terrible day"	*Example: "It is raining and I got caught in traffic"*	*Example: "I prefer sunny days and arriving on time"*

Part 3: Self-Judgement Tracking

Self-Judgement	Trigger	Compassionate Reframe	Effect of Reframe

Part 4: Daily Non-Judgement Practice

Day	Judgements I Noticed	How I Returned to Non-Judgement	Difficulty Level (0-10)
Mon			
Tue			
Wed			
Thu			
Fri			
Sat			
Sun			

Mindfulness Worksheet 6

One-Mindfully Practice

Do one thing at a time. When walking, walk. When eating, eat. When worrying, worry. Do each thing with complete attention. If other actions or thoughts arise, let go of distractions and return to what you are doing.

Key Principle
Concentrate your mind. If you find you are doing two things at once, stop and go back to one thing at a time. Let go of distractions and return your attention to the present moment, again and again.

Part 1: One-Mindful Activities Practice

Activity	Distractions That Arose	How I Returned to the Activity	One-Mindfulness Rating (0-10)
Morning routine			
Meal time			
Work/study task			
Conversation			

Part 2: Multi-Tasking vs One-Mindfully

Multi-Tasking Situation	How Could I Approach This One-Mindfully?

Part 3: Weekly Practice Log

Day	Activity I Did One-Mindfully	What I Noticed	Rating (0-10)

Mon

Tue

Wed

Thu

Fri

Sat

Sun

Mindfulness Worksheet 7

Effectiveness Practice

Focus on what works. Do what needs to be done in each situation. Let go of vengeance, useless anger, and righteousness that hurts you and does not work.

Key Principle
Play by the rules. Act as skilfully as you can, meeting the needs of the situation. Focus on being effective rather than being right. Ask: "Is what I am doing working to get me what I want?"

Part 1: Understanding Effective Action

Describe a recent situation where you "won the battle but lost the war" (you were right, but it was not effective):

What did being "right" cost you?

What would have been more effective?

Part 2: Right vs Effective Analysis

Situation	What Was Your Goal?	What Would "Being Right" Look Like?	What Would "Being Effective" Look Like?	Which Did You Choose?

Part 3: Weekly Effectiveness Log

Day	Situation Where I Chose Effectiveness	What I Did Instead of Being "Right"	Outcome
Mon			
Tue			
Wed			
Thu			
Fri			
Sat			
Sun			

Mindfulness Worksheet 8

Mindfulness Skills Summary and Integration

Use this worksheet to practise integrating all six mindfulness skills: Observe, Describe, Participate, Non-judgementally, One-mindfully, and Effectively.

The "What" Skills
Observe: Notice your experience. | Describe: Put words on the experience. | Participate: Enter fully into activities.

The "How" Skills
Non-judgementally: Without evaluating as good or bad. | One-mindfully: With full attention. | Effectively: Focus on what works.

Part 1: Integrated Practice Log

Observe	Describe	Participate	Non-Judgementally	One-Mindfully	Effectively

Part 2: Skill Strength Assessment

Skill	Current Strength (0-10)	How Will I Strengthen This Skill?
Observe		
Describe		
Participate		
Non-Judgementally		
One-Mindfully		
Effectively		

Part 3: Weekly Reflection

Which mindfulness skill was easiest to practise this week? Why?

Which skill was most challenging? What made it difficult?

How has practising mindfulness skills affected your daily life?

DISTRESS TOLERANCE

WORKSHEETS

Distress Tolerance Worksheet 1

STOP Skill Practice

Use this worksheet when you are in a crisis situation and need to prevent impulsive behaviour. STOP helps you pause before reacting.

STOP Skill

S - Stop: Do not react. Freeze. Do not move a muscle. | T - Take a step back: Take a break. Let go. Take a deep breath. | O - Observe: Notice what is happening inside and outside of you. | P - Proceed mindfully: Act with awareness. Consider your goals. Ask Wise Mind.

Part 1: STOP Skill Practice

S - Stop	T - Take a Step Back	O - Observe	P - Proceed Mindfully
What impulse did you stop?	*How did you step back? (breathing, leaving, etc.)*	*What did you observe? (thoughts, feelings, situation)*	*What effective action did you take?*

Part 2: Crisis Situation Analysis

Crisis Situation	What Happened When I Did NOT Use STOP	What Might Have Happened If I Used STOP

Part 3: Weekly STOP Practice Log

Day	Situation	STOP Steps Used	Outcome	Effectiveness (0-10)
Mon				
Tue				
Wed				
Thu				
Fri				
Sat				
Sun				

Distress Tolerance Worksheet 2

TIPP Skills for Changing Body Chemistry

Use TIPP skills when emotions are very intense and you need to quickly reduce their intensity. These skills work by changing your body chemistry.

TIPP Skills

T - Temperature: Use cold water on face to trigger the dive reflex. | I - Intense Exercise: Engage in intense physical activity for 20+ minutes. | P - Paced Breathing: Slow your breathing with longer exhales. | P - Paired Muscle Relaxation: Tense and release muscle groups.

Part 1: Temperature Practice

Date/Time	Emotion Before (0-10)	Method Used	Emotion After (0-10)
		☐ Cold water on face ☐ Ice pack ☐ Cold shower	
		☐ Cold water on face ☐ Ice pack ☐ Cold shower	

Part 2: Intense Exercise Practice

Date	Type of Exercise	Duration	Intensity Level	Effect on Emotions

Part 3: Paced Breathing Practice

Date/Time	Breathing Pattern Used	Duration (minutes)	Effect (0-10 calm)
	☐ 4-7-8 ☐ Box breathing ☐ Other:		
	☐ 4-7-8 ☐ Box breathing ☐ Other:		

Part 4: Paired Muscle Relaxation Practice

Muscle Group	Tension Level Before (0-10)	Tension Level After (0-10)

Face/Jaw		
Shoulders/Neck		
Arms/Hands		
Stomach/Back		
Legs/Feet		

Distress Tolerance Worksheet 3

ACCEPTS - Distraction Skills

Use ACCEPTS skills to distract yourself during a crisis until you can deal with the situation more effectively. These buy you time until the emotional intensity decreases.

ACCEPTS Skills

A - Activities: Engage in activities that require focus. | C - Contributing: Do something for others. | C - Comparisons: Compare to others less fortunate or to past difficult times. | E - Emotions: Generate different emotions. | P - Pushing away: Leave the situation mentally. | T - Thoughts: Occupy your mind with other thoughts. | S - Sensations: Use intense physical sensations.

Part 1: Personal ACCEPTS Toolkit

Skill	My Personal Options
Activities	
Contributing	
Comparisons	
Emotions	
Pushing Away	
Thoughts	
Sensations	

Part 2: ACCEPTS Practice Log

Date	Crisis Situation	Skill(s) Used	What I Did Specifically	Effectiveness (0-10)

Part 3: Reflection

Which ACCEPTS skills work best for you? Why?

Which ACCEPTS skills do you want to develop further?

Distress Tolerance Worksheet 4

IMPROVE the Moment Skills

Use IMPROVE skills to make a painful moment more tolerable. These skills help you cope when you cannot change the situation immediately.

IMPROVE Skills

I - Imagery: Use your imagination to feel better. | M - Meaning: Find or create meaning in the situation. | P - Prayer/Spirituality: Connect with your higher power or values. | R - Relaxation: Relax your body. | O - One thing in the moment: Focus on the present moment. | V - Vacation: Take a brief mental vacation. | E - Encouragement: Cheerlead yourself.

Part 1: Personal IMPROVE Toolkit

Skill	My Personal Strategies
Imagery *(safe place, coping images)*	
Meaning *(purpose, learning, growth)*	
Prayer/Spirituality *(values, connection)*	
Relaxation *(body scan, breathing)*	
One Thing *(present focus)*	
Vacation *(mental breaks)*	
Encouragement *(self-talk, affirmations)*	

Part 2: IMPROVE Practice Log

Date	Difficult Moment	Skill(s) Used	What I Did	Effect (0-10)

Distress Tolerance Worksheet 5

Pros and Cons of Crisis Behaviour

Use this worksheet to think through the advantages and disadvantages of both tolerating distress AND acting on crisis urges. Complete this BEFORE you are in crisis.

Part 1: Define the Crisis Behaviour

Crisis behaviour or urge I am analysing:

Part 2: Pros and Cons Analysis

ACTING ON CRISIS URGES	TOLERATING DISTRESS / NOT ACTING
PROS (Short-term benefits)	**PROS (Short-term benefits)**
CONS (Long-term costs)	**CONS (Long-term costs)**

Part 3: Wise Mind Decision

Looking at all the pros and cons, what does Wise Mind say is the most effective choice?

What skills will I use instead of the crisis behaviour?

Distress Tolerance Worksheet 6

Radical Acceptance Practice

Radical acceptance means fully accepting reality as it is in this moment, without judgement. It does not mean approval or giving up on change. Pain + Non-Acceptance = Suffering.

Key Principle

Radical acceptance is accepting reality as it IS, not as you want it to be. Rejecting reality does not change reality. Pain is part of life; suffering is optional. Acceptance is the only way out of hell.

Part 1: Identifying What Needs Acceptance

Reality I am struggling to accept:

How am I fighting against this reality? (anger, denial, bargaining, etc.):

What is the cost of not accepting this reality?

Part 2: Acceptance Practice

Acceptance Technique	My Experience Using This
Half-smile and willing hands	
Breathing into acceptance	
Imagining acceptance	
Allowing the world to be as it is	

Part 3: Weekly Acceptance Log

Day	What I Practised Accepting	Technique Used	Level of Acceptance (0-10)
Mon			
Tue			
Wed			
Thu			
Fri			
Sat			
Sun			

Distress Tolerance Worksheet 7

Turning the Mind

Turning the mind is choosing to accept reality. It is like coming to a fork in the road - you have to turn your mind toward the acceptance road and away from the rejection road, again and again.

Key Principle
Acceptance requires an act of choice. It is not automatic. You must make a commitment to accept. Then you must turn your mind toward acceptance again and again, each time you notice you have wandered down the road of non-acceptance.

Part 1: Identifying the Fork in the Road

What reality am I being asked to accept?

What does the rejection road look like? (behaviours, thoughts, feelings when rejecting)

What does the acceptance road look like? (behaviours, thoughts, feelings when accepting)

Part 2: Turning the Mind Log

Date/Time	What Triggered Non-Acceptance?	How I Turned My Mind	Cue/Reminder I Used	Times Turned Today

Part 3: Commitment Statement

My commitment to acceptance:

Distress Tolerance Worksheet 8

Willingness vs Willfulness

Willingness is doing just what is needed in each situation - wholeheartedly, without holding back. Willfulness is trying to control everything, giving up entirely, or refusing to make changes.

Key Difference
WILLINGNESS: Accepting what is, responding to life as it is. Acting effectively. Being open. | WILLFULNESS: Trying to fix everything, refusing to tolerate the moment, sitting on your hands when action is needed.

Part 1: Identifying Willfulness

Situation	How I Was Being Willful	The Cost of My Willfulness

Part 2: Practising Willingness

Situation	Willful Response I Wanted to Do	Willing Response I Chose Instead

Part 3: Willingness Techniques

Technique	How I Used It / What Happened

Willing hands (palms up, fingers relaxed)

Half-smile

Mindfulness of current thoughts

Asking "Am I being willful?"

Opposite action to willfulness

Distress Tolerance Worksheet 9

Self-Soothing with Five Senses

Self-soothing skills help you comfort yourself during difficult times. Use your five senses to create calming experiences.

Part 1: Personal Self-Soothing Kit

Sense	My Personal Self-Soothing Activities
VISION (things that are pleasing to look at)	
HEARING (sounds that calm or comfort)	
SMELL (scents that soothe)	
TASTE (flavours that comfort)	
TOUCH (textures and sensations)	

Part 2: Self-Soothing Practice Log

Date	Distress Level Before (0-10)	Sense(s) Used	Activity	Distress After (0-10)

Distress Tolerance Worksheet 10

Crisis Survival Plan

Complete this plan BEFORE you are in crisis. Keep it somewhere accessible so you can use it when needed.

Part 1: Warning Signs

Early warning signs that I am heading toward crisis:

Part 2: My Crisis Survival Skills

Skill Category	Specific Actions I Will Take
TIPP skills	
STOP skill	
ACCEPTS distraction	
IMPROVE the moment	
Self-soothing	
Radical acceptance	

Part 3: Support Contacts

Name	Relationship	Phone Number

Part 4: Professional Support

Therapist/Counsellor:	GP/Doctor:

Crisis Line: Samaritans 116 123 NHS 111 or A&E

Distress Tolerance Worksheet 11

Reality Acceptance Skills Summary

Use this worksheet to track your practice of all reality acceptance skills: Radical Acceptance, Turning the Mind, and Willingness.

Part 1: Weekly Reality Acceptance Practice

Day	Reality to Accept	Skill(s) Used	What I Did	Acceptance Level (0-10)
Mon				
Tue				
Wed				
Thu				
Fri				
Sat				
Sun				

Part 2: Skill Assessment

Skill	Ease of Using (0-10)	How Will I Strengthen This?
Radical Acceptance		
Turning the Mind		
Willingness		

Distress Tolerance Worksheet 12

Distress Tolerance Skills Integration

Use this worksheet to integrate all distress tolerance skills and create a comprehensive plan for managing difficult situations.

Part 1: Skills Summary Assessment

Skill	Confidence Level (0-10)	Practice Needed?
STOP		
TIPP		
ACCEPTS (Distraction)		
IMPROVE the Moment		
Pros and Cons		
Radical Acceptance		
Turning the Mind		
Willingness		
Self-Soothing		

Part 2: Weekly Reflection

Most helpful distress tolerance skill this week:

Situation where I successfully used distress tolerance skills:

Skills I want to focus on developing next week:

INTERPERSONAL EFFECTIVENESS

WORKSHEETS

Interpersonal Effectiveness Worksheet 1

DEAR MAN - Getting What You Want

Use DEAR MAN when you want to ask for something, say no to a request, or express an opinion. This skill helps you be effective in getting your objectives.

DEAR MAN Skills

D - Describe the situation. | E - Express your feelings and opinions. | A - Assert by asking or saying no clearly. | R - Reinforce by explaining consequences. | M - Mindful: stay focused on your goal. | A - Appear confident. | N - Negotiate: be willing to give to get.

Part 1: Planning Your DEAR MAN

Step	What Will I Say/Do?
D - Describe *(Just the facts)*	
E - Express *(Your feelings/opinions)*	
A - Assert *(Ask/say no clearly)*	
R - Reinforce *(Explain positive outcomes)*	

Part 2: HOW Skills

M - Mindful ***How will I stay focused on my goal?***	
A - Appear Confident *Body language, voice, eye contact*	
N - Negotiate *What am I willing to give to get?*	

Part 3: Practice Log

Date	Situation	What I Said	Outcome	Effectiveness (0-10)

Interpersonal Effectiveness Worksheet 2

GIVE - Keeping the Relationship

Use GIVE skills when maintaining or improving a relationship is your priority. These skills help you interact in a way that keeps the relationship positive.

GIVE Skills

G - Gentle: No attacks, threats, or judgements. | I - Interested: Listen and appear interested. | V - Validate: Acknowledge the other person's feelings and perspective. | E - Easy manner: Use humour, be light-hearted.

Part 1: Planning GIVE

GIVE Skill	How Will I Use This?
G - Gentle *No attacks or judgements*	
I - Interested *Show genuine interest*	
V - Validate *Acknowledge their perspective*	
E - Easy Manner *Light touch, humour*	

Part 2: Validation Practice

Person/Situation	What They Said/Did	My Validating Response

Part 3: Weekly GIVE Practice Log

Day	Relationship	GIVE Skill Used	Effect on Relationship	Rating (0-10)
Mon				

Tue				
Wed				
Thu				
Fri				
Sat				
Sun				

Interpersonal Effectiveness Worksheet 3

FAST - Keeping Your Self-Respect

Figure 12: FAST - Keeping Your Self-Respect

Use FAST skills when maintaining your self-respect is your priority. These skills help you act in ways that allow you to respect yourself afterwards.

FAST Skills
F - Fair: Be fair to yourself AND the other person. | A - Apologies: No excessive apologising. | S - Stick to values: Do not compromise your values. | T - Truthful: Be honest, do not lie or exaggerate.

Part 1: Planning FAST

FAST Skill	How Will I Maintain Self-Respect?
F - Fair *To yourself and others*	

A - Apologies
No over-apologising

S - Stick to Values
What are my values here?

T - Truthful
Be honest

Part 2: Identifying My Core Values

My core values that I will not compromise:

Part 3: Practice Log

Date	Situation	FAST Skill Used	How I Felt About Myself	Self-Respect (0-10)

Interpersonal Effectiveness Worksheet 4

Interpersonal Situation Planning

Use this worksheet to plan how to handle an upcoming interpersonal situation. Consider all three priorities: objectives, relationship, and self-respect.

Part 1: Situation Analysis

Describe the situation:

Who is involved?

Part 2: Priority Assessment

Priority	Importance Level (1-5)
OBJECTIVES: Getting what I want	
RELATIONSHIP: Maintaining/improving the relationship	
SELF-RESPECT: Keeping my self-respect	

Part 3: Skills Plan

Skills to Use	Specifically, I Will...
DEAR MAN (objectives)	
GIVE (relationship)	
FAST (self-respect)	

Part 4: Post-Interaction Reflection

What happened? How did it go?

What would I do differently next time?

Interpersonal Effectiveness Worksheet 5

Saying No and Setting Boundaries

Use this worksheet to practise saying no effectively whilst maintaining relationships and self-respect.

Part 1: Factors That Make Saying No Difficult

Factor	How This Affects Me
Fear of rejection	
Guilt	
Wanting to be liked	
Fear of conflict	
Not knowing what to say	
Difficulty tolerating others' distress	

Part 2: Saying No Practice

Request Made	What I Said	How I Felt	Outcome

Part 3: My Boundaries

Boundaries I need to set or maintain:

Interpersonal Effectiveness Worksheet 6

Interpersonal Skills Integration

Use this worksheet to integrate all interpersonal effectiveness skills and track your progress over time.

Part 1: Skills Assessment

Skill	Confidence (0-10)	Areas for Growth
DEAR MAN - Getting objectives		
GIVE - Maintaining relationships		
FAST - Keeping self-respect		
Saying no effectively		
Asking for what I need		
Validating others		

Part 2: Weekly Practice Log

Day	Interpersonal Situation	Skills Used	Outcome	Rating (0-10)
Mon				
Tue				
Wed				
Thu				
Fri				
Sat				
Sun				

Part 3: Reflection

What interpersonal success am I most proud of this week?

What interpersonal skills do I want to focus on next week?

EMOTION REGULATION

WORKSHEETS

Emotion Regulation Worksheet 1

Understanding Emotions

Use this worksheet to increase your understanding of emotions and their functions. Emotions are complex responses that involve thoughts, physical sensations, and action urges.

Why Emotions Matter
Emotions communicate to others and ourselves. They organise and motivate action. They can be self-validating. Understanding emotions is the first step to regulating them effectively.

Part 1: Emotion Identification

Emotion	Triggering Event	Thoughts	Body Sensations	Action Urge

Part 2: Functions of My Emotions

Emotion	What Is It Communicating?	What Action Is It Motivating?

Part 3: Emotion Myths vs Facts

Myth I Believe About Emotions	The Facts

Emotion Regulation Worksheet 2

Emotion Diary

Track your emotions daily to increase awareness and identify patterns. Notice the connection between events, thoughts, and emotional responses.

Daily Emotion Tracking

Day/Time	Emotion(s)	Intensity (0-10)	Triggering Event	Thoughts	What I Did
Mon AM					
Mon PM					
Tue AM					
Tue PM					
Wed AM					
Wed PM					
Thu AM					
Thu PM					
Fri AM					
Fri PM					
Sat AM					
Sat PM					
Sun AM					
Sun PM					

Weekly Patterns

Most frequent emotions this week:

Common triggers I noticed:

Emotion Regulation Worksheet 3

ABC PLEASE - Reducing Vulnerability

Use ABC PLEASE skills to reduce your vulnerability to negative emotions. Taking care of your body and mind makes you more resilient.

ABC PLEASE

A - Accumulate positive experiences. | B - Build mastery. | C - Cope ahead. | PL - Treat PhysicaL illness. | E - Balance Eating. | A - Avoid mood-altering substances. | S - Balance Sleep. | E - Get Exercise.

Part 1: ABC Skills

Skill	My Plan This Week
A - Accumulate Positives *(Pleasant activities)*	
B - Build Mastery *(Accomplish things)*	
C - Cope Ahead *(Plan for challenges)*	

Part 2: PLEASE Skills Tracking

PLEASE Skill	Mon	Tue	Wed	Thu	Fri	Sat	Sun
Physical health							
Balanced eating							
No substances							
Adequate sleep							
Exercise							

Emotion Regulation Worksheet 4

Opposite Action

Use opposite action when your emotion does not fit the facts OR when acting on the emotion is not effective. Act opposite to the action urge of the emotion, all the way.

When to Use Opposite Action
Use when: 1) The emotion does not fit the facts, OR 2) Acting on the emotion is not effective. Act opposite ALL THE WAY - not just behaviourally but also in posture, facial expression, and body language.

Part 1: Opposite Actions for Common Emotions

Emotion	Action Urge	Opposite Action
Fear/Anxiety	Avoid, escape, freeze	Approach, stay present, do what you fear
Sadness	Withdraw, isolate, be inactive	Get active, approach others, do things
Anger	Attack, criticise, be aggressive	Gently avoid, be kind, take a break
Shame	Hide, avoid, keep secrets	Make public, talk about it, repeat behaviour

Part 2: Opposite Action Practice

Emotion	Does It Fit the Facts?	Action Urge	Opposite Action I Took	Result

Emotion Regulation Worksheet 5

Check the Facts

Use Check the Facts to determine whether your emotional response fits the actual situation. Our interpretations often intensify emotions beyond what the facts warrant.

Part 1: Check the Facts Analysis

Question	My Answer
1. What emotion do I want to change?	
2. What is the prompting event? (Just the facts)	
3. What are my interpretations/assumptions?	
4. Am I assuming a threat? What is the actual probability?	
5. What is the catastrophe? Could I cope if it happened?	
6. Does my emotion fit the FACTS?	

Part 2: Reframing

Alternative interpretations of the situation:

What action fits the facts?

Emotion Regulation Worksheet 6

Problem Solving

Use problem solving when your emotion DOES fit the facts and you can change the situation. Focus on solving the problem rather than just managing the emotion.

Part 1: Define the Problem

What is the problem? (Be specific):

What emotion is this causing?

Part 2: Brainstorm Solutions

Possible Solution	Pros	Cons

Part 3: Action Plan

Solution I will try:

Steps I will take:

When will I do this?

Outcome (complete after trying):

Emotion Regulation Worksheet 7

Pleasant Activities Schedule

Plan and track pleasant activities to build positive emotions. Regular pleasant activities are essential for emotional well-being.

Part 1: My Pleasant Activities List

Short-Term Pleasant Activities (Quick, easy)	Long-Term Pleasant Activities (Goals, values)

Part 2: Weekly Pleasant Activities Schedule

Day	Pleasant Activity Planned	Did I Do It?	Mood After (0-10)
Monday			
Tuesday			
Wednesday			
Thursday			
Friday			
Saturday			
Sunday			

Emotion Regulation Worksheet 8

Building Mastery

Plan activities that give you a sense of accomplishment and confidence. Build mastery by doing things that are difficult but possible.

Key Principle
Do at least one thing each day to build a sense of accomplishment. Plan for success, not failure. Gradually increase the difficulty over time. Give yourself credit for what you accomplish.

Part 1: Mastery Activities by Life Area

Life Area	Mastery Activities I Can Do
Work/Education	
Home/Self-Care	
Health/Exercise	
Hobbies/Interests	
Relationships	
Personal Growth	

Part 2: Weekly Mastery Log

Day	Mastery Activity Completed	Difficulty Level (Easy/Medium/Hard)	Sense of Accomplishment (0-10)
Mon			
Tue			
Wed			
Thu			

Fri

Sat

Sun

Emotion Regulation Worksheet 9

Cope Ahead

Use Cope Ahead to prepare for difficult situations. Rehearse in your mind exactly how you will cope effectively with the situation.

Part 1: Situation to Cope Ahead For

Describe the upcoming difficult situation:

What emotions might come up?

Part 2: Coping Plan

Step	My Plan
1. Skills I will use BEFORE the situation	
2. How I will cope DURING the situation	
3. How I will cope AFTER the situation	
4. Backup plan if things get difficult	

Part 3: Mental Rehearsal

Imagine yourself in the situation, coping effectively. What do you see yourself doing?

Part 4: After the Situation

What happened? How did my coping plan work?

What would I do differently next time?

Emotion Regulation Worksheet 10

Letting Go of Emotional Suffering

Use mindfulness of current emotions to experience your emotions without being overwhelmed. Let go of emotional suffering by observing and accepting emotions.

Key Steps

1. Observe your emotion - notice it without trying to change it. 2. Experience the emotion as a wave - let it come and go. 3. Remember you are not your emotion. 4. Practice loving your emotion - do not push it away.

Part 1: Observing the Emotion

Observation	What I Notice
Name the emotion:	
Where do you feel it in your body?	
What is the quality of the sensation?	
What is the intensity (0-10)?	

Part 2: Riding the Wave

As you observe the emotion without acting on it, what happens to the intensity over time?

What thoughts or urges arise? Can you let them pass without acting?

Part 3: Practice Log

Date	Emotion	Initial Intensity	After Observing	What Helped

Emotion Regulation Worksheet 11

Building a Life Worth Living

Identify your values and goals to create a life that generates positive emotions naturally. Long-term happiness comes from living according to your values.

Part 1: Values Identification

Life Area	My Core Values	Am I Living This Value? (0-10)
Relationships		
Work/Career		
Health/Wellbeing		
Personal Growth		
Fun/Leisure		
Spirituality/Meaning		

Part 2: Goals Aligned with Values

Value	Long-Term Goal	Short-Term Steps

Part 3: Action Plan

One thing I will do THIS WEEK to live according to my values:

Emotion Regulation Worksheet 12

Emotion Model Analysis

Use this worksheet to analyse an emotional experience in detail. Understanding all the components helps you find intervention points.

Complete Emotion Analysis

Component	Description
1. Prompting Event (What happened?)	
2. Vulnerability Factors (What made me more reactive?)	
3. Interpretation (What was my interpretation?)	
4. Body Sensations (What did I feel physically?)	
5. Emotion Name (What was the emotion?)	
6. Action Urge (What did I want to do?)	
7. Action Taken (What did I actually do?)	
8. Aftereffects (What were the consequences?)	

Intervention Points

Where could I have intervened to change my emotional response?

What skills could I use next time?

Emotion Regulation Worksheet 13

Emotion Regulation Skills Integration

Use this worksheet to track your use of all emotion regulation skills and identify areas for continued growth.

Part 1: Skills Confidence Assessment

Emotion Regulation Skill	Confidence (0-10)	Practice Needed?
Understanding emotions		
ABC PLEASE (reducing vulnerability)		
Check the Facts		
Opposite Action		
Problem Solving		
Pleasant Activities		
Building Mastery		
Cope Ahead		
Letting Go/Mindfulness of Emotions		

Part 2: Weekly Practice Log

Day	Emotion Experienced	Skill(s) Used	Result	Rating (0-10)
Mon				
Tue				
Wed				
Thu				
Fri				

Sat	
Sun	

Part 3: Weekly Reflection

Most helpful emotion regulation skill this week:

Emotions I managed well:

Skills I want to focus on next week:

Mindfulness Worksheet 1a

Wise Mind Daily Check-In

Use this worksheet daily to check in with your three states of mind and practise accessing Wise Mind. Complete this each morning and evening for one week.

Key Principle
Wise Mind is the integration of Reasonable Mind and Emotion Mind. Regular check-ins help you recognise which state you're in and practise shifting to Wise Mind throughout the day.

Morning Check-In

Day	Current State of Mind	What Triggered This State?	Wise Mind Perspective	Intention for Today

Evening Reflection

Day	Predominant State Today	Moments of Wise Mind	What Helped Access Wise Mind?	Learning for Tomorrow

Weekly Insight: What patterns do you notice about when you access Wise Mind most easily?

Mindfulness Worksheet 1b

Wise Mind Decision-Making

Use this worksheet when facing important decisions. Wise Mind integrates logic and emotion to guide effective choices.

Key Principle
Important decisions benefit from consulting both Reasonable Mind (facts, logic, analysis) and Emotion Mind (values, gut feelings, intuition), then finding the Wise Mind synthesis.

Decision Analysis

Decision I need to make:

Reasonable Mind Says:	Emotion Mind Says:

What does Wise Mind suggest when I integrate both perspectives?

Values Check

Core Value	How Does Option A Align?	How Does Option B Align?

Decision Record

Date	Decision Made	State of Mind When Deciding	Outcome/Reflection

Mindfulness Worksheet 2a

Observing Emotions Calendar

Use this calendar to practise observing your emotions without reacting. Simply notice and name emotions as they arise throughout each day.

Key Principle
Observing emotions means noticing them without immediately reacting, judging, or trying to change them. Like clouds passing through the sky, emotions come and go.

Weekly Emotion Observation Log

Day	Morning Emotion	Afternoon Emotion	Evening Emotion	Body Sensations Noticed	Did I React or Observe?

Emotion Observation Practice

Emotion Observed	Intensity (0-10)	How Long Did It Last?	What Happened When I Just Observed?

What did you learn about your emotions this week from simply observing them?

Mindfulness Worksheet 3a

Describing Skills Checklist

Use this checklist to practise and track your describing skills. Describing means putting words on experience using facts, not judgements.

Key Principle
Effective describing sticks to observable facts: what you can see, hear, smell, taste, or touch. It avoids interpretations, assumptions, and judgements.

Describing Skills Self-Assessment

Skill	Not Yet	Sometimes	Often
I describe only what I observe			
I use specific, concrete language			
I avoid words like 'always' and 'never'			
I separate facts from interpretations			
I describe behaviour, not personality			
I label emotions without judgement			
I describe my own experience, not others' motives			

Practice: Convert Judgements to Descriptions

Judgement	Description (Facts Only)
He's so rude	
She's being difficult	
This is terrible	
I'm useless	
They don't care	

Mindfulness Worksheet 4a

Participating Calendar

Track your practice of fully participating in activities. Participating means throwing yourself completely into the present moment without self-consciousness.

Key Principle
Full participation means becoming one with the activity. You're not observing yourself from outside or worrying about how you look—you're completely immersed in the experience.

Weekly Participation Log

Day	Activity	Participation Level (0-10)	Barriers to Full Participation	What Helped Me Participate?

Flow State Tracking

Activity	Duration of Full Immersion	Self-Consciousness Level	How Did It Feel?

Which activities allow you to participate most fully? What conditions support your flow state?

Mindfulness Worksheet 5a

Non-Judgemental Stance Calendar

Use this calendar to track judgements and practise letting go of evaluative thinking. Notice judgements without judging yourself for having them.

Key Principle
A non-judgemental stance means observing without evaluating as good or bad. When you notice a judgement, simply acknowledge it and return to describing the facts.

Daily Judgement Tracking

Day	Judgements of Self	Judgements of Others	Judgements of Situations	Times I Returned to Non-Judgement

Judgement Release Practice

Judgement Noticed	Facts Behind the Judgement	Non-Judgemental Alternative	How Did Releasing Feel?

What patterns do you notice in your judgements? Are there particular triggers for judgemental thinking?

Distress Tolerance Worksheet 1a

STOP Skill Quick Reference and Checklist

Use this checklist during crisis moments. Keep it accessible for quick reference when emotions are intense.

Key Principle
STOP prevents impulsive reactions: Stop, Take a step back, Observe, Proceed mindfully. Use it whenever you feel an urge to react impulsively.

STOP Skill Checklist

Step	Action	Completed?
S - Stop	Freeze. Do not move. Do not react.	
T - Take a Step Back	Take a breath. Do not act impulsively.	
O - Observe	Notice what is happening inside and outside you.	
P - Proceed Mindfully	Consider your options. Act with awareness.	

Crisis Response Log

Date/Time	Crisis Trigger	Used STOP? (Y/N)	Outcome	What Would Have Happened Without STOP?

How has using STOP changed your crisis responses?

Distress Tolerance Worksheet 2a

TIPP Skills Weekly Calendar

Track your use of TIPP skills throughout the week. TIPP quickly changes your body chemistry to reduce emotional intensity.

Key Principle
TIPP skills work by changing your physiology: Temperature (cold water), Intense exercise, Paced breathing, and Progressive muscle relaxation rapidly reduce emotional arousal.

TIPP Weekly Practice Log

Day	Temperature Used	Intense Exercise	Paced Breathing	Progressive Relaxation	Effectiveness (0-10)

TIPP Effectiveness Analysis

TIPP Skill	Situations Where Most Helpful	How Quickly It Works	Notes
Temperature			
Intense Exercise			
Paced Breathing			
Progressive Relaxation			

Distress Tolerance Worksheet 3a

ACCEPTS Planning Worksheet

Plan your ACCEPTS toolkit in advance so you have ready-made distraction options during a crisis.

Key Principle
ACCEPTS skills distract you until you can address the crisis effectively: Activities, Contributing, Comparisons, Emotions (opposite), Pushing away, Thoughts, Sensations.

My Personal ACCEPTS Toolkit

ACCEPTS Skill	My Planned Options	Where to Access/How to Do
A - Activities		
C - Contributing		
C - Comparisons		
E - Opposite Emotions		
P - Pushing Away		
T - Other Thoughts		
S - Intense Sensations		

Quick Access List

List your top 5 go-to ACCEPTS strategies that work best for you: **1.** **2.** **3.** **4.** **5.**

Distress Tolerance Worksheet 6a

Radical Acceptance Daily Practice Calendar

Use this calendar to track daily radical acceptance practice. Accepting reality is a skill that requires repeated practice.

Key Principle
Radical acceptance is accepting reality exactly as it is in this moment. It does not mean approval—it means acknowledging what IS rather than fighting against facts.

Daily Acceptance Practice

Day	Reality I Practised Accepting	Acceptance Statements Used	Resistance Noticed	Moments of Acceptance

Acceptance vs Resistance Tracking

Situation	Time Spent Resisting	Time Spent Accepting	Which Felt Better?

What have you learned about the difference between acceptance and approval?

Distress Tolerance Worksheet 8a

Willingness vs Wilfulness Assessment

Use this worksheet to identify wilfulness and practise shifting to willingness. Willingness means accepting what is; wilfulness means refusing reality.

Key Principle
Willingness is doing what is needed in the situation. Wilfulness is trying to control or resist what cannot be controlled. Willingness opens doors; wilfulness keeps them shut.

Willingness Self-Assessment

Indicator	Never	Sometimes	Often
I accept situations I cannot change			
I do what the situation requires			
I let go of the need to control			
I stay open to alternatives			
I resist doing what works out of stubbornness			
I give up when things get hard			

Wilfulness to Willingness Log

Situation	Wilful Response	Willing Alternative	Outcome of Shift

Interpersonal Effectiveness Worksheet 1a

DEAR MAN Planning Checklist

Use this checklist to prepare for important conversations where you need to ask for something or say no.

Key Principle
DEAR MAN helps you be effective in getting what you want: Describe, Express, Assert, Reinforce, stay Mindful, Appear confident, Negotiate.

Conversation Preparation

What do I want from this interaction?

DEAR MAN Step	What I Will Say/Do	Prepared?
D - Describe	Describe the situation factually	
E - Express	Express how I feel about it	
A - Assert	Ask clearly for what I want	
R - Reinforce	Explain benefits of giving me what I want	
M - Mindful	Stay focused on my goal	
A - Appear Confident	Use confident body language	
N - Negotiate	Be willing to give to get	

Interpersonal Effectiveness Worksheet 2a

GIVE Skills Weekly Tracking Calendar

Track your use of GIVE skills to maintain and improve relationships. GIVE skills help you keep relationships whilst still getting what you need.

Key Principle
GIVE skills maintain relationships: be Gentle, act Interested, Validate, use an Easy manner. These skills ensure the other person feels respected.

Weekly GIVE Practice Log

Day	Person/Situation	Gentle?	Interested?	Validated?	Easy Manner?

GIVE Skills Self-Assessment

GIVE Skill	Strength (0-10)	Area to Improve	Practice Plan
G - Gentle			
I - Interested			
V - Validate			
E - Easy Manner			

Interpersonal Effectiveness Worksheet 3a

FAST Skills Self-Respect Assessment

Use this worksheet to evaluate and strengthen your self-respect in relationships. FAST skills help you maintain self-respect whilst interacting with others.

Key Principle
FAST skills maintain self-respect: be Fair, no Apologies (when not warranted), Stick to values, be Truthful. These ensure you respect yourself in relationships.

FAST Skills Self-Assessment

FAST Skill	Current Strength	Challenge Areas	Action Plan
F - Fair			
A - No Apologies			
S - Stick to Values			
T - Truthful			

Values Clarification

What are my core values that I will not compromise in relationships? 1. 2. 3. 4. 5.

Self-Respect Tracking

Situation	Did I Stay Fair?	Did I Stick to Values?	How Do I Feel About How I Handled It?

Interpersonal Effectiveness Worksheet 4a

Interpersonal Goals Planning

Use this worksheet to plan for interpersonal situations by identifying your goals and choosing appropriate skills.

Key Principle
Every interpersonal situation involves three potential goals: Objective (getting what you want), Relationship (maintaining the relationship), and Self-Respect (keeping your values).

Situation Analysis

Describe the situation:

Goal Type	My Goal	Priority (1-3)
Objective (What I want)		
Relationship (How I want them to feel)		
Self-Respect (How I want to feel about myself)		

Skills Selection

If Priority Is...	Use These Skills...
Objective highest	DEAR MAN
Relationship highest	GIVE
Self-Respect highest	FAST

Emotion Regulation Worksheet 1a

Emotion Identification Checklist

Use this checklist to help identify and name your emotions. Being able to accurately identify emotions is the first step in regulating them.

Key Principle
Naming emotions reduces their intensity. When you can identify and label an emotion, you activate the prefrontal cortex which helps regulate the emotional response.

Primary Emotions Checklist

Emotion	Present Now?	Intensity (0-10)	Body Sensations
Anger			
Sadness			
Fear			
Joy			
Disgust			
Surprise			
Shame			
Guilt			

Emotion Vocabulary Expansion

Basic Emotion	Mild Version	Moderate Version	Intense Version
Anger	Annoyed	Frustrated	Furious
Sadness	Disappointed	Unhappy	Devastated
Fear	Nervous	Anxious	Terrified
Joy	Content	Happy	Elated

Emotion Regulation Worksheet 3a

Opposite Action Planning Worksheet

Use this worksheet to plan opposite action for unjustified emotions. Opposite action changes emotions by changing what you do.

Key Principle

Opposite action works when the emotion doesn't fit the facts OR when acting on the emotion is not effective. Act opposite to the action urge, ALL THE WAY.

Opposite Action Reference Guide

Emotion	Action Urge	Opposite Action
Fear	Avoid, escape, freeze	Approach what you fear
Anger	Attack, criticise, yell	Gently avoid, take time out
Sadness	Withdraw, isolate	Get active, approach others
Shame	Hide, avoid	Make public, tell someone
Guilt	Avoid, punish self	Repair, make amends

Opposite Action Planning

Emotion I want to change:

Does the emotion fit the facts? (Y/N):

Is acting on it effective? (Y/N):

What is my action urge?

What is the opposite action I will take?

Opposite Action Practice Log

Date	Emotion	Opposite Action Taken	Did I Go All the Way?	Effect on Emotion

Emotion Regulation Worksheet 5a

Pleasant Activities Calendar

Track daily pleasant activities to build positive experiences. Regular pleasant activities build resilience against negative emotions.

Key Principle
Accumulating positive experiences is key to emotion regulation. Do at least one pleasant thing each day, even when you don't feel like it—especially when you don't feel like it.

Weekly Pleasant Activities Log

Day	Pleasant Activity	Duration	Enjoyment (0-10)	Effect on Mood

Pleasant Activities Menu

Quick (5-15 mins)	Medium (30-60 mins)	Extended (1+ hours)

My top 10 pleasant activities:
1.
2.
3.
4.
5.
6.
7.
8.
9.
10.

Emotion Regulation Worksheet 7a

PLEASE Skills Weekly Tracker

Track your PLEASE skills daily to reduce vulnerability to negative emotions. Taking care of your body helps regulate your emotions.

Key Principle
PLEASE skills reduce vulnerability: treat PhysicaL illness, balanced Eating, avoid mood-Altering substances, balanced Sleep, and Exercise. A healthy body supports emotional balance.

Weekly PLEASE Tracking

Day	Physical Health	Balanced Eating	No Substances	Good Sleep	Exercise	Overall Rating

PLEASE Goals

PLEASE Area	Current Status	Goal This Week
PhysicaL Illness		
Eating		
Avoid Substances		
Sleep		
Exercise		

Emotion Regulation Worksheet 9a

Check the Facts Worksheet

Use this worksheet to check whether your emotional response fits the facts of the situation. Often our emotions are based on interpretations, not facts.

Key Principle
Checking the facts helps determine if your emotion fits the situation. Ask: What is the emotion? What triggered it? What are my interpretations? What are the actual facts?

Fact-Checking Process

What emotion am I experiencing?

What triggered this emotion?

What are my interpretations/assumptions about the situation?

What are the FACTS (only what I can observe, no interpretations)?

Is there another way to interpret this situation?

Does my emotion fit the facts? (Y/N)

Does the intensity fit the facts? (Y/N)

Fact-Checking Log

Situation	Initial Emotion	After Checking Facts	Change in Intensity	Learning

Emotion Regulation Worksheet 11a

Build Mastery Activities Log

Track activities that build a sense of competence and mastery. Doing things that make you feel capable helps build resilience against negative emotions.

Key Principle
Build mastery by doing things that make you feel competent and effective. Choose activities that are challenging but achievable. Success builds confidence.

Weekly Mastery Log

Day	Mastery Activity	Difficulty Level	Accomplishment Feeling (0-10)	Notes

Mastery Activities by Life Area

Life Area	Activities I Can Do	Next Challenge
Work/Study		
Home/Daily Living		
Physical		
Social		
Creative/Hobbies		

What new skill or activity would I like to master in the next month?

www.ingramcontent.com/pod-product-compliance
Lightning Source LLC
LaVergne TN
LVHW020412220926
848484LV00016B/2550/J
* 9 7 8 1 9 1 9 3 6 5 6 9 5 *